St. Louis Community College

Forest Park
Florissant Valley
Meramec

Instructional Resources
St. Louis, Missouri

Playing with Power
in Movies, Television,
and Video Games

Playing with Power
in Movies, Television,
and Video Games

From Muppet Babies
to Teenage Mutant Ninja Turtles

Marsha Kinder

UNIVERSITY OF CALIFORNIA PRESS
BERKELEY LOS ANGELES OXFORD

University of California Press
Berkeley and Los Angeles, California

University of California Press, Ltd.
Oxford, England

© 1991 by
The Regents of the University of California

Library of Congress Cataloging-in-Publication Data
Kinder, Marsha.
Playing with power in movies, television, and video games : from Muppet Babies to Teenage Mutant Ninja Turtles / Marsha Kinder
p. cm.
Includes bibliographical references and index.
ISBN 0–520–07570–6 (alk. paper)
1. Motion pictures and children. 2. Television and children. 3. Motion pictures and television. 4. Intertextuality. 5. Cognition in children. 6. Video games. I. Title.
PN1992.63.K5 1991   91–11252
302.23′4′083—dc20   CIP

Printed in the United States of America

9 8 7 6 5 4 3 2 1

*To the loving memory
of my dear friend and former
collaborator
Beverle Ann Houston*

and

*To my son,
Victor Aurelio Bautista,
who inspired this project*

Contents

Preface

This book is addressed to a wide range of readers—to those concerned about their children's interaction with Saturday morning television, Nintendo video games, and cult heroes like Teenage Mutant Ninja Turtles; to those curious about how children acquire the ability to understand narrative and how this ability has been affected by mass media like television and video games; to those interested in American popular culture and corporate mergers in the multinational entertainment industry; and to those engaged with issues of gender and with the relationship between cognitive and psychoanalytic theory. Readers who are less interested in theory may prefer initially to skip over most of the first chapter and begin with the section "A Preliminary Case Study: Where Did Big Bird Go?" (p. 24), perhaps returning to the theoretical groundwork upon finishing the book.

This volume started out as an essay for the television issue of *Quarterly Review of Film and Video* that Nick Browne was assembling in honor of the late Beverle Houston, who was my closest friend and colleague and longtime collaborator. After consulting with Nick on possible topics, I decided to bring together two projects that I had been thinking about for some time: a case study of how television had affected my son's entry into narrative, and an exploration of inter-

ix

textuality as a means of commodity formation. That essay then turned into a scholarly paper for an innovative panel on animal representation organized by Anne Friedberg for the Society of Cinema Studies—a context that led me to develop the sections on animal masquerade and to elaborate on Teenage Mutant Ninja Turtles. It was Tania Modleski who first suggested that this project warranted a book. Ernest Callenbach, my wonderful editor at University of California Press and longtime friend and collaborator at *Film Quarterly*, shared the opinion and was largely responsible for making it happen. I owe special thanks to all four of these colleagues for helping me develop the project from essay to book.

I also want to thank several other colleagues and friends who read parts of the manuscript and gave many helpful suggestions for its improvement: Rosalie Newell, Margaret Morse, Rick Berg, Patricia Marks Greenfield, Lili Berko, Sue Scheibler, Jon Wagner, and the USC students in my graduate seminar on narrative theory.

At the University of Southern California, I am grateful to the Institute for the Study of Women and Men for giving me a faculty summer research grant to do empirical studies in conjunction with this project, and to Sharon Bowman at the Anna Arnold Bing Day Care Center for allowing me to observe and interview some of her students. I am deeply indebted to my wonderful research assistants Walter Morton and Michael Sinclair, who documented these empirical studies on video, and particularly to Walt Morton, who did editing and additional photography. I am also grateful to all the marvelous children who participated in these interviews, including my son, Victor, and his friends Erik Schneider, Jeff Lund, Mia Robinson, Matthew Kalmus, and Erica and Danny Rabins.

I would also like to thank CBS for providing me with demographics and tapes of some of their Saturday morning programs; Universal Studios and New Line Cinema for press kits and stills from *The Wizard* and *Teenage Mutant Ninja Turtles*; and Jim Henson Productions and United Media/Mendelson Productions for stills from *Muppet Babies* and *Garfield and Friends*. I also owe thanks to my friend Stephan Gerber and to Robert Chen, Steve Ricci, Michael Wilmington, and Owen Costello for helping me obtain additional materials.

I also want to acknowledge my brilliant, muscular, and prolific friend John Rechy, who always acknowledges me in his books and who frequently accuses me of writing on texts that are "unworthy" of my powers of analysis.

Most of all, I want to thank my husband, Nicolás Bautista, for his patience and good-humored support during the months when I was obsessed with this project.

1

Foreplay and Other Preliminaries

"A long time ago there were no toys and everyone was
bored. Then they had TV, but they were bored again.
They wanted control. So they invented video games."
                                        Victor Aurelio Bautista

According to my eight-year-old son, Victor, who is a reluctant moviegoer as well as our household Nintendo cham-
pion, the history of entertainment is driven by the pleasure
principle—the alleviation of boredom and the pursuit of
control or mastery. Cinema (which he omits entirely from
his minihistory) is clearly expendable.

Apparently, postmodern kids like Victor need to be *sold*
on the concept that movies still have an essential place in the
entertainment system. Both Saturday morning television
and home video games perform this job of selling by refig-
uring cinema not as a medium that is obsolete, but as what
Beverle Houston calls "a prior discourse" that can be parodied, recycled, and mastered.[1] Thus, even *before* children go
to the cinema, they learn that movies make a vital contribution to an ever-expanding supersystem of entertainment,
one marked by transmedia intertextuality.

Intertextuality, Dialogism, and Sliding Signifiers

The term *intertextuality* was first introduced by Julia Kristeva,
elaborating on Mikhail Bakhtin's concept of dialogism. Ac-

1

cording to Bakhtin, "The linguistic significance of a given utterance is understood against the background of language, while its actual meaning is understood against the background of other concrete utterances on the same theme, a background made up of contradictory opinions, points of view and value judgments."[2] In contemporary media studies, intertextuality has come to mean that any individual text (whether an artwork like a movie or novel, or a more commonplace text like a newspaper article, billboard, or casual verbal remark) is part of a larger cultural discourse and therefore must be read in relationship to other texts and their diverse textual strategies and ideological assumptions. As Robert Stam puts it, "In the broadest sense, intertextuality or dialogism refers to the open-ended possibilities generated by all the discursive practices of a culture, the entire matrix of communicative utterances within which the artistic text is situated, and which reach the text not only through recognizable influences but also through a subtle process of dissemination."[3] Thus, even if the author or reader of a particular text is not consciously aware of the other texts with which it is connected, those texts still help to structure its meaning.

In this book I will focus primarily on intertextual relations across different narrative media. As a means of structuring events within patterns of space, time, and causality, narrative creates a context for interpreting all perceptions. Narrative maps the world and its inhabitants, including one's own position within that grid. In acquiring the ability to understand stories, the child is situated as a perceiving, thinking, feeling, acting, speaking subject within a series of narrative fields—as a person in a family saga, as a spectator who tunes in to individual tales and identifies with their characters, and as a performer who repeats cultural myths and sometimes generates new transformations. Ever since television became pervasive in the American home, this mass medium has played a crucial role in the child's entry into narrative. My study explores how television and its narrative conventions affect the construction of the subject.

In assimilating and redefining that "prior discourse" of cinema, both Saturday morning television and home video games cultivate a dual form of spectatorship. They position young spectators to combine passive and interactive modes of response as they identify with sliding signifiers that move fluidly across various forms of image production and cultural boundaries, but without challenging the rigid gender differentiation on which patriarchal order is based. Although the meanings of all signs tend to be multiple and slippery, by *sliding signifiers* I refer specifically to those words, images, sounds, and objects that—like the pronouns *I* and *you*, or the adverbs *here* and *there*—blatantly change meaning in different contexts and that derive their primary value precisely from that process of transformation.

This combined mode of spectatorship helps to account for the extraordinary success of that commercial supersystem of transmedia intertextuality constructed around Teenage Mutant Ninja Turtles, those ultimate sliding signifiers who transgress every important border, except gender. Within this Turtle network, young players are encouraged to define themselves not in opposition to the alien Other but as voracious consumers—like Pac-Man, who defeats enemies by eating them. Thus, like the protean Turtles, who imitate old masters (both the Italian Renaissance artists after whom they are named and the Japanese ninja warriors whose martial arts skills they practice), children are learning to function as transformative mutants.

In adapting both this transcultural legacy and themselves to a new supersystem in which they prove their own mastery, the Ninja Turtles dramatize the interrelated processes of *as-*

similation and *accommodation*—concepts central to Jean Piaget's theory of genetic epistemology. Piaget claims that "in order to know objects, the subject must act upon them, and therefore transform them"; in turn, the subject is transformed, in a constant process of "reequilibration."[4] In this book I will demonstrate how children's television and home video games construct consumerist subjects who can more readily assimilate and accommodate whatever objects they encounter, including traditional modes of image production like cinema and new technological developments like interactive multimedia.

Consumerist Interactivity

We are now on the verge of an interactive multimedia revolution that is already placing cinema, television, VCR's, compact disc players, laser videodisc players, video games, computers, and telephones within a consolidated supersystem combining home entertainment, education, and business. Journalists are prophesying that "through the marriage of computers and film," soon "people will be able to pick up the fiber-optic phone line, access any listing, say, in the Paramount or ABC libraries, punch in a code and, within minutes, have *Singin' in the Rain* or a documentary on civil-rights violations flash across a wall-sized, high definition screen."[5] The latest developments in interactive media (such as Compact Disc Interactive, developed by Sony and Philips, and Digital Video Interactive, developed by General Electric and Intel Corporation) promise consumers that, with the purchase of an electronic device (which, like a Nintendo home video game system, can be hooked up to any television set) and the use of a remote control unit or "joystick," they will be able to access and combine a wide range of graphics, video images, sounds, words, and data bases. The vast range of applications for this cutting-edge technology in science, business, education, and entertainment can already be seen and played with at interactive multimedia galleries like Tech 2000 in Washington, D.C.

We have already seen the rise of popular interactive TV programs like "America's Funniest Home Videos," the success of which was made possible by the wide availability of affordable video-8 camcorders of high quality. On this show the audience not only votes for their favorite video, but also provides the entertainment by documenting their own experience. Like public access programming on cable television, such developments have the potential to democratize the video medium—a potential most fully realized in the recent Eastern European revolutions, where populist video both documented and participated in the making of history. In the United States, roving spectators with camcorders are increasingly documenting the impromptu violence they happen to witness in urban streets (as in the case of black motorist Rodney Glen King, whose severe beating by several policemen in Los Angeles in March 1991 was captured by a passing observer and broadcast on national television—an instance of video vérité that led to charges being brought against some of the officers and a bitter political struggle to force Police Chief Daryl F. Gates to resign). Yet on American prime time, this democratic potential is being used primarily to document comical pratfalls staged in the home for prizes, fame, and fun. Although home video and pirate radio have been celebrated in such recent films as *sex, lies, and videotape* (1989) and *Pump Up the Volume* (1990), where they function both as masturbatory fantasy and as a means of politicizing depressed housewives and teens, in the United States the democratic potential of interactive mass media has largely been appropriated by commercial interests.

In an analysis of interactive television of the 1980s,

Andrew Pollack concludes: "So far, the only interactivity that appears to be developing into a successful business is the simplest approach, requiring no special equipment in homes . . . allowing viewers to order merchandise on shopping networks, by calling an '800' telephone number or to respond to questions on television by calling a '900' number." Although he focuses on quiz shows like *Jeopardy* and *Wheel of Fortune*, which encourage viewers to play along, prize competitions in which one predicts the next music video or the quarterback's next call, and viewer voting contests for the best outcome of a mystery show or the funniest home video, he acknowledges that interactive television may have a better chance in the 1990s because "years of exposure to video games and computers mean that consumers now are more acclimated to interactivity." Pollack nevertheless warns that the success of these systems will be determined by "how well such services can attract and serve advertising."[6]

The more experimental interactive developments in modern media are beyond the scope of my project. Rather, I will focus here on how Saturday morning television and home video games, and their intertextual connections with movies, commercials, and toys, help prepare young players for full participation in this new age of interactive multimedia— specifically, by linking interactivity with consumerism.

Cognitive Theory and the Gendered Spectator/Player

To theorize about these new interactive media, we cannot restrict ourselves to the passive models of spectatorship rooted in psychoanalysis (which have tended to dominate film studies) but must also consider cognitive theory. To this end, I will use Piaget's theory of genetic epistemology, which foregrounds the interrelated processes of assimilation and accommodation in the cognitive development of the child; the empirical work of Arthur Applebee, which applies this model (as well as the cognitive theories of L. S. Vygotsky and Jerome Bruner) to the child's interaction with narrative; and the writings of Seymour Papert, who applies Piaget's model to the child's interaction with computers.

In *The Child's Concept of Story: Ages Two to Seventeen*, Applebee describes two modes of responding to narrative that can be found in early childhood and that develop collaboratively through later cognitive phases. This combination evokes the dual player/spectator position constructed for children by Saturday morning television and home video games. According to Applebee, in the "interactive participant role" (already observable in the infant's earliest dealings with the physical world), the child as perceiving/acting subject responds "piecemeal" to narrative discourse, and visual and verbal representations generate immediate concrete action, enabling the infant to handle, survive, or control events. In the "spectator role" (observable by age two and a half), the various systems of representation become fully involved and integrated as an "aesthetic" experience; the perceiving subject now responds to the whole.[7] Like Piaget, Applebee assumes that "as children mature, they do not pass out of one mode of response into another, but integrate their older structures into a new and more systematic representation of experience."[8] Although focused primarily on the spectator response, his study suggests that the interactive participant role is what drives the major shifts to later cognitive stages.[9]

Piaget's theory of genetic epistemology distinguishes four principal stages of cognitive development, which follow the formation of sensorimotor intelligence:

> After the appearance of language or, more precisely, the symbolic function that makes its acquisition possible

(1½–2 years), there begins a period which lasts until nearly 4 years and sees the development of a symbolic and preconceptual thought.

From 4 to about 7 or 8 years, there is developed, as a closely linked continuation of the previous stage, an intuitive thought whose progressive articulations lead to the threshold of the operation.

From 7–8 to 11–12 years "concrete operations" are organized, i.e. operational groupings of thought concerning objects that can be manipulated or known through the senses.

Finally, from 11–12 years and during adolescence, formal thought is perfected and its groupings characterize the completion of reflective intelligence.[10]

Within each new cognitive stage, Piaget claims that "the fundamental factor of development" is *equilibration*, which he defines as "a sequence of self-regulations whose retroactive processes finally result in operational reversibility."[11] According to Piaget:

> A mental operation is reversible when, starting from its result, one can find a symmetrically corresponding operation which will lead back to the data of the first operation without these having been altered in the process. . . . If I divide a given collection of objects into four equal piles, I can recover the original whole by multiplying one of my quarters by four: the operation of multiplication is symmetrical to that of division. Thus every rational operation has a corresponding operation that is symmetrical to it and which enables one to return to one's starting-point.[12]

These self-regulations involve a constant rebalancing of the assimilation of sensory input with the accommodation of the subject and his or her developing mental structures for grouping data. This ongoing process leads "from certain states of equilibrium to others [that are] qualitatively different" and requires the subject to "pass through multiple 'non-balances' and reequilibrations."[13] Applebee suggests that the collaboration between the unifying tendencies of the spectator mode and the analytic tendencies of the interactive mode facilitates this process of reequilibration.

In allowing space for ideology (or what Applebee calls the social structuring of the subject's "construction of reality"), this cognitive approach acknowledges the cultural production of differences in gender, race, ethnicity, and class. Yet unlike the psychoanalytic model, it does not perceive gender differentiation as the linchpin to subject formation within the patriarchal symbolic order—an assumption that has been essential to much of the best feminist film theory over the past fifteen years. Although some might claim that this "omission" helps to clear the way for transition to a more equitable coding of gender, I believe that it actually only "naturalizes" patriarchal assumptions, which continue to flourish in postmodernist media like computers, video games, and television.

The acknowledgment of gender differentiation in subject formation is crucial to the software I will be examining here (video games, TV programs, and movies), where traditional gender roles are increasingly reinforced rather than transgressed. In analyzing the mass toy market as "one of the strongest early influences on gender," Susan Willis observes:

> There is much greater sexual division of toys defined by very particular gender traits than I'd say has ever existed before. . . . Walk into any toy store and you will see, recapitulated in the store's aisle arrangement, the strict distinction and separation of the sexes along specific gender lines: Barbies, My Little Ponies, and She-Ras in one aisle; He-Man, the Transformers, and ThunderCats in another.[14]

Unfortunately, these same divisions are also found in Saturday morning television programs and commercials and in home video games and arcades. I will therefore position this cognitive approach within a larger framework of poststructuralist feminism, which explores the specific ways in which the gendered subject and his or her representations of reality are constructed within a social field. In so doing, I hope to avoid the indifference to feminist issues that is sometimes associated with cognitive theory and postmodernism. For I strongly agree with Lynne Joyrich that "it is only by calling attention to the specificity of gender and a gendered spectatorship (even while exploring the numerous practices and discourses that impinge upon and complicate this notion) that we can avoid the apolitics of an indifferent post-feminism."[15]

Toward a Synthesis of Psychoanalytic and Cognitive Theory

I accept Applebee's assumption that "theoretical argument" is a form of transactional discourse: we must respond to it interactively, challenging individual arguments and judging it piecemeal instead of embracing it whole, as if it were a poetic discourse. I will argue here for an interactive dialogue between psychoanalytic and cognitive theory—that is, for the appropriation from both models of ideas particularly useful for theorizing this dual form of gendered spectator/player positioning at this moment in history. Although, like David Bordwell, I believe "that principles of cognitive psychology and rational-agent social theory could cooperate to produce a constructivist theory of interpretation," I agree with Edward Branigan that such a theory is not necessarily incompatible with certain key principles from the psychoanalytic paradigm, particularly those that have been formative in the development of feminist film theory.[16] Like Louis Althusser,

I draw only on that part of the Freudian/Lacanian model that theorizes subject formation within the social context of the nuclear family under patriarchal capitalism (a perspective that exposes the ideological implications of subject positioning not generally addressed by cognitive theory).

In his highly influential essay "Freud and Lacan," Althusser credits French psychoanalyst Jacques Lacan with developing the semiotic potential in Freud's writings—by emphasizing Freud's discovery of the "discourse of the unconscious" and by going even further to claim that the unconscious is "structured like a language." According to Althusser, then, the primary object of psychoanalysis is the way culture structures the unconscious (the way it transforms the "small" animal into a gendered human adult), and Lacan's "most original" contribution was to give us a "conceptual hold on the unconscious" by showing that this "transition" from biological to human existence is achieved within the "Symbolic Order" (or what Althusser calls "the Law of Culture").

> Lacan demonstrates the effectiveness of the Order, the Law, that has been lying in wait for each infant born since before his birth, and seizes him before his first cry, assigning to him his place and role, and hence his fixed destination. . . . This is the beginning . . . even where there is no living father, of the official presence of the Father (who is Law). . . . So the Oedipal phase is not a hidden "meaning" . . . [or] a structure buried in the past. . . . [Rather it] is the dramatic structure, the "theatrical machine" imposed by the Law of Culture on every involuntary, conscripted candidate to humanity.[17]

When combined with the historical perspective of Althusser's own Marxist paradigm, this Lacanian theory of subject formation comes to explain the primary function of ideology: the "interpellation" of individuals into a symbolic order that constructs them as human gendered subjects who will bear their father's name and who will unconsciously help to reproduce the existing power relations of their culture.

> Ideology . . . "recruits" subjects among the individuals . . . or "transforms" the individuals into subjects . . . by that very precise operation which I have called *interpellation* or hailing, and which can be imagined along the lines of the most commonplace everyday police (or other) hailing: "Hey, you there!" . . . [If] the hailed individual . . . turn[s] round . . . , he becomes a *subject*. Why? Because he has recognized that the hail was "really" addressed to him, and that "it was *really him* who was hailed" (and not someone else).[18]

As many of Althusser's critics have observed, the subjects he describes are entirely passive—a condition that belies his own questioning of ideology and its operations.

The dual spectator/player position I am presenting here contradicts this Althusserian notion of a totally passive subject. In some ways it is analogous to the ambivalent stance that Lacanian film theorist Christian Metz adopts in his influential essay "Story/Discourse: Notes on Two Kinds of Voyeurism": "the ambivalent coexistence of this anachronistic affection with the sadism of the connoisseur who wants to break open the toy and see into the guts of the machine."[19] Yet whereas Metz sees the active mode of spectatorship as suited for a sophisticated analyst like himself, Piaget conceptualizes it as operative in the early acquisition of narrative; to him it is an essential component in the continuing process of cognitive development and an important vehicle for assimilation and accommodation.

Although many cognitive theorists tend to dismiss psychoanalytic premises because they have not been empirically verified, Applebee seems to accept the synthesis of the two models. For example, in discussing an empirical study from 1963 based on 360 stories collected from two- to five-year-old children in a New Haven nursery school, Applebee reports that "the original investigators analyzed these [narratives] from a neo-Freudian perspective, using them as a means to explore latent theories or crises of developmental importance." Without in any way challenging the study's findings, Applebee supplements them with a cognitive analysis of the children's assumptions "about what a story is, how it is organized, and how it can be 'used' or varied in response to different problems."[20] The implication is that, because of the different kinds of questions raised, the two paradigms address the material at different levels of inquiry; yet both make valuable and compatible contributions to theories about the child's physical and mental development. In a sense, then, psychoanalysis (like cinema) is treated as a "prior discourse," which is being assimilated within an interactive cognitive model.

This process of assimilation is more explicit in Seymour Papert's popular *Mindstorms: Children, Computers, and Powerful Ideas*. Although firmly grounded in Piaget's model of genetic epistemology, Papert's study also draws on Winnicott's psychoanalytic theory of transitional objects (which mediate between inner psychic reality and the external world) and on theories of computation and artificial intelligence, to explore how the computer (that "Proteus of machines") can challenge our standard assumptions about developmental psychology and learning. In the narrow sense, Papert defines artificial intelligence (AI) as a branch of advanced engineering, which aims at "extending the capacity of machines to perform functions that would be considered intelligent if performed by people." Yet he uses the term in the broader sense—that is, as a cognitive science, like linguistics and psychology, but one that "draw[s] heavily on theories of computation [of how mathematical and logical operations are performed or of how large masses of coded information are processed] . . . to give concrete form to ideas about thinking that previously might have seemed abstract, even metaphysical." In contrast to deductive and knowledge-based approaches, he claims that computation theory provides "a dynamic model" for how intellectual structures change, and that "while psychologists use ideas from AI to build formal, scientific theories about mental processes, children use the same ideas in a more informal and personal way to think about themselves."[21] Thus it is hardly surprising that he also attempts to give "concrete form" to certain psychoanalytic ideas about child development.

At one point Papert speculates that the oedipal crisis (so central to psychoanalysis) might actually accelerate the child's development of *conservation* (a crucial cognitive ability theorized by Piaget). Usually acquired around the age of seven, conservation enables the child "to understand that objects or quantities are 'conserved' and remain constant despite changes in their appearance (e.g., one cup of milk is the same amount whether poured into a tall, thin glass or a wide, shallow bowl)."[22] Observing that such changes in appearance are frequently generated by new contexts or operations that require constant reequilibration, Papert applies these cognitive dynamics not only to abstract numbers and concrete substances like milk, but also to members of the nuclear family:

> Conservation might even be derived from the model of a father not quite succeeding in imposing order on the family. It is possible to speculate, though I have no evidence, that the emergence of conservation is related to the child's

oedipal crisis through the salience it gives to this model. I feel on firmer ground in guessing that . . . it is related both to structures that are firmly in place, such as the child's representation of authority figures, and to germs of important mathematical ideas, such as the idea of "cancellation."[23]

By implying analogic relations between the mathematical idea of cancellation and the oedipal fear of castration, Papert positions the opposing cognitive and psychoanalytic models within a new, larger structure that nevertheless "conserves" Piaget's crucial notion of equilibration. In this way Papert helps us to see the essential role that conservation plays in subject formation, particularly in a culture that fetishizes protean change.

A synthesis of psychoanalytic and cognitive approaches is also attempted in *Narratives from the Crib*, a fascinating collection of nine complementary analyses (by a linguist, a psychoanalyst, and several developmental psychologists) of the presleep monologues of a two-year-old girl named Emily, as well as of the dialogues she has with her father just beforehand.[24] Taped by her parents over a fifteen-month period (between her twenty-first and thirty-sixth months), these amazing discourses reveal the "special status" of narrative "in the integration of affect, cognition, and action"—a conclusion with which all nine analysts agree, despite their theoretical differences.[25]

Reenvoicement and the Sleep-bargaining Genre

Integrating linguistic, cognitive, and psychoanalytic perspectives, John Dore provides the broadest and most provocative analysis in *Narratives from the Crib* in a chapter titled "Monologue as Reenvoicement of Dialogue."[26] Exploring the social function of Emily's monologues in the context of the nuclear family, he claims that they "reenvoice" issues from the nightly presleep dialogues the child has with her father. These infantile monologues, Dore suggests, demonstrate a primal form of intertextuality in language development—a process that "replaces" (or perhaps mediates between) Skinner's idea of imitation, where children merely repeat what they have heard, and Chomsky's notion of "sentence creativity," where new combinations are generated.[27] Borrowing the concept of "reenvoicement" (that is, the combination of "the voices of authority" with "one's own internally persuasive voice") from Bakhtin's theory of dialogism, Dore positions this intertextual process within the social unit of the family as conceptualized by Gregory Bateson—that is, as "a kind of cybernetic system of feedback loops."[28] Thus Dore concludes:

> Emily's monologues can be viewed as trial-and-error productions, hierarchically organized in terms of certain linguistic units, operating as self-corrective feedback mechanisms, and adapting to related models of language forms used by her parents in the wider system of language they all share. . . . [Thus] any control she may be able to exercise over her monologues is strictly constrained by the properties of the larger family system. . . . Her monologues will inevitably be "maps" of her parents' larger maps.

Or, as Dore puts it more succinctly, "language acquires children as much as children acquire language."[29]

Providing an "ethnographic" description of the social struggle that takes place during the nightly "scene of putting the child to bed," Dore observes: "The dialogues negotiate the conditions for going to sleep. The central fact for Emily is that she must sleep alone, and the father, whose 'job' [of putting her to sleep] this is, must leave the room." Defining genre as "a functional format for organizing content, style and structure simultaneously," and claiming that "genre . . . is what most deeply organizes Emily's speech," Dore calls this particular interaction "the sleep-bargaining scenario." As such, he argues, it is "often actualized by a complex weave of genres" and thus is itself a more complex genre (like the novel) that has the capacity to assimilate and restructure others. Within this specific narrative genre, Emily's role is to use language interactively to keep her father from leaving her bedside, "by continually questioning him, eliciting repetitions, crying, pleading and otherwise delaying him."

> The emotional significance for Emily here is enormous. It is not only that she may feel abandoned by her parents each time she must sleep; at a critical, transitional point in the collection of our data a baby boy is born into the family. The mother is nursing him, which is apparently why the father is handling Emily at sleep time. All of this contributes to the considerable emotional impetus motivating Emily's talk, in both dialogues and the monologues. . . . I suggest that the emotionally charged style of her monologues is due to these conflicts, which may accelerate her growth.[30]

Although Dore explains why the father (rather than the mother) is putting Emily to bed, he does not fully explore the significance of this substitution—especially since the infant usually hears the maternal voice first, even while still in the womb. There is even some empirical evidence that female voices on television are more appealing to preschool spectators than those of males—probably because they echo that of the mother.[31] Building on Lacan's essay "The Mirror Stage," Kaja Silverman observes in *The Acoustic Mirror*:

> The mother performs a crucial role during the subject's early history. She is traditionally the first language

teacher, commentator, and storyteller—the one who first organizes the world linguistically for the child, and first presents it to the Other. The maternal voice also plays a crucial part during the mirror stage, defining and interpreting the reflected image, and "fitting" it to the child. Finally, it provides the acoustic mirror in which the child first hears "itself." The maternal voice is thus complexly bound up in that drama which "decisively projects the formation of the individual into history," and whose "internal thrust is precipitated from insufficiency to anticipation." Indeed, it would seem to be the maternal rather than the paternal voice that initially constitutes the auditory sphere for most children, although it is clearly the latter which comes to predominate within the superego.[32]

One question that could be raised by this substitution of the father (for the mother) in the sleep-bargaining ritual is whether it might accelerate the introjection of the superego (a process that Freud claimed was rarely successfully accomplished in female subjects).

Nevertheless, in Emily's reenvoicement of the voice of her father, she performs like a precocious Scheherazade, whose desperate situation demands inventiveness and drives her across L. S. Vygotsky's "zone of proximal development" (the gap between what a child performs alone and the level of potential development as determined by adult guidance).[33] Her nightly monologues become a form of serial wordplay with a set of social and linguistic rules that enable her to channel her desire and function as a speaking subject; these achievements then help to accelerate her cognitive and emotional development. Vygotsky claims: "The essential attribute of play is a rule that has become a desire. . . . In short, *play gives a child a new form of desires*. It teaches her to desire by relating her desires to a fictitious 'I,' to her role in the game and its rules. In this way, a child's greatest achievements are possible in play, achievements that tomorrow will become her basic level of real action and morality."[34]

Within a cognitive perspective such as this, Freud's description of the child's introjection of the voice of the father as a censorious superego and Lacan's description of the subject's ascension to the symbolic order through the Name-of-the-Father can both be incorporated as pivotal "reequilibrations" involving assimilation and accommodation. Thus, just as Papert credits the oedipal crisis with accelerating the acquisition of certain cognitive skills, apparently Dore credits reenvoicement of dialogues with the father with accelerating the acquisition and regulation of narrative and launching the oedipal plot. Roland Barthes also observes:

> Although we know scarcely more about the origins of narrative than we do about the origins of language, it can reasonably be suggested that narrative is contemporaneous with monologue, a creation seemingly posterior to that of dialogue. At all events, . . . it may be significant that it is at the same moment (around the age of three) that the little human "invents" at once sentence, narrative, and the Oedipus.[35]

Because of its pivotal position at the infant's first entry into narrative, the sleep-bargaining genre becomes a metaphorical analogue for the whole project of narrative—a meta-narrative like the *Arabian Nights*, which indeed may be a sophisticated elaboration of the genre. I wonder whether the serial structure and emotional power of other complex narratives are also partly rooted in their intertextual connections with this sleep-bargaining genre. For example, in Marcel Proust's *A la recherche du temps perdu*, the narrator's primal scene is a sleep-bargaining *drame du coucher* in which the mother seductively withholds her bedtime kiss; in Doris Lessing's *Briefing for a Descent into Hell*, the sleep-bargaining ritual between parents and child is portrayed as the basis of larger political struggles; and in Mañuel Puig's *Kiss of the Spider Woman*, sleep bargaining becomes a potent vehicle for intertextual hybridization, not only between literature and film and between melodrama and propaganda, but also between the rival discourses of Freud and Marx. The metanarrative status of the sleep-bargaining genre may also help to explain why spectators derive so much pleasure from the segmented, serialized structure of movie sequels, video games, and especially television, which functions as a nightly bedtime discourse for millions of viewers. In all of these sleep-bargaining fictions, it is language and its capacity to generate an indefinite number of combinations and an endless flow of narratives that keep the speaker conscious and in control and that postpone sleep as an analogue for premature death.

"Fort/Da" Games and the Freudian Master Plot

Within a psychoanalytic model of psycho-sexual development, this sleep-bargaining genre could in turn be perceived as merely a variation on the game of "fort/da," in which the child controls the loss (or potential loss) of a desired object (such as a parent) by using both verbal language and concrete "transitional" objects like toys. "Fort/da" is the famous game of a wooden toy on a string devised by Freud's eighteen-month-old grandson, who repeatedly threw the toy forward saying, "Fort" (gone), and then retrieved it saying, "Da" (back). In both *Beyond the Pleasure Principle* and *The Interpretation of Dreams*, Freud stated that this game was the child's means of controlling and thereby gaining pleasure from the otherwise painful absence of his mother: "in their play children repeat everything that has made a great impression on them in real life and . . . in doing so they . . .

make themselves master of the situation."[36] He saw his grandson's game as an active means of expressing and thereby binding a complex knot of contradictory feelings. Through this displacement of his feelings about his mother onto the toy, the child was able not only to stop the displeasure caused by her absence, by making the desired object reappear, but also to express the hostility he felt toward her for leaving him, by violently throwing the toy away. Apparently this game strategy was so successful that when the mother died a short time later, the child, Freud claimed, took the loss very well.

In *Reading for the Plot*, Peter Brooks proposes a theory of reading narrative based on the "master plot" in *Beyond the Pleasure Principle*; he describes a movement in Freud's theory "from a postulate of repetition as the assertion of mastery (as in the passage from passivity to activity in the child's game) to a conception whereby repetition works as a process of *binding* toward the creation of an energetic constant-state situation which will permit the emergence of mastery and the possibility of postponement."[37] Within the developmental context of a life-story, this "constant-state situation" could also be read as another example of Piagetian equilibration.

Like many cognitive theorists, Brooks defines narrative as one of the "systems of understanding that we use in our negotiations with reality,"[38] yet he draws on the psychoanalytic paradigm to argue that this "dynamic psychic process" is motored by desire. Adopting Freud's "master plot," he claims that all narratives are driven by Eros (the totalizing force that seeks to combine things into new unities and ever greater wholes) and Thanatos (the death instinct that drives toward the end, the proper death). Although frequently treated as antagonists, Brooks emphasizes that Freud's Eros and Thanatos are both conservative forces that try to restore an earlier state of things and thus both inexorably lead toward "quiescence, death, and nonnarratability." In contrast, the middle of the narrative—with its elaborations, suspensions, and repetitions—seeks to prolong life by avoiding the short circuits of a premature or inappropriate death. Thus Brooks claims that "it is no accident that most of the great examples of narrative are long and can occupy our reading time over days or weeks or more" and that the *Arabian Nights* with its serial structure is a "metaseductive" solution designed "to keep desire alive, to prolong and renew the intersubjective and interlocutionary relation" of the narrative exchange.[39]

The Reenvoicement of Mass Media in Sleep-bargaining Rituals

This "master plot" driven by Eros and Thanatos is, I believe, first narrativized (for most subjects) in the nightly sleep-bargaining rituals between parents and child—whether played out in interactive dialogues and games, or in stories told by the parents, or in the child's reenvoicement of these struggles in monologues, tears, and dreams. Dore acknowledges that the sleep-bargaining genre is not necessarily restricted to verbal interaction: "We must appreciate that this entire activity could be accomplished silently; placing her in the crib and exiting through the door could do it. And this scene must indeed be done this way in other cultures, in other families, and perhaps at times in this family. However, the encouragement of talk is a primary ethnographic fact in this family's life."[40]

I also believe that within our postmodernist culture and at various developmental stages of this ongoing generational struggle between parents and child, other media situated in the home such as television and video games substitute for the parents in those sleep-bargaining rituals and "dialogues with the father" and thus become primary models for the child's discursive repertoire. This substitution is hardly surprising: according to the National Institute of Mental Health, children spend far more time looking at video screens than interacting with parents or teachers.[41] These "talking toys" provide the child both with a compelling multisensory enunciation of the patriarchal symbolic order (what Jerome Bruner calls the culture's "canonicality")[42] and with a powerful means of reenvoicing cultural values. Such reenvoicements can be achieved not only through monologues, but also through a dialogic system of intertextuality (involving language, play, and commercial exchange), which positions the child as an active consumer whose desires are directly addressed. Not surprisingly, the "promissory genre" that Dore finds so frequently in the speech of Emily's father during their dialogues recurs as a dominant discursive format of both television commercials (with their repeated promises of pleasure) and video games (with their systems of immediate rewards and punishments). These domesticated mass media thus replace the family as the "collective mind" or the "primary cybernetic system of feedback loops."

In the following chapters I will explore how television and video games teach children to recognize and recombine popular narrative genres and thereby facilitate intertextual reenvoicement. We can only speculate on what kinds of narratives will be generated by such reenvoicements; but already metanarratives like *The Arabian Nights* and *A la recherche du temps perdu* are being succeeded by proliferating supersystems such as *Super Mario Brothers, Back to the Future,* and *Teenage Mutant Ninja Turtles*—with all of their protean sequels, adaptations, and marketing spinoffs.

Like Applebee, Papert, and Dore, I adopt for my project the very strategy of cognitive restructuring I describe—by combining psychoanalytic and cognitive models of spectatorship and methodologies from various disciplines into a single system, by creating a minisystem of intertextual versions (the conference paper, the journal article, the book),[43] and by starting with a case study of a "unique" subject (my son, Victor) and then repositioning that experience intertextually within increasingly larger networks of spectatorship, entertainment, and history.

A Preliminary Case Study: Where Did Big Bird Go?

In a scenario of their early months and years together, the mother's eyes are drawn to the shimmering set, and very soon the eyes of the infant as well. . . . In their very bedroom, the infant is forced through her to confront this third term, the television and its representational practices. Thus the television substitutes itself partly for other institutions and discourses which constitute the Name-of-the-Father.[44]

When my former collaborator Beverle Houston wrote this paragraph, I was bringing up baby. My son, Victor Aurelio Bautista, was born in November 1982, and we spent many hours at home together in front of that "shimmering set." I decided to observe my son's interactions with television and its effect on his ability to read narrative, and to write what Gregory Ulmer calls a "mystory" (evoking "mystery" and "mastery" as well as biography)—that is, "a kind of personal periodic table of cognitive elements" that shapes one's creativity and demonstrates "the equivalences among the discourses of science, popular culture, everyday life, and private experience."[45] In this way, I would be responding to Susan Willis's call for "professional women and their children . . . [to] work together in critical pursuits."[46]

Yet my notes on Victor's interaction with television lack precise dating, partly because I could never bring myself to the point of total "objective detachment," as Freud did with little Hans (the son of a colleague) in his celebrated case study or with his own grandson in his famous theorization of "fort/da."[47] Although our culture might tolerate a male behaviorist like B. F. Skinner experimenting with his own children, a woman doing the same is ordinarily condemned as a "bad mother." As Susan Suleiman has noted, in patriarchal culture and its psychoanalytic literature "the good and even the good-enough (Winnicott) mother is characterized . . . above all by her exclusive and total involvement with her child. . . . *Mothers don't write, they are written*."[48] Thus, in writing as a mother who studies her child and reads him as a text, I chose to "tender" the book to my son—perhaps as an extension of the parent/child sleep-bargaining dialogue or, as Suleiman suggests, as "a propitiatory offering . . . to appease the crying child" who always protests (at least in the mother's guilt-ridden imagination) when she is writing instead of attending to his needs.[49]

In attempting such a project, I followed the example of Ruth Weir's ground-breaking 1962 study of her son Anthony's crib talk, a work that also inspired the more "objective" *Narratives from the Crib*, where the parents collected the tapes and helped to decipher their daughter's language but did not analyze the data.[50] Unlike these two studies, which focus primarily on spoken language and present a systematic examination of data, my observations are anecdotal and concern my son's interaction with mass media. Like Papert's description of his childhood experience with gears (the key transitional object that helped to shape and cathect his early mental model of reality) in the foreword to *Mindstorms*, my records are more ethnographic in nature. Yet I hope that they might also raise questions that warrant further empirical investigation.

Victor was born prematurely at only twenty-eight weeks

of gestation, weighing a little less than two and a half pounds. He spent his first two months in an incubator in the neonatal intensive care unit at UCLA Medical Center in a twenty-four-hour atmosphere of bright lights, loud radio music, and noisy beepers warning of deviant heartbeats—an experience that may have made him particularly receptive to multisensory mass media. My husband and I were able to visit him at least twice a day, and fortunately Victor developed normally, suffering no permanent side effects. Yet because of his "extreme prematurity," Victor was a subject in "Project Infant," a developmental intervention study by Doctors Lela Beckwith and Arthur Parmelee at UCLA, and my own narrative account of the pregnancy and birth was included in *The Premature Labor Handbook*.[51] Thus, the description included here of his interaction with mass media has intertextual relations with these other texts in which Victor already appears as a subject.[52]

When Victor came home from the hospital at two months, he slept in a small cradle in our bedroom; in the room was a TV set and a large mirrored closet in which the TV image was reflected. Thus, wherever one looked, the TV image was always visible. I would usually nurse Victor in that room, frequently with the television set turned on.

When Victor was around a year old (shortly after he had begun to say recognizable words), when I would push him in his stroller (one of the most effective ways of putting him to sleep) I would listen to his presleep monologues, which frequently consisted of a catalogue of names (Mommy, Daddy, Victor, Sister, Granny), as if he were listing members of a category or paradigm.[53] Sometimes the list would include a fictional character from TV like Big Bird.

Shortly after Victor's second birthday we went to a relative's house where he met his cousin Rachel for the first time. As soon as we got home, he ran to the family photo albums and found Rachel's picture, which he had seen many times before. Since the age of one he had spent a great deal of time going through these photos, which seemed to function for him as a grid of visual signifiers—images defining family and friends and the position of his own imaginary signifier within this social structure. I wondered whether this passion for reading visual images was influenced by his experience of having watched so much television as an infant, during and before the "mirror stage"—a crucial step in subject formation theorized by Jacques Lacan, where the infant (between six and eighteen months of age) first recognizes and mistakenly idealizes its own imago (or imaginary signifier) in the mirror, usually next to that of the mother holding it.[54] I also wondered what impact the simultaneous experience of TV spectatorship and the mirror stage might have on an infantile viewer: is their connection stronger and more inevitable (than the connection between the mirror stage and film viewing), based as it is not merely on analogy but also on historical juxtaposition, a switch from metaphor to metonymy? And is this effect intensified by having an ordinary mirror present, in which both the TV image and the infantile spectator can be reflected?

Shortly after this incident of finding Rachel's picture, Victor showed similar glee in recognizing the face of Bill Cosby on a billboard and clearly said, "Jell-O," even though the billboard was advertising another product. He had previously seen Cosby on TV commercials for Jell-O; clearly, then, television was a grid for mapping other signifying systems outside the home (both verbal and visual signifiers). Indeed, it was already inaugurating him into advertising discourse as a consuming subject.

Up to about twelve months (when, according to Piaget, "there are no permanent objects, but only perceptual pictures which appear, dissolve, and reappear"),[55] Victor's favorite TV images were the HBO logo, commercials, music videos, and any other images with strong graphics, fast cutting, multicolors, and loud music. During this period, when "infants watch sporadically," his attention had to be captured by aggressive formal elements.[56] Gradually over the next six months as he began to pay attention to the television over longer stretches of time, he started taking pleasure in recognizing the images of certain characters who appeared very frequently, such as Michael Jackson in music videos and Big Bird on "Sesame Street."[57] It was as if he were adding these figures to the catalogue of names he had recited in his stroller and of faces he had studied in the family albums. He had no trouble recognizing Big Bird as the star: the distinctiveness of his size, shape, and color made him easy to distinguish from other characters.

Whenever the image cut away from Big Bird, Victor would ask with anxiety: "Where Big Bird go?" This question evoked not only Brooks's statement that all narratives are obituaries that account for a death, but also Piaget's observation that "the 'permanence' of an object begins with the action of looking for it when it has disappeared at a certain point A of the visual field."[58] It also made me wonder whether early interaction with the televisual image generates a lingering ambiguity between fluid perceptual images and permanent objects. Moreover, Victor's anxiety made me realize that, in learning how to read editing conventions, my son had already experienced the castrating power of the cut. He had no means of mastering that game of presence and absence—not, that is, until he learned how to use the remote control unit, which inaugurated a new, more pleasurable version of "fort/da." Sometime between the age of eighteen and twenty-four months, Victor became very absorbed in playing with the remote control "joystick," as if (like the misrecognition of his own idealized image in the mirror stage) it enabled him to develop an exaggerated sense of his own motor control and of his own empowerment in the world. Eventually we took the joystick away from him for fear he would break it—a remedy that in retrospect seems suspiciously castrating.

Victor's anxiety over an object's disappearance also occurred repeatedly in one of his favorite sleep-bargaining rituals. Practically every night just before we would leave him alone in his own bedroom (where he had been sleeping since the age of six months), my husband or I would carry Victor to the window to look for the moon. Whether it was present or absent, Victor would repeatedly say "Moona" (conflating the English word *moon* with the Spanish *luna*, which my husband, a native speaker of Spanish, used in these rituals). It was as if the chanting of this word was magical, like the joystick, for it had the power to create continuity among all the nights when the ritual was performed—whether in English or in Spanish, whether with me or with my husband, in whatever stage of the lunar cycle. On those nights when the moon was *not* visible, Victor seemed to use the word to call forth its referent, or to fill in for its absence.

At twenty-three months, around the time when Victor was beginning to make sentences, we took him to a movie theater to see Walt Disney's *Pinocchio* but had to leave because he was more interested in running up and down the aisles than in watching the big screen. In contrast to his experience with television, where he enjoyed considerable latitude in selecting what he would watch (perhaps a bit more than is customary for a child of his age), here he had no control over what images he was seeing; my husband and I chose the movie and the theater, and there was no remote control unit for him to manipulate. It therefore makes perfect sense that he would turn his attention to testing his developing motor skills by interacting with the physical space of the theater.

Children of my generation were usually introduced to the moving image when our parents first took us to the cinema; thus moviegoing tended to remain for us a rich source of fantasy. But to kids like Victor who are raised on television, moviegoing frequently translates into a frightening loss of power. In contrast to television, the oversized movie images and overbearing sounds demand their undivided attention for long stretches of time and deprive them, not only of control over what they perceive, but also of periodic retreat into a comforting domestic background.

The first movie that captured Victor's attention was *The Empire Strikes Back* (an episode in the *Star Wars* trilogy), which he watched on television. It was a week when the film had blanket circulation on most of the cable stations, so whenever we changed the channel, we entered a different part of the narrative. This unusual form of segmentation enabled Victor's response to become more interactive.

Applebee maintains that in the interactive mode, "techniques of transactional symbolism" lead us to "judge [a text] step by step, and act on it piecemeal. . . . We qualify, accept, or challenge the argument, offer a new perspective, or simply express our pleasure or disgust." When we take on the role of spectator, in contrast, "poetic techniques ask us to consider a work as a whole"; that is, "we look on, testing our hypotheses about structure and meaning, but we do not rush in to interrupt—to do so would obscure the relationships and spoil the effect of the whole."[59] He claims empirical studies of youngsters' early interactions with stories demonstrate that "young children respond to each incident separately with no rise or fall of interest over long stretches of the plot."[60] Or, as the National Institute of Mental Health report puts it, "Young children remember discrete scenes and events better than the relations between the scenes."[61] I suspect this disinterest in plot can be explained in part by the findings of D. S. Hayes and D. W. Birnbaum, who in a 1980 study demonstrated that preschoolers tend to pay more attention to the visual aspects of television and to ignore large portions of the audio—a mode of selective spectatorship that undermines the comprehension of linear continuity.[62] Summarizing ten years of empirical studies, the National Institute of Mental Health concludes: "At very early ages, children already demonstrate active and selective viewing strategies, for example, watching animation, turning away from dialog they do not understand, turning back when music or sound effects suggest lively action or 'pixillation' (animated activity). Age factors as well as properties of the medium interact to determine how children develop useful viewing strategies."[63] Apparently, at age two Victor was not quite ready for the "wholeness of discourse" that cinema required and was far more comfortable with the interactive mode facilitated by the highly segmented structure of television.

Victor enjoyed this segmentation (which can be reproduced with greater spectator control on VCR's and laser disc players) partly because it made it easier for him to recognize his favorite characters. Whenever the Wookie appeared, Victor would say: "Leave it. I want see Wookie." He loved this inarticulate id figure, just as he also loved the Cookie Monster on "Sesame Street," Animal on "Muppet Babies," and Slimer on "Ghostbusters." Victor also watched for the castrating patriarch Darth Vader, saying, "He's dark." He loved searching for these two characters, whom he would recognize and name, as if he were mastering their images and the categories to which they belonged. Eventually he asked me to name other characters, even extras, saying: "Who's that? Who's that?" Each time we watched the film, he would add new qualities to each character, as if he were constructing what Roland Barthes calls a "semic code" (a cluster of adjectival characteristics that are associated with and grouped under a proper name of a character or place).[64] First there were proper nouns, next the association with adjectives like "dark," and then he added verbs: "Wookies hug," "Darth Vader talks and walks" (and on "Sesame Street," "the Cookie Monster eats cookies," "the Count counts," and so forth). Applebee observes: "By two-and-a-half, the earliest age at which we have many records, this use of language in the spectator role includes the shaping of experience as well as of language."[65] Similarly, in her introduction to *Narratives from the Crib*, Katherine Nelson points out that all the contributors to the volume agreed that Emily's early monologues helped her make sense out of three domains of experience: not only (1) the outside world of people, things, and events and (2) herself as a speaking/perceiving/thinking/feeling/acting subject, but also (3) language itself with its linguistic and narrative forms.[66]

Victor began to follow the narrative line when he started watching video tapes on our VCR. He would pick one movie and obsessively watch it over and over, learning all the characters and mastering the narrative, and then move on to another—in a manner very similar to the way he would later consume home video games. The first movie that he watched obsessively was Gene Kelly's musical version of *Jack and the Beanstalk*, which softens the oedipal conflict by adding a character who mediates between father and son. (Kelly plays the bean salesman who accompanies Jack on his quest, helping him to best the Giant and cut down the phallic stalk; ultimately he woos Jack's mother and presumably becomes the boy's father.) Even more than in *Empire*, Victor was most interested in parent/child couples—fathers and sons, mothers and sons—naming and following them, and worrying whenever any of them disappeared from the screen.

This tape was soon displaced by *Tubby the Tuba, Modern*

Times, The Circus, The General, Sherlock Jr., Follow that Bird, The Muppets Take Manhattan, The Red Balloon, Dumbo, Lambert the Lion, Pinocchio, and *Tom and Jerry Cartoons.* Victor would frequently repeat lines of dialogue from these tapes in regular conversations and reconstruct scenes while playing with little plastic toys. Following each viewing, he would ask many questions, especially about the characters' emotions and motives (for example, "Why was the man running after Miss Piggy?" "Why was she angry?"). If he had a book of the same story, after watching the film version he would want my husband or me to read it to him every night before bedtime—the sleep-bargaining ritual. He liked seeing various versions of the same story and took great pleasure in noticing the smallest deviation and in making up his own variations. As Barthes observed: "Rereading is no longer consumption, but play (that play which is the return of the different). If . . . we *immediately* reread the text, it is in order to obtain, as though under the effect of a drug . . . , not the *real* text, but a plural text: the same and new."[67]

This stage of obsessive repetitions through various signifying systems seemed to provide Victor with models for generating his own sentences and stories about events in his own life, and he was especially eager to have these narrative elements incorporated into bedtime stories (whether told by him or by us, his parents) as if (like the chanting of the word *moona*) these narratives would assure him of continuity and equilibrium in the midst of growth and change. Echoing Barthes, Brooks claims: "An event gains meaning by its repetition, which is both the recall of an earlier moment and a variation of it: the concept of repetition hovers ambiguously between the idea of reproduction and that of change, forward and backward movement."[68] This reenvoicement behavior is consistent with the empirical findings summarized by Applebee: "From a very early age these discussions [of events important to children] begin to be subsumed within the conventional, culturally provided frame of the story mode; even the two-year-olds studied used at least some of the conventions studied in 70 percent of their stories."[69]

As soon as Victor began to master the narratives, he started censoring certain tapes that had formerly been his favorites. He claimed that *Jack and the Beanstalk* had "ugly parts" (the scene where the Giant captures Jack), as did *The Muppets Take Manhattan* (the part where a mugger chases Miss Piggy in the park, a sequence about which he had asked many questions). He preferred watching animated cartoons, perhaps because their "fluid images" could be more easily distinguished and distanced from "permanent objects" in real life. An exception was "Dennis the Menace," which he preferred to watch in live action rather than in animation, possibly because the farcical violence typical of cartoons is virtually omitted from the live-action series.[70] Victor also liked black-and-white silent comedies (what he called "quiet films") by Chaplin and Keaton, possibly for the same reason that he liked cartoons—that is, because, as in animation, their blatant stylization enabled him to remove the characters and their violent actions from his own sphere. Now at age eight, Victor prefers video games over television, and television shows over video tapes and movies, and still loves to control the joystick while interacting with his two favorite modes of image production. While watching television he enjoys the unpredictability of what will be broadcast, even if it turns out to be a rerun he's already seen. In November 1990, his five favorite TV shows were "The Simpsons," "America's Funniest Home Videos," "Teenage Mutant Ninja Turtles," "Looney Tunes," and "Inspector Gadget."

Emerging Questions

These observations of Victor's interaction with television made me wonder about the impact of seeing an imaginary world so full of rich visual signifiers before having encountered their referents or acquired verbal language. Although the interiorization of images based on perception and imitation precedes language acquisition in any culture, does early exposure to television accelerate the transformation of mental images into communicative symbols?[71] Does it encourage the sliding of the signifier, so that by the time one first encounters, say, an elephant in the zoo, the living animal is merely another signifier for the image already seen on TV in documentaries and animated cartoons—that is, merely part of the paradigm of elephant signifiers? Does early television exposure lead to the primacy of the visual signifier over the verbal signifier and the referent? Does it help efface the referent in postmodernist culture? Does it contribute to the postmodernist claim that the simulacrum or imitation is preferable to the real?

I also wondered whether early exposure to television accelerates the process described by D. W. Winnicott of "decathecting transitional objects"—as when the infant's most cherished teddy bear or blanket loses its privileged status (as the unique symbol of that intermediate territory between inner psychic reality and the external world) by having its meaning "spread out over . . . the whole cultural field." Does the television become a concrete embodiment of that cultural field, in its proliferation of transitional phenomena (both the televisual images and the remote control unit) that help the infant "to accept difference and similarity" as it makes the "journey from the purely subjective to objectivity"?[72] Does such use of the television as a purveyor of transitional phenomena help to fetishize the TV image in later life, that is, by empowering it to play a key role in subsequent versions of the sleep-bargaining ritual, to allay anxiety, to act as a soporific, and to provide pleasure linked with oral eroticism?

Although television may "hail" infants as consuming subjects (as Beverle Houston has argued), are these children not also learning at an early age how to play "fort/da" power games with the image—how to switch the channel, fast forward, and choose the desired tape? And would this experience not make them far more responsive to the interactive spectatorship offered by video games than to the passive spectatorship and imaginary plenitude offered by cinema? According to Winnicott, what makes play so "immensely exciting . . . is always the precariousness of the interplay of personal psychic reality and the experience of control of actual objects. . . . To control what is outside one has to *do* things, not simply to think or to wish. . . . Playing is doing."[73]

Victor's explanation for the popularity of video games that opened this chapter is consistent with Winnicott's definition of play and with the empirical reports gathered by Patricia Marks Greenfield in *Mind and Media*, who claims that all the children she interviewed (between ages eight and fourteen) "were unanimous in preferring the games to television" and "were also unanimous about the reason: active control." Whereas she concludes that "video games are the first medium to combine visual dynamism with an active participatory role for the child,"[74] I believe this combination is already in play on Saturday morning television.

Things to Come

In the chapters that follow I will argue that the widespread introduction of television into the home since the 1950s has affected the process of subject formation, enabling the television set to function both as a mirror (in the Lacanian sense) and as an ideological state apparatus (in the Althusserian sense—that is, as a social apparatus that transmits and reproduces the dominant ideology, not through blatant propaganda or restrictive censorship imposed by repressive laws and enforced by violent means, but primarily through widely accepted cultural practices, such as religion, education, and the arts).[75] Moreover, the particular conventions of American commercial television, with its blatant emphasis on intertextuality, segmentation, and flow and with its pervasive popularity worldwide, have led subjects to see themselves as highly adaptable transformers or sliding signifiers—that is, to perceive their imaginary signifier as marked by an idealized protean malleability rather than by an idealized unity as in the Lacanian matrix. While this protean malleability may have appeared and been promoted in earlier periods, particularly through the transformative media of animated cartoons and comic books and through the mixed form of the reflexive comic novel (which is now perceived, partly under the growing influence of Bakhtin, as having several postmodernist characteristics),[76] not until such malleability became a dominant characteristic of a popular mass medium like television did it become a powerful means of reproducing the postmodernist subject. For in being positioned within the home and in assimilating earlier narrative forms such as movies, novels, comic books, and cartoons, the television medium shapes the infant's entry into narrative. Also, by appropriating functions that once were performed by what Althusser considers the most powerful ideological state apparatuses of earlier eras—the family, the education system, and the church—the television medium has become the most powerful ideological state apparatus in this late phase of postindustrial capitalism.[77]

These dynamics partly explain why television is so widely perceived as a postmodernist medium, or at least as a medium that contributes to the postmodernist condition, and why, within this context, intertextuality functions as a powerful vehicle of commodity formation. In this process, the newly emerging subject comes to perceive himself or herself as a gendered commodity around which a whole commercial nexus is organized—just like Garfield, the Muppet Babies, and other TV personalities with whom the child is led to identify. Further, the child comes to believe that this nexus is activated and extended whenever he or she consumes a product. In short, television teaches viewers that commercial interactivity empowers precocious consumers by enabling them to assimilate the world as they buy into the system.

This process of reproducing the postmodernist subject and its dynamic of commercial empowerment is now being intensified and accelerated in home video games, in commercial transmedia supersystems constructed around figures like Teenage Mutant Ninja Turtles, and in multinational corporate mergers like Sony's recent takeover of Columbia Pictures and Matsushita's acquisition of MCA/Universal. In these expanding networks of synergy, connectivity, collectability, restructuring, new world orders (and other postmodernist buzzwords), children, corporations, and countries are learning that transmedia intertextuality is a powerful strategy for survival.

2

Saturday Morning Television: Endless Consumption and Transmedia Intertextuality in Muppets, Raisins, and the Lasagna Zone

> At the ideological level, the goal [of cinema] is to reinforce the unified subject as an intermediate step in reproducing a certain social world. This is not the definitive work of television. Its function is more directly linked to consumption, which it promotes by shattering the imaginary possibility over and over, repeatedly reopening the gap of desire.
>
> *Beverle Houston, "Viewing Television: The Metapsychology of Endless Consumption"*

In a groundbreaking essay that distinguished how spectator positioning operates in American commercial television as opposed to mainstream narrative cinema, Beverle Houston explored psychoanalytic discourse on cinema and television theory, altering both models to create a new paradigm that addressed the complex relationship between these two modes of image production within the cultural field.[1] She was particularly drawn to films like *King of Comedy*, *Poltergeist*, and *Videodrome*, which present television as a dangerous medium and dramatize the competitive relationship between these mass media. For in the final analysis, movies and television have been pivotal in constructing or reinforcing two

39

very different conceptions of subjectivity: the unified subject, associated with modernism and cinema; and the decentered consumerist subject, associated with postmodernism and television.

In this chapter I wish to show how many of the concepts Houston articulated in her essay are explicitly addressed in Saturday morning television, as if it were teaching young viewers not only how to gain pleasure by pursuing consumerist desire, but also how to read the intertextual relations between television and cinema as compatible members of the same ever-expanding supersystem of mass entertainment.

Transmedia Intertextuality and the Child

The most casual glance at Saturday morning American network television yields many examples of transmedia intertextuality among television, movies, and toys. Even in the early days of radio and television, the purchase of a sponsor's product or a program-related premium (like the Captain Midnight decoder offered in 1942, or the Captain Video board game and Cisco Kid writing tablet offered in 1950) was frequently used to rate a show's popularity, but by the 1980s this intertextuality and its commodification had been greatly elaborated and intensified. The most extreme case was the so-called program-length commercial, half an hour of TV cartoons specifically designed to sell a new line of toys (increased sales of which sometimes brought profitable kickbacks to the stations that aired them).[2] Such shows were made possible by the deregulation of American broadcasting in the 1980s and, more specifically, the elimination by the Federal Communication Commission (FCC) of its ban against product-based programs in 1984. In 1987, however, the courts ordered the FCC to investigate this phenomenon, an inquiry that the Children's Television Act of 1990 (passed on October 18, 1990) required be concluded by March 1991 (that is, within 180 days after the act became law).[3]

The TV spinoff from a successful movie (and vice versa) is a more generally accepted form of tie-in, perhaps because the profit motive is less blatant, even though spinoffs frequently involve ancillary toys and crossovers into commercials. Recent examples can be found on all three major networks: "Teenage Mutant Ninja Turtles" and "Dink, the Little Dinosaur" (from *The Land Before Time*) on CBS, "The Karate Kid" on NBC, and "Beetlejuice," "Slimer and the Real Ghostbusters," and "The Wizard of Oz" on ABC. Although such intertextuality is not restricted to children's programming but pervades all of commercial television (as John Fiske and Mimi White have demonstrated most convincingly),[4] I believe that it probably has the greatest impact on young children. Even when young viewers do not recognize many of the specific allusions, they still gain an entrance into a system of reading narrative—that is, a means of structuring characters, genres, voices, and visual conventions into paradigms, as well as models for interpreting and generating new combinations. As Althusser has argued, while most subjects (both youngsters and adults) remain unaware of the ideological implications of their own schemata or the degree to which they have been shaped by their culture, this very lack of awareness helps to naturalize those cognitive categories, making it more difficult for the subject to see beyond them.[5]

Applebee claims that with each new story we assimilate we must accordingly alter, or accommodate, the schemata, genre, or category to which we assign it, an act that necessarily changes our "representations of experience." He argues that "we *build* the world through our accumulated record of experience, our systems of implications of previous activity" and that the "adequacy of these representations is a crucial factor in determining our ability to function in that world," that is, "to understand and to some extent control what happens to us."[6]

While this cognitive process continues to operate in adults, early childhood is when the basic categories for the "construction of reality" and their organization into "hierarchic systems" are established. Piaget claims that the first major shift into an operational mode of thought occurs around age seven, and Applebee applies this perception specifically to the child's understanding of narrative.

> As children become aware of their responses to a story, they begin to classify them into categories with clearly marked attributes. It is these categories which seem to be evaluated, rather than the specific details of the story itself. . . . The selection of attributes sometimes seems "analytic," focusing on parts of a work such as its "rhyme" or "rhythm," but these are used to define a class (of "works that have rhyme". . .) rather than as a means of exploring the structure of a particular work. Other attributes which children select tend to be situational; content is treated literally rather than as embodying a point or message of a wider generality. Stories are enjoyed because they are about "cowboys" or "families" or "trains," not because they are about "how families work" or "problems of good and evil."[7]

Yet as Dore has shown in his analysis of Emily's presleep monologues in *Narratives from the Crib*, even in the speech acts of a two-year-old one can find the assimilation and development of "not only the components of grammar (phonology, syntax, and semantics) but also the process of genre (of thematic construction, of stylistic rendering, of discursive processes)."[8] Dore claims that using "the notion of speech genre as the largest manageable unit of linguistic functioning" will help us discover the "deep functions" of language.

Although he acknowledges that "genre performance is less fixed, less stable, and less computational than grammar," he states that it is more clearly socially determined and so more clearly reveals how children are "acquired" by language. "Our field needs at least a more deeply interactionist view of language development. . . . We need a theory of what happens *between* speakers and, especially, a theory of the interaction between how the child acquires language cognitively and how a society acquires the child functionally."[9]

This explanation is precisely what Dore hopes to achieve with his theory of speech genres and what I hope to achieve with the following analysis of genre and intertextuality in children's television programming. I believe that the extensive emphasis on genre and intertextuality in Saturday morning television helps to facilitate cognitive development, yet at the same time it associates this developmental progress with consumerism (a connection that the child retains in later life), thereby enabling our consumerist culture "to acquire the child functionally." As Susan Willis observes:

> Children learn and want to be consumers at an ever earlier age. . . . Today, two- and three-year-olds request toys regularly. They know exactly what they want and the brand names as well. . . . It does not matter whether the child actually buys the toy or merely voices desire: "I want that!" In advanced consumer society, . . .we consume with our eyes, taking in commodities every time we push a grocery cart up and down the aisles in a supermarket, or watch TV, or drive down a logo-studded highway.[10]

As we saw in chapter 1, my son Victor's first recognition of Bill Cosby on a billboard already marked him as a two-year-old consumer; he has remained eager to buy Jell-O or any other product promoted by this familiar paternal celebrity, no matter whether Cosby appears in commercials, in his "picture page" reading promos, in his own popular TV series, or in movies like *Ghost Dad*. Thus within patriarchal consumer culture, Cosby extends the "dialogues with the father," which Victor interactively reenvoices both at home and in the marketplace. The pervasive intertextuality in children's television also enables the shows to address viewers of different generations and to retain spectators as they mature, by offering new meanings and new cognitive pleasures, especially in reruns. This dynamic is seen explicitly on Nickelodeon, the so-called "children's network," particularly in their ads for syndicated "classics" like "Lassie," "Mister Ed," "Green Acres," and "Bewitched."

The dynamic is especially strong in the revival of "Looney Tunes," where intertextual allusions from Warner Brothers cartoons made in the thirties, forties, and fifties are recontextualized in the ever-expanding commercial intertextuality of the 1980s and 1990s. Writing about the original Warner Brothers cartoons, Martin Rubin has argued that "this tendency toward explicit intertextuality reached its most intense and overt form" in the late 1930s and early 1940s, which was "a transitional period for the WB cartoon—between the Fleischeresque amorphousness and secondhand Disneyisms of the early '30s . . . and the fully developed personality animation of the mid-'40s and after." Thus he claims that intertextuality helped to create distinctive "stars"—"the contemporary, streetwise personae of the WB characters," in contrast to the "eternal, mythologized comic archetypes" of Disney's Mickey Mouse and Donald Duck. Rubin acknowledges that most of the "topical references to popular songs, sayings, movies, plays, radio shows, books, magazines, celebrities, political figures, advertising slogans, etc." are no longer recognizable to spectators today, a fact that makes the cartoons more easily appropriable to the new consumerist context.[11] This appropriation has generated numerous new products bearing the image of Road Runner, Coyote, and Bugs Bunny, which are designed to compete in toy stores and video shops with similar ware featuring not only Disney's Mickey and Donald, but also more contemporary stars like Muppet Babies, Roger Rabbit, and Teenage Mutant Ninja Turtles. A similar case of cultural reinscription is found in "PeeWee's Playhouse," where the intertextual meanings of inset Fleischer cartoons from the 1930s are transformed by their new postmodernist context, blurring historical distinctions or at least making them seem insignificant.

This commodified multigenerational structure calls into question the rigid boundaries that John Fiske draws between intertextuality and direct allusions:

> The theory of intertextuality proposes that any one text is necessarily read in relationship to others and that a range of textual knowledges is brought to bear upon it. These relationships do not take the form of specific allusions from one text to another and there is no need for readers to be familiar with specific or the same texts to read intertextually. Intertextuality exists rather in the space *between* texts.[12]

While I agree that the recognition of specific allusions is not an essential condition for all intertextual relations, to exclude it (as Fiske suggests) is unfortunate, for that would prevent us from seeing how intertextuality can function as a form of commodity formation. Within particular social and economic contexts, the recognition of specific allusions makes certain intertextual relations pay off—especially at the point of purchase.

Saturday morning television also undermines the distinction Fiske makes between horizontal forms of intertextuality (among primary texts) organized around genre or character, on the one hand, and vertical intertextuality "between a primary text, such as a television program or series, and other texts of a different type that refer explicitly to it" (such as publicity, station ID's, journalistic articles, and criticism), on the other.[13] The conflation of these various forms of intertextuality into a single commercial system erases the boundaries between primary and secondary texts, enabling primary texts (such as television series and video games) to function as promotional material for other primary texts (such as movies and toys), and vice versa. It was precisely this kind of conflation that made possible the program-length commercial. Thus, the problem of decommodifying children's television cannot be addressed simply by limiting the amount of commercial time that broadcasters can sell or by demanding a crackdown on the program-length commercial—two of the regulations introduced by the Children's Television Act of 1990. Although well intentioned, these measures are merely "Band-Aid" solutions. As long as children's programming is firmly embedded in the larger intertextual structures of American commercial television, it will reproduce consumerist subjects. To supplement these legal measures, perhaps what is needed is an educational program in elementary and secondary schools on how to read media images interactively, a program that enables children to understand how meaning is constructed and encourages them to question and negotiate those readings that are privileged by the text and its corporate sponsors.

Saturday CBS Fun

Within specific shows designed for children, the intertextual relations among movies, television, and other media are complex. On four successive Saturdays (September 30, October 7, 14, 21, 1989) I taped CBS's morning programming—what was then called "Saturday CBS Fun" (it was renamed "Kids' TV" in the fall 1990 season). On the West Coast and in the Midwest, this "strip" of children's television begins at 7:00 A.M. (on the East Coast it begins at 8:00 A.M.) and extends to 11:30 A.M., unless preempted by sports (see table 1). I decided to tape CBS rather than the other networks because that is the channel my son, Victor, usually watches on Saturday mornings.

What I found was a fairly consistent form of transmedia intertextuality, which positions young spectators (1) to recognize, distinguish, and combine different popular genres and their respective iconography that cut across movies, television, comic books, commercials, video games, and toys; (2) to observe the formal differences between television and its prior discourse of cinema, which it absorbs, parodies, and ultimately replaces as the dominant mode of image production; (3) to respond to and distinguish between the two basic modes of subject positioning associated respectively with television and cinema, being hailed in direct address by fictional characters or by offscreen voices, and being sutured into imaginary identification with a fictional character and fictional space, frequently through the structure of the gaze and through the classical editing conventions of shot/reverse shot;[14] and (4) to perceive both the dangers of obsolescence (as a potential threat to individuals, programs, genres, and media) and the values of compatibility with a larger system of intertextuality, within which formerly conflicting categories can be absorbed and restrictive boundaries erased.

I also found that in featuring animal (or other forms of nonhuman) protagonists, many of these programs dramatize subject formation, or what Althusser called "the extraordinary adventure which from birth to the liquidation of the Oedipal phase transforms a small animal conceived by a man and a woman into a small human child."[15] By encouraging

Table 1
Saturday Morning Network Programming

Fall Season, 1989 (West Coast schedule)

	CBS	NBC	ABC
7:00	Dink the Dinosaur	Alf Tales	Scooby Do
7:30	Muppet Babies	Camp Candy	Gummi Bears
8:00	"	Captain N	Winnie the Pooh
8:30	PeeWee's Playhouse	Karate Kid	Real Ghostbusters
9:00	California Raisins	Smurfs	"
9:30	Garfield & Friends	"	Beetlejuice
10:00	"	Chipmunks	Bugs & Tweety
10:30	Rude Dog & Dweebs	Saved by the Bell	"
11:00	Raggedy Ann & Andy	Sports	Sports

Fall Season, 1990 (West Coast schedule)

	CBS	NBC	ABC	Fox
6:00	2 the Point	Young People's Special	Black Sheep Squadron	ThunderCats
6:30	Kidquiz	Krypton Factor	"	Popeye & Friends
7:00	Muppet Babies	Camp Candy	Winnie the Pooh	Zazoo U
7:30	"	Captain N & Super Mario Brothers 3	Wizard of Oz	Bobby's World
8:00	TMNT*	"	Ghostbusters	Tom & Jerry
8:30	"	Gravedale High	"	Attack of the Killer Tomatoes
9:00	Garfield & Friends*	Kid 'n' Play	Beetlejuice	Piggsburg Pigs
9:30	"	Chipmunks Go to the Movies	New Kids on the Block	Fun House
10:00	Bill & Ted's Adventures	Saved by the Bell	Bugs Bunny & Tweety Show	Captain Planet
10:30	PeeWee's Playhouse	The Guys Next Door	"	Batman
11:00	Sports	Saturday videos	Little Rosey	Soul Train

*On the East Coast and in the Midwest, "Garfield and Friends" precedes "TMNT". This order is reversed on the West Coast because the three-hour time difference frequently leads to more sports preemptions and the network wants to protect the higher-rated program.

young spectators to identify with nonhumans, these programs represent a form of masquerade that (consistent with
Mary Ann Doane's theorization of female spectatorship)
produces "a certain distance between oneself and one's image" and, in this case, a distance from the entire process of
subject formation and gendering.[16] On Saturday morning
television, this masquerade is facilitated by the choice of
creatures whose gender is not immediately distinguishable to
an untrained eye; the patriarchal act of naming thus blatantly constructs them as subjects by simultaneously individ-
uating them from their species and designating their gender. In this way, young viewers learn that television and its
advertising discourse are powerful agents of the gendering
process and that during the vulnerable period when their
own gender identification is being established, the most effective way for them to play an active role is by choosing
their own clothes and toys.

Let me cite a concrete example. Victor used to enjoy playing with toy ponies at a friend's house—until he saw them
featured in the "My Little Pony" commercials, where they
were being fondled exclusively by little girls (in hyperfeminine clothes) who combed their colorful manes, as if they
were equine Barbies. He thus learned that the gendering of
toys is determined not by direct experience (that is, not by
observing which children actually found them fun to play
with), but by how they are represented in TV commercials
and other marketing practices.

This gendering process also extends to inanimate toys—
even to those once considered appropriate for both sexes.
For example, a recent commercial for "Dream Builder"
shows two little girls playing with a building set designed
specifically for their gender, the implication being that all
other similar toys are intended exclusively for boys. If the
young female viewer already owns a set of building blocks,

then, it instantly becomes inappropriate and therefore obsolete. Thus, this advertiser makes the product more desirable to its target audience by commodifying the gendering process: by renaming the toy and dressing it up in a female masquerade that is just as hyperfeminine as the clothes worn by the little girls in the commercial. Since all of these toys are designed and promoted as objects of identification for the youngsters who consume them, it is apparent that these children are being constructed as commodified gendered subjects in precisely the same way.

Within the advertising discourse on Saturday morning television, this exaggerated emphasis on choosing "appropriately" gendered products is also associated with the movement toward adolescence, implying that consumerism is a form of growth. In many of these commercials young viewers are frequently positioned to identify with sliding signifiers who fluidly change age, size, voice, and form before their eyes and ears. As Susan Willis observes, "Young children anticipate adolescence both consciously and unconsciously . . . [and] in consumer society their anticipations are met more quickly and easily by commodities than by social institutions like family and schools. Commodities offer the young child a means to articulate his or her notions about the transition to adolescence."[17] Although several commercials show preteens consuming products (like Barbies, soft drinks, and cereals) that instantaneously transform them into adolescents, this process is perhaps most resonant in the campaign for milk (that wholesome product that "does a body good"), for there it blatantly appropriates, fetishizes, and commodifies a "natural" substance that is linked to the infant's original object of desire: the mother's body.

Appropriating Mother's Milk

As if illustrating the dynamics of Lacan's mirror stage, these ads for milk playfully dramatize "the deflection of the specular *I* into the social I." They feature a growing child who is painfully aware of what Lacan would call physical "insufficiencies" and who is anticipating a magical transformation into the "Ideal-I" that he or she first saw in the mirror. Moreover, the "misrecognition" of this idealized image "appears to him [or her] above all in a contrasting size . . . that fixes it."[18]

In at least two commercials in this series a young boy stands in a mirror relation to another figure who embodies his present and future object of desire (the mature female he would like to possess, the mature male he would like to rival and replace). As he gulps down his milk, the boy is magically transformed into the idealized imaginary signifier that someone else imagines he must become if he is ever to fulfill those desires—that is, the mature, muscular signifier of phallic power. Thus, in an act of ventriloquism, the sponsor and the medium (the absent enunciators) (1) speak to him as the future commodified subject they are helping him become, (2) design and groom his imaginary signifier and that of his object of desire, (3) transmit to him the culture's assumptions about what is "good" for his body (not only protean protein, but also heterosexual coupling and the reproduction of the nuclear family), and (4) position these transformative images within an oedipal miniplot that is driven by desire (that is, the young boy's desire to grow up as quickly as possible so he can become the phallus that the desirable older female desires). As Lacan puts it, "If the desire of the Mother *is* the phallus, the child wishes to be the phallus in order to satisfy that desire."[19]

In these commercial narratives that flaunt their powers of

gendering, milk is naturalized as a fetishistic substitute for the primary signifier of desire—in other words, for the father's phallic power, which (in patriarchal culture and Lacanian theory) arrogantly replaces the mother's body as the original object of desire. Thus, milk curiously comes to stand for the phallus rather than the breast ("the tube of plenty" rather than "the boob tube"), and the television medium is revealed as the perfect replacement for the Lacanian mirror. For, as Beverle Houston reminds us, while television's endless flow of text suggests the flow of milk from the mother's body, its representational practices and "magical enunciation—at once diffuse, sourceless, but directly demanding"— partly substitute for the Name-of-the-Father.[20]

Eating Fellini

These patterns of transmedia intertextuality and commodified masquerade are clearly demonstrated on two CBS shows (which were broadcast back to back on Saturday morning, October 14): "The California Raisins" and "Garfield and Friends." Amazingly, both shows included a cartoon character who not only parodied Federico Fellini as the symbol of film culture on the wane, but also boasted a name that evoked a desirable edible (Rasperini and Fettucini). In both instances, too, the nonhuman protagonists were at first highly respectful of this auteur, yet ultimately sought to assimilate him and his cinematic model into their own brand of stardom, demonstrating the superior versatility and consumptive power of both themselves and their medium, TV animation.

In the segment of "Garfield and Friends," the lasagna-loving feline is "discovered" by an egomaniacal Italian film director named Federico Fettucini (to the accompaniment of music from the soundtrack of *8½*). Garfield is cast (and dressed) not in the starring role that he imagines (in a fantasy sequence evocative of the auteurist imaginary that is the source of creativity in *8½*), but in the anonymous role of stunt double, which enables him to assume multiple identities yet undermines the pride he takes in his own uniqueness. To get revenge, Garfield changes the script and usurps the role of director, recasting himself as auteur. This resolution demonstrates that in television the magnetic aura belongs not to the writer or director, whose name is rarely known, but to a character like Garfield (or Bill Cosby), who functions as a commercial nexus around which a whole array of products can be marketed.

Such commercial systems of intertextuality are easily extended outside the home to urban space, where stuffed Garfields and other animal icons cling to car windows and where birthday parties are increasingly designed around a popular media personality like Garfield, whose image is reproduced in the celebrity guest, birthday cake, party favors, and loot bags. These birthdays can later be read diachronically (particularly when documented on home video), both in terms of the child's developmental chain of transformative masquerades and as a minihistory of pop culture. These systems have also appropriated an ever-proliferating stream of banal products like lunch boxes, which were recently featured in a television exhibit at the National Museum of American History in Washington, D.C., tracing the fickle rise and fall of popular TV stars and genres (from western hero Wild Bill Hickcock in 1955 to sci-fi ThunderCats in 1986) while demonstrating some stability in rapidly changing social formations like the family, school, and consumption. According to *Standard and Poor's Industry Survey* of toys for 1989:

The most successful marketing strategy during the 1980s was the use of storylines and animated television programs to promote new products, which increased consumers' brand awareness. . . . Companies have also succeeded in boosting both brand awareness and sales by licensing their products' logos and likenesses, which now appear on everything from briefs to lunchboxes. Product proliferation has also helped. By offering a broad line of related products and accessories, as opposed to only a few toys based on a product concept, companies have also been able to increase the sales of popular toys by encouraging what the industry calls "collectability."[21]

In the "California Raisins" episode, an Italian producer-director named Federico Rasperini (who mimics other Italian filmmakers besides Fellini, such as Sergio Leone and Carlo Ponti) wants to direct a rock video starring the Raisins (who, incidentally, rose to TV stardom from commercials), but he does not know how to work in this new medium. Feeling sorry for him because he has invested his own money in the project and because they (erroneously) assume he is broke, the good-hearted Raisins accept his offer. Although they all agree on the Motown classic "Stop, in the Name of Love," Rasperini (in his quest for an ever more lavish cinematic spectacle) keeps changing the genre (from western, to swashbuckler, to circus show, to horror film, and so forth), and consequently the mise-en-scène and costumes keep changing as well. Their video is also sabotaged by the Raisins' rival, Lick Broccoli, a British heavy-metal singer who wants to replace them as star and change the style of the music. As a result, Rasperini's video is not ready for the premiere. The Raisins come to his rescue, deciding to let their "live" performance (in direct address) control the clip and to incorporate the previous filmed versions as inserts, thus utilizing the visual modulation, fast editing, and pastiche structure characteristic of the music video genre. This solution also realizes one of the dreams of that ultimate postmodernist filmmaker, Raul Ruiz: "You can have many films inside of one. It's one of my dreams to make a film that begins in the time of *Ivanhoe* and would end as a western. The story would not change, the actors would not change. Only the film would change. That would be fantastic."[22]

This program trains junior spectators how to distinguish, combine, and consume different genres in both media, for as Fiske insists, "Genre is a means of constructing both the audience and the reading subject."[23] Dore perceptively observes, "The learning of genre requires more repetitions and routine productions, indeed even ritualizations, of varieties of talk in context than does grammatical thinking,"[24] and this is precisely what this episode of "The California Raisins" provides. But beyond this cognitive function, the program also leads kiddie spectators to prefer video (with its live broadcasting, direct address, instantaneous electronic editing, and heavy reliance on computer animation) over film. It suggests historical reasons why international auteurs like Fellini have chosen to direct music videos and why they were not entirely successful. It presents a discourse on ethnicity, linking Italians with European elitist high modernism and black Americans with postmodernist pop culture. As Fiske argues:

> Highbrow, elitist works of art are typically valued for their unique qualities. . . . Understanding works of art generically, however, locates their value in what they have in common, for their shared conventions form links not only with other texts in the genre, but also between text and audiences, text and producers, and producers and audiences. Generic conventions are so important in television because they are a prime way of both understand-

ing and constructing this triangular relationship between producer, text, and audience.[25]

An Intertextual Reading of Three Empirical Studies

Although one might predict that the appearance of a Fellini-like figure on two successive shows would increase a child's recall of these narratives, Perry Thorndyke claims precisely the opposite in a 1977 study on the comprehension and memory of narrative discourse: "For successively presented stories, . . . repeating story structure across two passages produced facilitation in recall of the second passage, while repeating story content [e.g., the same character in a different set of actions] produced proactive interference."[26] Since Thorndyke's experiment was selectively designed to measure the recall of structure *apart* from content, he considers the reduction in plot recall an "interference." Yet his own findings imply that the conflict between similarities and differences in structure *and* content leads the subject to a more complex restructuring, which I would read not as interference, but as what Piaget calls "conservation." Thorndyke acknowledges: "When these same characters were engaged in a different set of actions and relationships in the second story, a new hierarchy encoding the relationships had to be constructed in memory."[27] I believe that it is precisely this restructuring of hierarchies of relations and categories (or, in Piaget's terms, "reequilibrations") that serves as a cognitive basis for genres and is fostered by intertextuality.

Another empirical study of children's recall of narrative structure, by Jean M. Mandler and Nancy S. Johnson, challenges Piaget's assumption that errors in remembering the temporal sequence of events "were due to a failure to comprehend chronological, causal and distinctive relations"; instead, these researchers argue that more attention must be given to the structure of the specific stories (which might include not only narrative structure, which is the focus of their own study, but also the mode of image production and intertextual relations with other stories). They acknowledge:

> There is considerable anecdotal evidence that young children often adequately recall stories and plots of television cartoons. . . . The uncertain evidence in this area of study suggests again that the structure of the materials being used must be carefully examined before we can reach a sound conclusion about children's reproduction of temporal and causal sequences.[28]

The heavy reliance on intertextuality in Saturday morning TV cartoons, I would argue, helps to facilitate not only the comprehension and recall of stories, but also the development of more complex schemata of what stories are like, with their highly complex patchwork of similarities and differences in plots, characters, iconography, mise-en-scène, and modes of image production.

One of the most fascinating empirical studies of children's responses to television narratives was conducted by Patricia Marks Greenfield and her associates, who tested 110 first- and second-graders on their ability to generate "creative" narratives after having been exposed to toy-based television cartoons and/or program-related toys. The children were randomly divided into three groups: an experimental group that was exposed to the TV/toy tie-ins and two control groups that were not. In a pretest, the subjects were asked to tell a story using one of two sets of toys: "program-related" Smurfs or "neutral" Trolls. Then they participated in either watching a "toy-based" Smurf cartoon on TV or playing a "neutral" game of connect-the-dots. Finally, they were asked to tell another posttest story (using either Smurf toys or Trolls), which was analyzed for "transcendent imagination" (that is, "the number of imaginary items supplied by the child, as opposed to what was already supplied in a given stimulus situation").[29]

The investigators hypothesized that "product-based television and related toy products would stimulate the earlier, more imitative and context-dependent forms of imagination, while inhibiting the more creative and independent forms that develop later." Their findings demonstrated that "it is clearly the combination of product-based television and thematically-related toys that is most inhibiting to creative imaginations." When the two influences were examined independently, they found that, "overall, TV, both with and without program-related toys, stimulated imitative imagination, while inhibiting creative imagination."[30]

These interpretations of the data are somewhat compromised by the definition of "transcendent imagination" on which they are based. The investigators argue that "imitative imagination," which they define as the child's ability (usually appearing at the end of the second year of life) to "mentally recreate an entity or action from a preceding situation," is the "earliest manifestation of imagination" in Piaget's scheme of representational development; therefore, they claim, it can be used as a foil to the true, more mature "transcendent imagination," where the child supplies new imaginary items. Although presented as a universal definition of creativity, "transcendent imagination" is actually based on a historical notion associated with romanticism and high modernism, a notion that was not widely held either during the Enlightenment, which preceded these periods, or during our own postmodernist era, which followed. For example, during the eighteenth century, when parodic adaptations of classical works were considered highly creative, one finds the British poet Alexander Pope defining "true wit" in "An Essay on Criticism" (1711) as "what oft was thought, but ne'er so well expressed"; and the brilliant satirist Jonathan Swift in *The Battle of the Books* (1704) lavishly praising the nobility of writers (like Pope and himself) who draw wisdom and beauty from ancient authors the way the bee draws pollen from the flowers, but harshly condemning moderns who pride themselves for originality, like the arrogant spider spinning from his own "Excrement and Venom" and "producing nothing . . . but Flybane and a Cobweb." Greenfield's definition of "transcendent imagination" is equally incongruous in our own postmodernist period, where hybridization, simulacra, and what Fredric Jameson calls "pastiche" are dominant creative modes.[31] Even Vygotsky argues for the importance of imitation, which enables children to "go well beyond the limits of their own capabilities" and thereby functions as a crucial link between learning and development.[32] A child's reworking of material from mass media can be seen as a form of parody (in the eighteenth-century sense), or as a postmodernist form of pastiche, or as a form of Bakhtinian reenvoicement mediating between imitation and creativity.

At one point in their study Greenfield and her associates acknowledge some "conceptual difficulty" in their "definition of creative and imitative imagination." The issue arises when one of their subjects uses "Smurfs to build their story around Teenage Mutant Ninja Turtles" (who are not in the study). Although their experimental design leads them to count this response in the "highly creative" category of "new imaginary items," they acknowledge that since it comes from other media sources, "It is probably more accurate to say that television and program-related toys change the *source* of imagination, rather than its creativity or quantity."[33] The concept of intertextuality might provide a more effective framework for reading these important data, which may help to explain how we arrived at our postmodernist condition and how it is currently being reproduced in our children.

In *The Limits of Interpretation*, Umberto Eco tries to explain the current refocusing of theoretical inquiry from innovation to repetition:

> Before, mass mediologists tried to save the dignity of repetition by recognizing in it the possibility of a traditional dialectic between scheme and innovation (but it was still the innovation that accounted for the value, the way of rescuing the product from degradation). Now, the emphasis must be placed on the inseparable scheme-variation knot, where the variation is no longer more appreciable than the scheme.[34]

Reminding us that "the concept of absolute originality is a contemporary one, born with Romanticism," and that it is "possible to describe the model of a Greek tragedy as a serial" and "the whole of Shakespeare [as] a remake of preceding stories," Eco nevertheless concludes that we may be witnessing "the birth of a new public that, indifferent to the stories told (which are in any case already known), only relishes the repetition and its own microscopic variations."[35] From this perspective, "a true and real genetic mutation" is more likely to be found in the audience than in the text—which is precisely what I am arguing here.

To demonstrate in detail how television helps children to acquire this postmodernist conception of creativity, I will present a reading of two other cartoon programs: the "Green Ranger" episode from "Muppet Babies," broadcast on September 30, 1989, and the "Lasagna Zone" episode from "Garfield and Friends," broadcast on October 7, 1989. Although these two episodes are representative of their respective series, they display transmedia intertextuality and commodified masquerade more complex than those found in the Fellini examples previously discussed. I have deliberately avoided selecting an episode from "PeeWee's Playhouse," since that show's postmodernist subversion of the borders between genres, genders, races, and species has already been analyzed elsewhere in considerable detail by myself and others.[36]

"The Green Ranger": The Anxiety of Obsolescence

"Muppet Babies" is an animated "prequel" spinoff from Jim Henson's Muppets, who are featured (in live action) on the classic PBS children's series "Sesame Street," as well as in their own dramatic feature films and products. (The successful proliferation of the Muppet image led the Disney organization to negotiate for the rights to use them in their movies and theme parks, but this takeover deal fell through late in 1990 after Henson's death and resulted in bitter countersuits.) Currently in its seventh season on CBS, "Muppet Babies" has already produced ninety-nine episodes, an unusually high number, particularly since its current ratings are lower than in the past. (For comparative ratings of selected CBS shows on Saturday morning television, see table 2.)

Segmented into two separate half-hour episodes (so that it is easier to tune in or out at the midpoint), "Muppet Babies" presents the nursery adventures of eight baby animals of varied species—Kermit the Frog, Ralph the Dog, Fuzzy the Bear, Gonzo the Blue Weirdo, Animal the Infant, Skeeter and Skooter the co-ed twins, and Miss Piggy. There is no mention of their families nor any explanation of why they are always in the nursery with their human nanny, whose head we never see. She remains an ambiguous figure, perhaps to enable a wide range of kiddie viewers to cast her as significant other in their own varied family scenarios.

As if dramatizing Piaget's assumption that assimilation

Table 2

*Comparative Ratings (in Points) and Audience Share (in Percent)
for "Muppet Babies," "Garfield and Friends," and "Teenage
Mutant Ninja Turtles," Fall Season 1990–91*

	Muppet Babies	Garfield	TMNT
Household rating	2.5 (14%)	4.5 (18%)	6.2 (23%)
Women, 18 and older	.7 (22%)	1.3 (23%)	1.6 (19%)
Men, 18 and older	.5 (15%)	1.0 (15%)	1.4 (15%)
Teens, 12–17	1.2 (8%)	3.2 (11%)	5.8 (14%)
Children, 2–11	4.6 (55%)	8.1 (51%)	12.1 (52%)
Kids, 2–5	4.3 (37%)	8.5 (42%)	13.6 (45%)
Kids, 6–11	4.9 (63%)	7.9 (58%)	11.1 (55%)

*Source: Nielsen Index for National TV Rating:, for the period September 10, 1990
to December 9, 1990.*

and accommodation drive cognitive development and creative invention (as opposed to mere imitation), "Muppet Babies" celebrates interactive fantasy, in contrast to a passive reliance on high-tech toys. It constructs a space that Winnicott (one of the most influential psychoanalytic theorists of play) would describe as "the intermediate area . . . allowed to the infant between primary creativity and objective perception based on reality-testing"; like the mother's breast, this intermediate space fosters "the *illusion* that there is an external reality that corresponds to the infant's own capacity to create."[37] Winnicott's emphasis on this "area's" connection with the mother makes all the more significant the nurturing presence of the headless nanny (whose breasts are frequently visible, even if her maternity is denied), for she invariably encourages the Muppets in their play and sometimes even "enriches" their games with concrete objects from her own "toy chest." She is the "responsible person" described by Winnicott, who must be present to alleviate the frightening aspects of play.[38]

To represent this "intermediate space" of the Muppets' creative play, the series repeatedly intercuts between excerpts from live-action movies or TV programs and animated footage in the nursery, integrating the two discourses (through the wizardry of high-tech computer animation). Thus, the series consistently presents a running commentary on the relationship between movies and television and how they train youngsters to read narratives interactively.

For example, the opening title sequence (repeated every week) includes images of Kermit as Indiana Jones swinging on a rope, as in *Raiders of the Lost Ark*; battle footage à la *Star Wars* (the film that helped promote the use of computer animation for special effects and that pioneered the marketing strategies of recycling and recombining old movie genres and creating product tie-ins for young consumers); Miss Piggy winning an Oscar, a spectacle that evokes both films and the TV coverage of this event; and Miss Piggy and friends on the yellow brick road. This shifting of scenes requires the constant redressing both of Muppets and mise-en-scène and also effaces historical distinctions between a 1940s classic like *The Wizard of Oz* and the two recent George Lucas blockbusters, both of which generated their own series of sequels. Most important, this opening dramatizes the system of substitutions that facilitates ego identification with fictional characters and imaginary worlds, and therefore is essential to both "creative play" and spectator positioning: animals filling in for humans, children filling in for adults, cartoon characters filling in for live-action actors, TV characters filling in for film stars, TV filling in for cinema. These substitutions help to establish the key paradigms and analogical/hierarchical sets that will guide kiddie spectators in reading specific episodes of "Muppet Babies." They also evoke Lynne Joyrich's description of television's postmodernity: "Constantly shifting its placement of the subject (as it moves between a number of interrupted fragments), television seems to revel in a pure celebration of difference—a process that is ultimately equal to its reverse formulation, an agenda of absolute indifference."[39]

Significantly, even in this opening "celebration of difference," traditional gender boundaries remain firmly in place. Consistent with Doane's argument,[40] the two female Muppets present the two options constructed for the female spectator by patriarchal cinema: the transvestite position (where girls identify with male characters or their female variants) is occupied by Skeeter, an androgynous female twin; and the more potentially subversive female masquerade is performed by the narcissistic, aggressive Miss Piggy. Conveniently for advertisers, the gendering of both female roles is tied directly to costuming (either as a functional difference that distinguishes Skeeter from her twin brother, or as a form of excess that characterizes the incomparable Piggy). Thus, costumes become interchangeable software, like Barbie's clothes, and another cultural code to be mastered by young spectators of both genders.

Entirely omitted from the opening title sequence is the third female character in the series: the headless Nanny. Hélène Cixous has described the figure of the decapitated female as a displacement of male castration anxiety onto the woman, particularly if she fails "to submit to masculinity as culturally ordered by the castration complex."[41] In this instance, the decapitated matriarch is stripped not only of her reproductive powers, but also of her racial specificity, though her "headlessness" evokes the Aunt Jemima–type maid from the old Tom and Jerry cartoons. Moreover, her consistent costuming in brightly colored striped stockings and baggy skirt and sweater vaguely suggests a subordinate class position—as a hired nanny rather than a biological granny. Despite her stabilizing presence, her ambiguity makes her parental authority easily appropriable by patriarchal characters featured in specific episodes.

The "Green Ranger" episode opens with live-action, black-and-white film footage of a cowboy standing on a rock and spying on the scene below (which we do not yet see), as a male offscreen voice says, "Hmm, looks like they got some trouble at the Rusty Spur." Then there is a cut to the object of the cowboy's gaze: a still drawing of a ranch in black-and-white, with horses and other important items highlighted in color. The camera cuts back to a closer shot of the cowboy, who whistles, and then to the new object of his gaze and address—his horse, which he jumps onto and rides out of the frame; we now hear the male voice-over sing the Range Rider's theme song: "Anytime, anywhere, when help is needed, I'll be there."

This segment introduces us not only to the iconography of the western genre (the setting, cowboy hero, horse, ethos, and lingo), but also to cinema's suturing structure of the gaze (where the possessor of the look is shown to be a controlling *man* of action, whereas the object is immobile, domesticated, subhuman). It also teaches us how to read pictures: how color and movement draw our eyes to the most important objects and actions, and how words help to anchor our interpretation of images. This process of reading images is made explicit in a later sequence, when Kermit announces that he doesn't know how to read and Skooter (as if coaching a Renaissance courtier) tells him: "You look at pictures, don't you? Everything's drawn out for you, nice and simple like. It's as simple as falling off a horse."

From this opening black-and-white film sequence we move to an animated version of the western (which mediates between the still drawing and the live-action footage). This

fluid movement between animation and live action also occurs in other TV series ("Super Mario Brothers," for instance) and is simulated by the animated performance of
PeeWee Herman. In each case the combination facilitates
the kind of transgressive identification across other borders
(of genre, generation, race, culture, and species) that was
demonstrated in the opening title sequence and that is the
specialty of the Muppet Babies and presumably of their pee-
wee spectators. In addition to the stable costs of animated
films (which now seem moderate, in contrast to the spiraling
costs of live-action movies), this postmodernist superfluidity
may help explain the "cartoonmania" of the late 1980s and
early 1990s, which some are calling the "new Golden Age" of
animation.[42]

In the Muppets' animated version of the western, we see
a green Kermit in cowboy outfit look into a saloon as a male
voice-over asks: "What in tarnation is going on in there?"
When the camera zooms in for a closer look, we see a ball,
a doll, and other toys that do *not* belong in the western genre
fly out of the saloon, and the voice-over quips hermeneuti-
cally: "Seems more like a question of what's coming out of
there." We follow Kermit's gaze and person into the saloon,
where the other Muppets are arguing as they play cards—
the two activities on which we segue (by means of a dissolve)
back into the nursery, where Kermit, wearing the same cowboy hat, sits before an animated blue TV set watching the
black-and-white live-action western, smiling with pleasure.
When the image cuts from Kermit watching TV to the object
of his gaze (the fictional world of the Roy Rogers western),
we are firmly sutured into identification with Kermit, from
whose point of view we have been watching the western and
whose fantasy recreation we soon will reenter.

Within the fictional world of the western, we see the same
live-action cowboy as before, but as he gets off his horse the

Inside his interactive fantasy (which was generated by watching TV), Kermit, a would-be western hero, learns how to mount a horse by watching his idol, the animated headless Range Rider. ©Henson Associates, Inc., 1987.

image changes to color animation (colored figures against a black-and-white background) and the blue frame of the TV set disappears. Once inside the saloon, an animated Range Rider (whose head we never see) mediates the argument among the Muppets, sounding suspiciously like Nanny: "What seems to be the problem here?" In case we've missed these visual and verbal associations with the matriarchal guardian, he adds: "Seems to me we're going to have to sort this one out with your nanny." This body shot of the heroic ranger draws our attention to his groin (rather than to his breasts, as in similar shots of Nanny). Although these headless body shots emphasize the signifiers that distinguish these two characters by gender, their formal similarity and the dialogue simultaneously identify them as members of the same paradigm: adult authorities. As in the Thorndyke experiment, the combination of similarities and differences leads the young subject to a more complex restructuring of cognitive categories.

At this point in the story, Kermit, who has been watching his hero in action, breaks out of the cinematic suture, proclaiming the "moral" to us in direct address: "The Range Rider doesn't like cheating!" On the surface, the blatant message of "The Green Ranger" concerns how to define the hero: as a *male* who instinctively helps others without self-consciousness or vanity. This is what Kermit learns from watching his favorite TV show, through both identification with and direct address from its hero. This moral would probably satisfy the 1990 Children's Television Act, which requires stations to serve "the educational and informational needs of children." Yet the episode teaches children many other things besides.

Perhaps most important, it explains how a genre (or TV series) can be replaced or recycled. Kermit is devastated when he discovers that this is the last episode of "The Range Rider" (which in turn is actually a composite of several classic westerns, including "Roy Rogers" and "The Lone Ranger"), for the program is being replaced by a soap opera called "As the Toast Burns." But we also learn from this episode that the iconography of the western still survives in television. The ongoing card game (which is carried over from the western fantasy to the nursery) is still found on the never-ending game show genre; the heroic horse is still featured on "Mister Ed" (a show that is brought to mind by the talking horses in Kermit's western fantasy and that is now in syndication for a new generation on the children's cable network, Nickelodeon); the desert landscape and chase narrative are still central in Road Runner cartoons (which are included in the newly resyndicated "Looney Tunes" on Nickelodeon, and which are evoked when Animal plays

"Road Crawler" as an homage to *his* favorite western hero);
the western clothes and jargon (if not the ethos) could at that
time still be found on prime-time soaps like "Dallas" (which
is parodied when Miss Piggy Sue Ewing plays "a modern
cowgirl with beauty, brains, and a great head for business
. . . just like on nighttime TV"); and the western is still a
popular generic motif in music videos (what Kermit calls
"songs written about stuff you never did").

This "lesson" in survival through compatibility is presented in the form of a catalogue (of various Muppets offering their own favorite version of the western genre and
their interactive notion of how to make Kermit a western
hero), which ruptures the coherence both of the narrative
line and of Kermit's unifying point of view. This catalogue
structure implies that, like any genre, the western is an open
system that allows room for both assimilation and accommodation, or in Fiske's terms, "a shifting provisional set of
characteristics which is modified as each new example is
produced."[43] It also evokes what Roland Barthes calls
"the extension of a paradigm onto the syntagmatic plane"—
a form of "semiotic transgression" around which "a great
number of creative phenomena are situated" (and perhaps
an elaborate version of what Victor was doing in his stroller
when he was stringing together all the names he knew *before*
he knew how to make a sentence).[44]

In trying to console Kermit for the loss of his hero (this
"reopening of the gap of desire" over which he has no control), Nanny explains TV's structural dynamics of reruns,
syndication, and cancellations: "Well that show's been running since I was a little girl. They probably ran out of episodes to rerun. . . . You can't ride the range forever, you
know . . . someone new always seems to come along." By
supporting Brooks's claim that extended serialization merely
postpones the inevitable end of all narrative, this speech im-

plicitly addresses the deeper fears that underlie Kermit's separation anxiety, for absence and economic obsolescence can easily be read as aging, castration, and death.[45]

The "Green Ranger"'s recuperative model is a generational discourse well suited to a successful prequel that reverses the aging process and that now, in its seventh season, is proliferating in syndication even as it anticipates the threat of cancellation. It presents a consumerist oedipal narrative that conflates several familiar paradigms: a young "green" hero displaces the retiring Range Rider the way sons traditionally displace fathers, patriarchs eventually displace nannies, new TV shows annually displace cancellations, and television historically displaces cinema. Thus, not only does this episode help children structure a diverse set of categories into complex hierarchic systems, but it also fosters a creative use of transmedia intertextuality to forestall obsolescence and death.

"The Lasagna Zone": The Anxiety of Endless Consumption

"Garfield and Friends" (broadcast October 7, 1989) also contains episodes that treat the anxiety of obsolescence—such as the opening segment, where Binky, "the most popular kid show host on TV," is suddenly replaced by "Bowling for Meatloaf" because it's "more intellectual than a clown show"; or the "Garfield quickie" that follows, where Booker reflexively asks: "What do you get when you cross a lasagna-loving cat with a bunch of zany farm animals?" and Sheldon replies: "You get picked up for another season!" Yet the "Lasagna Zone" episode is far more representative of the series as a whole, in that it focuses both on Garfield's constant alternation between extreme boredom and anxiety and on his dual consumerist obsessions with eating and watching TV ("Microwave lasagna and a TV set—what more could

anyone ask out of life!"). Beverle Houston theorizes the connection thus: "In its endless flow of text, [television] suggests
the first flow of nourishment in and from the mother's body,
evoking a moment when the emerging sexual drive is still
closely linked to—propped on—the life-and-death urgency
of the feeding instinct. . . . It is no accident that the main
textbook in American television studies is called *The Tube of
Plenty*."[46]

Like "Muppet Babies," "Garfield and Friends" constantly
alludes to other TV shows and movies, but it also focuses on
the tension TV creates in positioning its spectator both as a
unique individual with distinctive tastes, like Garfield (who is
thus distinguished from other feline media stars like Heathcliff, Tom, and Sylvester), and as part of a mass audience
with common appetites. This opposition is reflected in the
program's title, which pairs the unique Garfield with his
anonymous friends (who nevertheless include a creative pig
named Orson, a name that evokes the unique Orson Welles).
In the opening title sequence, where Garfield is featured as
star performer before a chorus line of "friends," he aggres-
sively confronts his viewer(s) in direct address: "Hey you
with the gum, I hope you've got enough for everybody.
[Then, in voice-over:] Here are some commercials, and then,
more of ME!" Like Miss Piggy, the narcissistic Garfield
flaunts his mask of uniqueness, as if to guard against the
postmodernist erasure of boundaries.

This opposition between the individual and the species is
intensified by the choice of an animal as protagonist. In his
discussion of totemism, Claude Lévi-Strauss quotes Henri
Bergson as saying:

> "To recognize a man means to distinguish him from other
> men; but to recognize an animal is normally to decide
> what species it belongs to. . . . An animal lacks concrete-
> ness and individuality, it appears essentially as a quality

and thus essentially as a class." It is this direct perception of the class, through the individuals, which characterizes the relation between man and the animal or plant, and it is this also which helps us to understand "this singular thing that is totemism."[47]

Our consumer culture has developed a new form of totemism in which we alleviate anxiety and gain an illusory sense of empowerment by bestowing our conception of human individuality onto animals—by giving homes to them (rather than to orphans or the homeless, who themselves are frequently treated as an animal species devoid of individuality); by letting them substitute for missing members of the dysfunctional family; by interpellating them as icons of uniqueness with unusual names like Heathcliff, Garfield, and Orson; and by transforming them into voracious consumers for whom we are always buying new products and with whom we therefore increasingly identify. This process is intensified when animals appear in the doubly domesticated realm of television, where they are often identified by excesses of human desire coded as "functional difference" (like Coyote's obsession with Road Runner, the Turtles' passion for pizza, and Garfield's lust for lasagna), particularly since desire—as opposed to instinctual drive—helps to distinguish humans from other animals. By identifying with such anthropomorphized creatures, spectators acknowledge their own slipperiness as signifiers—as both animal *and* human—while still affirming their "uniqueness" as the animal that possesses the functional difference of human subjectivity.

Identification with animals is especially appealing to kiddie spectators, who, like Animal, Cookie Monster, and Slimer, are still in the process of what Althusser calls "the long forced march which makes mammiferous larvae into

human children, *masculine or feminine subjects.*"[48] In one experimental study where ninety-six third-graders (with a median age of eight and a half) were asked to respond to two
stories, one with human characters, the other with animals,
74 percent of the children preferred the animal stories, perhaps because they were less emotionally involving and therefore aroused less anxiety about "good" versus "bad" (that is,
socially disapproved) behavior.[49] Even for us adults in our
congealed subject positions, identification with animals helps
us regain some of the lost fetal flexibility that is so central to
a popular toy genre like transformers, to the current craze
for Teenage Mutant Ninja Turtles, and to a character like
Sheldon in "Garfield and Friends," a chick only half out of
his shell. Instead of evoking a single individual or species,
these creatures suggest a system—of evolution, reproduction, biological development, acculturation, or transmedia
intertextuality. Identification with such creatures serves as
an entrance into these larger systems, where traditional
boundaries are ambiguous. In describing our age of cyborgs,
for example, Donna Haraway claims: "The dichotomies between mind and body, animal and human, organism and
machine, public and private, nature and culture, men and
women, primitive and civilized are all in question ideologically."[50]

Animal signifiers also help us to see beyond the waning
nuclear family and the growing influence of the single
mother by "naturalizing" alternative models for human
bonding. Consider the buddy relationship between Garfield
and his bachelor owner, John; the loyal pack or gang on
"Heathcliff," "California Raisins," and "Teenage Mutant
Ninja Turtles"; the multiracial nursery on "Muppet Babies"
(which reminds one of day care or a foster home); and the
integrated neighborhood on "Sesame Street," including numerous species that do not easily fit into a single nuclear

The little chick Booker and his brother Sheldon, who is a transformer only half out of his shell, star in the quickie that follows "The Lasagna Zone." ©1989 United Feature Syndicate.

family (an issue that is the thematic focus of the Muppet movie *Follow that Bird*).

These instabilities of the subject and its oscillations between pleasure and anxiety, passivity and control, are the focus of "The Lasagna Zone." In this clever parody of "The Twilight Zone," we are entreated (in direct address) by a cartoon Rod Serling to "consider, if you will, the case of one Garfield the cat," who, after dropping lasagna on his owner John's new satellite dish, "finds himself in the wrong end of that cathode ray tube." Garfield's entry into the TV screen parodies the celebrated dream sequence from *Sherlock Junior*, where Buster enters the fictional world of the movie he's projecting. In "The Lasagna Zone," this bizarre premise generates TV parodies within a film parody within a TV

An animated Rod Serling, as on-screen narrator, describes Garfield's entry into "The Lasagna Zone." ©1989 United Feature Syndicate.

parody—a multilayered structure like lasagna and like the TV supertext (which "Garfield and Friends" reproduces with its unpredictable segmentation).

Garfield's anxious entry into the "lasagna zone" (that intermediate space between reality and play) can also be read as a variant of the sleep-bargaining genre. After a dialogue with John, who urges him to go to bed and who warns against staying up all night, Garfield continues the dialogue with the TV set, in a liminal state between waking and sleep. Compulsively consuming more images and lasagna to keep himself awake and alive, he projects his bedtime fears of castration, obsolescence, and death onto the TV set and its stream of images, those transitional objects with which he totally identifies. Thus, not only does Garfield consume TV, but TV consumes Garfield. As Brooks predicts, the repetition compulsion seeks "to master the flood of stimuli," yet every switch of the dial brings a new short circuit, and every new fiction threatens him with another premature death.[51]

Once Garfield is inside the diegetic imaginary of television, with its paradoxical combination of endless flow and constant interruptions, the sequence focuses on the television medium itself. The source of the image is not the light beam from a nearby projector, as in cinema, but a signal that comes from outer space. (Earlier, when Garfield was adjusting the satellite dish, he remarked: "I want to watch a western . . . I'll point it toward Texas.") The segmentation of TV programming is intensified by the changing of channels through the remote control unit, which is manually operated by Garfield's canine friend, Odie, though Garfield tells him (through direct address) when to push the button.

John's satellite dish receives over one hundred channels and the pace of the channel switching keeps accelerating; there is no escape for Garfield. Each program proves more boring in its familiarity, and each new fictional world more threatening than the previous one. Garfield's coherence as a signifier is destabilized by a series of grotesque masquerades, and his assimilation and accommodation of the TV image are thrown off balance. Garfield becomes a black-and-white monster in a Frankenstein movie, a "colorized" football receiver chased by the opposing team, a macho cowboy in a card game (where the betting of two horses, two pianos, and two mayors recalls a surreal image from Buñuel's *Un Chien andalou*), a ballerina in pink tutu in *Swan Lake*, a survivor on a deserted island about to be eaten by a gorilla, a participant in the Binky clown show, and a bargain in a used-pet emporium ("Here's a 1978 wide-bodied pussy cat with all the standard equipment—whiskers, claws, fleas, the works!").

While Garfield's masquerade as a ballerina may seem to

When Garfield is inside the fictional world of television, he speaks to his privileged canine spectator Odie in direct address and at one point actually faces him, as in a mirror relation. ©1989 United Feature Syndicate.

undermine the rigid gender boundaries that are ordinarily reinforced in children's programming, this female role is presented as merely one of a series of monstrous or perilous subject positions to be rejected. Within this catalogue, the one identification that appropriately proves impossible to evade is that of a commodity—for after awakening and returning to his spectator position, Garfield retains the plaid muffler, one of the accessories he acquired (and one of the best visual puns) in the used-pet emporium.

Before Garfield can escape from the TV set, though, the remote control unit breaks down, as if revealing the falseness of its promise of empowerment. Consequently, Garfield is forced to keep running as the background images con-

Garfield's appearance as a ballerina in tutu with a chorus line is one of the rare moments when his gender is compromised. ©1989 United Feature Syndicate.

tinue to change at an accelerated pace, placing him on Gilligan's island, in a toothpaste commercial, the weather report, the home shopping channel, an episode of Booker and Sheldon from his own "Garfield and Friends," and so on. Finally Garfield shouts, "Odie, help, my vertical hold is slipping," and images roll by in an indecipherable blur, ending this montage sequence that so clearly extends the vertical axis of a paradigm onto the syntagmatic plane.

Such transformative intertextuality is even more intense in the fall 1990 season of "Garfield and Friends," which premiered on CBS in its new 9:00 A.M. time slot on Saturday, October 13, with a range of parodies including "The Hound of the Arbuckles," "Moby Duck," "Odilocks and the Three Cats," and "Quack to the Future." Even the toys advertised

Garfield's hand in a card game is called with two horses, two mayors, and a piano, an image that evokes one of the most subversive moments from Buñuel's surrealist classic *Un Chien andalou.* ©1989 United Feature Syndicate.

between these segments were promoted for their protean ability to be interactively transformed by young consumers—for instance, Barbies with "cool cut hair" that can be bobbed and restored, and "Baby Uh-Ohs" with changeable diapers. Appropriating the theme of active imagination from "Muppet Babies," the new Garfield show varies this credo by linking it primarily to books (rather than to television, movies, and toys), yet in fact the show demonstrates television's powers of home delivery not just for literature, but for movies and any other product.

The theme of creative imagination is explicitly introduced in the first episode, where, after a mysterious technical breakdown prevents Garfield from watching a Sherlock

Holmes movie on TV, John tells him that books (in this case, the Conan Doyle novel on which the movie was based) are better than TV or movie adaptations because they allow you to use your own imagination to fill in the pictures. Yet this statement also implies that (in contrast to books) the visual mass media provide a better analogue for the human imagination at work—an idea that is reinforced when Garfield, instead of finishing the Conan Doyle novel, chooses to go to sleep "and have a dream sequence." In simulating dreams (the ultimate adaptive medium that internalizes consumerist desire for external products), television displays its full transformative powers, both as a source for and adaptation of dreams and other audiovisual media. In Garfield's personal dream adaptation of "The Hound of the Baskervilles," he plays a brainy Dr. Watson to an obtuse Sherlock Holmes, whose character owes more to the animated TV star Inspector Gadget (whose cases are actually solved by his clever dog, Brain) than to Conan Doyle's brilliant detective. Garfield's master, John Arbuckles, plays the client in search of his lost dog, who sounds suspiciously like Odie. After Garfield awakens from his dream, he finds the missing Odie entangled in the TV antenna wire—thus solving two mysteries at once. But Master John, like Inspector Gadget, takes all the credit. Ironically, then, in adapting the classic literary source, both Garfield's dream and his TV series make us reread Sherlock Holmes through the filter of the parodic TV detective Inspector Gadget (not vice versa), for the subversive Garfield identifies with and therefore privileges the underdog/undercat/undermedium, which prove to be superior after all.

The theme of creative adaptation is also explicitly echoed in Orson's song celebrating imagination that introduces the second episode. In this parody of *Moby-Dick*, Orson the pig, playing Ishmael, alludes to other familiar whale tales like Pinocchio and the biblical story of Jonah. Yet instead of

sticking with the parody of the whale tale, the episode turns
into a series of imaginative generic transformations, determined not by TV channel switching as in "The Lasagna
Zone" or by movies, television, and toys as in "Muppet Babies," but by the books Orson *chooses* to read. By projecting
a series of adventure books onto the syntagmatic plane of
the narrative, the episode establishes a paradigm of monsters, whose members (whale, dinosaur, polar bear) all prove
highly adaptable to the television medium. But when Orson
tries to escape from this paradigm by picking a coloring
book as a "safe choice," he inadvertently positions coloriza-
tion as a monster, whose roots can be traced back to coloring
books and animation and which now threatens the status of
personal choice in movies and television. Thus the intertextual connections among commodities combined in a series
prove far more powerful than individual choice—a paradox
that is central to all commercial television and especially to
advertising discourse. This disavowal of the consumer's
choice is also echoed in Garfield's precommercial tag line,
where he threatens to kill the pet dog of any spectator who
dares switch to another channel.

Despite these overt threats to the viewer in the new season, nowhere is the anxiety of subject positioning more intense than in "The Lasagna Zone," for in that episode John's
repeated warning comes true: by obsessively watching too
much television, Garfield has become one himself—a malleable receiver, a consumable object of exchange with a broken "joystick." This spectator position, Beverle Houston has
persuasively argued, describes how the female subject has
been theorized under patriarchy (a perspective that makes
Garfield's female masquerade in pink tutu more resonant):

> The sliding from the imaginary pleasure of mastery
> through the passivity of being ourselves the object of di-

rect address and the seductive gaze; the attendant re-
duced stake in an apparent coherence of the signified; the
multiple identifications called for in the movement from
fiction to fiction and mode to mode; finally, the forced
acceptance of painful delay, deferral, waiting—these characteristics put all of television's spectators into the situation provided for the feminine in theories of subjectivity
as well as in her actual development and practice in patriarchy.

At times, Houston's analysis of television's unique form
of spectator positioning precisely defines Garfield's plight:
"Rather than suturing the viewer further into a visually re-
evoked dream of plenitude [as in cinema], it keeps the ego
at a near-panic level of activity, trying, virtually from moment to moment, to control the situation, trying to take some
satisfaction, to get some rest from the constant changes
. . . taking something like pleasure in the terror of desire
itself."[52]

Whereas Garfield's desperate situation results from his accidental entry into a warp zone, this "near-panic activity to
control constant changes" exactly describes how video games
ordinarily position the active player, for there "warp zones"
and multiple worlds are built into the system and "games
and their organization . . . forestall the frightening aspect of
playing."[53] Although Houston argues that "in its suggestion
of better possibilities, the channel changer reiterates lack
. . . [and] further weakens our chance of immersion,"[54] one
could also argue that the remote control box (or "joystick")
potentially performs a sex change on spectator positioning,[55] changing the TV viewer from a passive watcher to an
active player (or, put in Applebee's cognitive terms, from the
spectator mode that responds to the whole to the interactive
mode that responds piecemeal).

In this pivotal sequence, then, the meaning of "the twilight zone" is expanded beyond mere allusions to earlier texts like the Rod Serling sci-fi series and Buster Keaton's *Sherlock Junior* to include a rich intertextual prefiguring of the constructed "virtual reality" (VR) one finds in video games and in the latest interactive multimedia (the kinds of VR that were also prefigured in films as diverse as *Celine and Julie Go Boating* [1974], *Looker* [1981], and *Total Recall* [1990] and were greatly elaborated in William Gibson's popular novel *Neuromancer* [1984]). I am thinking, for example, of the Mandala System by Vivid Effects (on exhibit in Tech 2000), where an on-line video camera records the live performance of the player and the sounds that he or she makes on imaginary instruments, then instantly integrates them within a prerecorded music video now being displayed; or of VPL's electronic helmet, goggles, and glove that enable a player to perceive, enter, and manipulate a three-dimensional VR world of computer-generated images with a mere turn of the head or twist of the hand; or of the new systems, developed with funding from the telephone industry, where two players can meet and interact in a fantasy VR environment of their choice—a technology with great potential for transforming telephone sex. Originally developed for tank warfare and for repairing spaceships in outer space, these experiments with VR promise to expand the same illusory freedoms that early cinema granted its oppressed urban spectators, with similar ideological effects—at least as described by Walter Benjamin: "Our taverns and our metropolitan streets, our offices and furnished rooms, our railroad stations and our factories appeared to have us locked up hopelessly. Then came the film and burst this prison-world asunder by the dynamite of the tenth of a second, so that now, in the midst of its far-flung ruins and debris, we calmly and adventurously go traveling."[56]

Watching and Playing

Both "Garfield and Friends" and "Muppet Babies" (as well as other shows on Saturday morning television) create the impression that watching TV can be an empowering, humanizing interactive experience that combines watching with *playing*. As Lynn Spigel has observed, the interactive possibilities of television were recognized and promoted in the early days of television and also in early films about TV (such as *International House*, an amazing film from the 1930s in which W. C. Fields shoots boats on a TV screen, as if he were playing a Nintendo game).[57] This interactive illusion is strengthened on Saturday morning television by the recurring image that introduces commercial breaks in some of the CBS shows, where children are shown manipulating levers and power buttons in a studio control room as scenes from "Muppet Babies" and "PeeWee's Playhouse" appear on the monitors. While such strategies can be read as merely another example of television's deceptive manipulation of young consumers, one might also argue that they encourage the kind of negotiated readings posited by Stuart Hall and the Birmingham School, where generational subgroups actively appropriate images from mass culture.[58] Indeed, this latter approach is more compatible with Applebee's cognitive model of the "interactive participant role" than with the passive mode of spectatorship associated with psychoanalysis (especially with the Lacanian and Althusserian models).

In any event, this interactive spectatorship may lead children to prefer television over movies and to see it as more competitive (or compatible) with Nintendo's captivating home video games, where spectator positions are preprogrammed to make youngsters feel empowered through interactive play. In the world of Nintendo and its rival systems, players are almost invariably positioned as active, growing, male consumers—whether they identify with the voracious Pac-Man, who is empowered to devour more enemies whenever he munches fruity energizers; or with the humble Mario and Luigi, who are instantly transformed into giant Super Brothers whenever they consume a Super Mushroom; or with the mutated Ninja Turtles, whose martial arts powers are enhanced whenever they eat pizza. Firmly positioned within traditional patriarchy, all three options seem to be merely elaborate variations on Popeye's reliance on spinach, yet with the crucial supplement of interactivity and the corollary that consumption is a form of growth. These video games, I believe, are so compelling not only because they use oral symbolism and offer partial and multiple reinforcement (as some behaviorists have argued),[59] but also because they simulate the phallocentric humanist synthesis of assimilation and accommodation that Schiller ascribed to the "play drive":

> With the play drive . . . man will combine the greatest fullness of existence with the highest autonomy and freedom, and instead of losing himself to the world, will rather drive the latter into himself in all of its infinitude of phenomena, and subject it to the unity of his reason. . . . Man . . . is only fully a human being when he plays.[60]

3

The Nintendo Entertainment System: Game Boys, Super Brothers, and Wizards

> It is a whole new medium, an immensely powerful agent for the dissemination of culture. Eleven million of them have been sold in the United States in just over three years, and by the end of the year they are expected to be in nearly 20 million American homes. Nearly 50 million of the indispensable game cartridges are expected to be sold this year alone.
>
> "The Nintendo Kid," *Newsweek*

Although many American toy companies claim that home video games are just a passing fad, they are proving to be a new mass medium with extraordinary co-optive power.[1] The first successful totally electronic video game in the United States was Pong, a coin-operated entertainment designed in 1971 by three young electrical engineers working for Ampex—Nolan Bushnell, Ted Dabney, and Al Acorn. That same year they founded their own company, Atari, which released the game in 1974, selling over ten thousand units; another ninety thousand copies were sold by other manufacturers. Pong was soon installed not only next to pinball machines in the arcades, but also in airports, bus stations, cocktail lounges, laundromats, restaurants, and other public places across America. Because of its compactness, mobility, and decreasing price, by mid-decade Pong was gaining popularity in the home as well. In 1976, Bushnell, having already bought out his partners, sold Atari for some $30 million to Warner Communications, a conglomerate that could afford to invest in research and development and in more effective distribution for home use. The very next year the company introduced the first successful "programmatic" home video package, the Atari Video Computer System.[2]

Thus the stage was set for the first U.S. boom in home video games, which began in 1979 when Atari, Midway, Mattel, Cinematronics, Sega, and others introduced more challenging games, including some designed by Japanese companies like Namco and Taito. At this point Atari's main competition was Midway, the licensed producer for three of the Japanese-designed top-selling games in the United States: Pac-Man, Galaxian, and Space Invaders. By 1982, books were being published on video games, which boasted of the new medium's ability to surpass movies in the marketplace:

> In the United States alone, consumers spend more on video games—about $9 billion a year, including some $8 billion for coin-op and $1 billion for home games—than on any other form of entertainment, including movies and records. One game alone, Atari's awesome Asteroids, earned about as much just in its best year ($700–800 million) than the biggest money-making film of all time, *Gone With the Wind*, has made in four decades of screenings.[3]

Yet after a three-year boom, with annual sales peaking at $3 billion in 1982, a glut of poorly designed home video games flooded the American market, causing Atari to lose close to $600 million. The plunge, which began in 1983 and fell another 60 percent in 1984, bottomed out in 1985, when video games seemed totally dead.

Nintendo Enters the Market

The first year of the crash, 1983, was precisely when Nintendo, a hundred-year-old, Kyoto-based firm that formerly made playing cards, toys, and arcade games like Donkey Kong, introduced its Famicon, the Family Computer home video game system. Quickly beating out the rival systems of Sony and Matsushita in Japan, Nintendo sold 2.1 million units in the first eighteen months of sales and soon controlled 95 percent of that market, with a 33 percent penetration of all Japanese households. As Fumio Igarashi observed, "With an enormous base of 7 million users, the Famicon considerably outnumbers the 4 million personal computers in current use in Japan"—a fact with tremendous implications for other interactive tie-ins. Igarashi reports:

> According to Nintendo, not only securities firms providing stock market quotations but also banks, mail-order businesses, and various types of data-base firms can be expected to link up. Nippon Telegram and Telephone Corp. (NTT), which has seen rough going for its featured new media, the CAPTAIN videotex system, is said to be giving serious consideration to the possibility of linking it with the Famicon network.[4]

Such linkages are made possible by a forty-eight-pin computer cable connector that is on the bottom of every Nintendo set, hidden under an easily removable protective panel.

In 1985, when the U.S. home video game market was at its nadir, Nintendo came to America to revive the craze, spending $30 million in advertising to convince retailers and consumers that their games were different. The potential was still good, for a very high proportion of American youngsters had already played video games and so were prime targets for the revival.[5] Indeed, within five years Nintendo controlled 80 percent of the market, which was back up to the 1982 peak level of $3 billion (just for game cartridges), and a joint venture with AT&T was rumored (along similar lines as those proposed for NTT in Japan).[6] With total sales reaching $5 billion, Nintendo's U.S. income for 1989 represented a 40 percent increase over the previous year, giving the company a 20 percent share of the entire U.S. toy market.[7] By the end of 1989, one out of every five homes in the United States had a Nintendo system; by the end of 1990, the company estimated it would be in one out of three.[8]

The best article on Nintendo to date is by David Sheff, who visited both the home office in Kyoto and the American headquarters in Redmond, Washington, and who is one of the few persons to recognize the scope of their enterprise. Sheff claims that "Nintendo has its sights set on a goal that IBM and its rivals have long assumed would be theirs: the first universal home computer. . . . In American homes, by the end of this month [December 1990], there will be almost 30 million Nintendo sets, as compared with 6 million Macintoshes and 18 million IBM and IBM-compatible personal computers." Thanks to the computer cable connector at the bottom of every Nintendo set, moreover,

> Your video game system . . . can be connected to a modem, keyboard and auxiliary storage devices. . . . When connected to a 1½ inch thick gray box that hooks up to the connector (available early in 1991 and expected to cost roughly $150), the Nintendo system becomes a networking terminal. Plug in a phone line, and you'll be able to shop, call up movie reviews, buy pork bellies, do research, make airline reservations, order a pizza. The networks also will allow new forms of game play, such as competitions between Nintendo players throughout the country, and eventually the world.

According to Sheff, Fidelity Investments of Boston has already contracted with Nintendo to provide on-line stock quotations to subscribers, and AT&T is still negotiating; "but the biggest potential business for Nintendo is in multimedia entertainment systems."[9]

The keys to Nintendo's success in the video game market were superior technology and close control over compatible software. Costing somewhere between $80 and $150, their Famicon is a graphics computer with expanded memory and the same kind of eight-bit microprocessor that is used in the Apple IIC and Commodore 64 personal computers, by means of which it can produce excellent fast-moving graphics in fifty-two colors and "handle 64 times more data than earlier systems."[10] This little box, with dual control panels for two players, turns any television set into a machine that can accommodate nearly a hundred highly sophisticated games, which cost from $20 to $55 each and which work only on the Nintendo system.

Nintendo used the "razor marketing theory," introduced into the toy industry in 1959 by Mattel with the Barbie doll—a strategy of focusing on the development and sale of software (whether a game cartridge, a Barbie outfit, or a razor blade) that is compatible only with the company's unique hardware. Moreover, the hardware is purposely kept inexpensive to enhance marketability of the whole system and to generate continuing sales of new software to the same customers. The failure to provide enough software of high quality was what caused Sony to lose the VCR market to VHS (despite its technical inferiority to their own Betamax system) and what led to the 1983 crash of the U.S. home video game market. To avoid repeating this mistake, Nintendo licensed thirty-four independent companies to compete in developing game cartridges of high quality. Thus far the most successful game has been "Super Mario Brothers," which, introduced in September 1985, sold over 2.5 million copies in the first four months and which, like the movie *Star Wars*, has already generated two sequels ("Super Mario Brothers 2" and "3"). Most important, in the American market (but not the Japanese), Nintendo incorporated a patented proprietary chip into each of the games designed by its licensees: "The chip ensures that only cartridges authorized by Nintendo work on its machines. Nintendo also bars its licensees from marketing game titles for competing machines, such as those made by Atari and Tonka Corp.'s Sega Div."[11] This strategy was so successful that it was challenged in the courts. In December 1988, Tengen Inc., a former licensee based in California, brought an antitrust lawsuit against Nintendo, which responded with a countersuit for patent infringement. In 1989 Atari brought a $100 million lawsuit against Nintendo for preventing competitors from making game cartridges that would work on Nintendo's hardware.[12]

These suits have not slowed Nintendo's attempts to expand its share of the market. There are now two successful Super Mario Brothers TV shows: the original nationally syndicated program, "The Super Mario Brothers Super Show," which in Los Angeles is aired on the Fox channel on weekday mornings and on a cable station on weekday afternoons, and currently ranks fourth among nationally syndicated children's programs; and a new NBC Saturday morning show based on "Super Mario Brothers 3" called "Captain N—The Game Master," which is the top-rated Saturday morning cartoon for six- to eleven-year-olds. There is also a magazine called *Nintendo Power*, which provides tips on how to play the games and previews of new games to come, with a paid circulation of two million; a national game-counseling hot line, which handles fifty thousand calls a week; a network of over 250 fan clubs; and a dazzling array of product tie-ins, including a cereal, a fruit juice, and a line of boutique clothes in Toys 'R' Us, in addition to the usual toys, lunch boxes, and activity books. In 1989, Nintendo also introduced a miniaturized portable computer called "Game Boy," which can be hooked up to a friend's system for "a two-player challenge" and which has its own compatible games (the most successful so far being "Tetris" and "Super Mario Land"). Nintendo also offered consumers three super-interactive alternatives to the joystick: a Power Glove, from Mattel; U-Force, from Broderbund Software; and Nintendo's own Power Pad. Each costing around $70, these products promise not only to increase a player's control but also to enhance identification by putting the player "inside the action." Nintendo has also promised consumers a new "Super Computer" to compete with the sixteen-bit system already being marketed by Genesis. Sheff, who saw this Super Computer previewed in Kyoto with "Super Mario Brothers 4," reports:

> The game seems three-dimensional, and there appear to be four backgrounds moving at different speeds, with far more objects moving at once. . . . The picture itself is more movie-like, and the background sounds are stereophonic. . . . Instead of using four colors at a time out of a bank of 52, the system can select up to 256 out of 32,763 colors. It produces super-high resolution (twice that of other 16-bit systems). Built in is the ability to create, move and rotate very large, highly realistic characters. Like its more gently powered ancestor, it has the capability for future expansion built in—but this system is ready to hook up to CD and CD-ROM players, laser disc players, modems and other computer terminals.[13]

In developing and promoting such products, Nintendo confidently assures its consumers: "Now, you're playing with power!"

We're Off to See The Wizard

Like Saturday morning television, video games teach young players not that movies are obsolete, but that they have a new (though perhaps subordinate) role to play in the ever-expanding system of entertainment. A film like Universal's *The Wizard* (1989, the directorial feature debut of UCLA film school graduate Todd Holland) provides one concrete model of what that new role might be. Far from figuring video as a dangerous medium (like the films about television that Beverle Houston considered), *The Wizard* fetishizes video games—both their hard- and software. In fact, the film could be read as a ninety-minute commercial for the Nintendo system—especially for products like the Power Glove (which was a hot seller in the 1989 Christmas season) and "Super Mario Brothers 3" (the third game in the series). Although this game was not yet available in the stores when the film opened in December, by the end of 1990 it had sold seven million copies, which made it the top-selling video game in the U.S. market. Of course, this use of movies as a site of product placement and as an alternative advertising medium is not unique to *The Wizard* but is a common phenomenon of the 1980s—as has been persuasively argued by Mark Crispin Miller.[14] What *is* unique here is the centrality of the product promotion, as if designed to teach young spectators that such commercial intertextuality is the cultural norm.

A thirty-eight-page, full-color magazine *Pocket Power* (published by Nintendo and distributed free at the theater ticket counter) featured a cover story on *The Wizard* which makes it clear that these products are the real "stars" of the movie. In this advertising brochure thinly disguised as a magazine, one anonymous article tells us that writer-producer David Chisholm "compared the game to the sequel of a big movie hit. Fans are anxious for it ["Super Mario Brothers 3"] because it is even bigger and better than the original." The magazine also uses the young human stars to endorse the game products, telling us that "the cast were ecstatic knowing they were the first to get a glimpse of Super Mario Bros. 3." The strongest endorsement comes from the best-known child actor in the movie, Fred Savage (star of ABC's hit series "The Wonder Years," which *The Wizard*'s co-producer Ken Topolsky also produces): " 'I never played anything like it before,' said Fred. 'I can't wait until it comes out and I can buy it!' "[15]

Other video game magazines, such as the bimonthly *Game Player's Buyer's Guide to Nintendo Games*, make us see that cinema can play a vital role by preselling young players on stories that are being adapted by Nintendo—that is, by suturing them into identification with its superheroes. Currently, Nintendo has game versions of *Predator*, *Total Recall*, *Dick Tracy*, *Who Framed Roger Rabbit?*, *Top Gun*, *Platoon*, *Rambo*, *Robocop*, *The Karate Kid*, *Jaws*, *Goonies*, *Friday the 13th*, *Back to the Future*, and *Indiana Jones and the Temple of Doom*. When video game magazines describe these adaptations, they frequently warn players not to be disappointed by the differences (that is, by the loss of the unified imaginary). For example: "Like most Nintendo versions of hit movies, *Back to the Future* doesn't exactly duplicate the film, but rather strings together a series of arcade-type situations suggested by aspects of the story. You assume the role of Marty McFly, who is thrown back in time 30 years." Or: "Step into Arnold Schwarzenegger's shoes by assuming the role he played in the movie. . . . *Predator* manages to preserve something of the excitement of the movie, but the connection mainly serves as a pretext for a long series of challenges and difficulties in keeping with the Nintendo tradition."[16] Perhaps this structural difference is one reason why NES came out with an expensive suturing apparatus like the Power Glove and why Saturday morning TV shows like "Muppet Babies" and "Garfield and Friends" and movies like *The Wizard* so pointedly combine spectator and interactive modes of positioning: this combination is a powerful draw, particularly with young spectators who still must rely on equilibration to master more advanced stages of operational thought.

The Wizard also promotes Universal Studio's theme parks—both the one in Los Angeles, where a key sequence of the movie is set (and whose pitch is *"Live* the movies!"), and the one in Orlando, Florida, where (according to a commercial that accompanied the feature) you can "ride a movie." Movie tie-in rides are also in operation at Disney theme parks; one of the best is "Star Tours," designed by George Lucas, in which a small movie theater is transformed into a spaceship that simulates an interactive spectator position for 3-D action sequences from *Star Wars.*[17] Even the original Disneyland in Anaheim, California, will apparently be undergoing an expensive refurbishing over the next ten years, involving the addition of "a slew of rides based on hit movies—including *The Little Mermaid,* the *Indiana Jones* series and the upcoming *Dick Tracy,* giving Disneyland a more glitzy, Hollywood flavor." The plans include in addition a Muppets stage show and a 3-D Muppets movie, another 3-D movie developed by George Lucas, and a new theme area called Hollywoodland, which will feature simulacra of Hollywood Boulevard and the Hollywood sign, two new rides that "have patrons careening through scenes from the hit movie *Who Framed Roger Rabbit,*" and rides that have already proved successful in Florida—"the Great Movie Ride, which lets customers travel through recreations of movie classics, and Superstar TV, in which selected patrons will be able to appear in classic episodes of *I Love Lucy* or the *Johnny Carson Show.*"[18]

The Wizard helps us to see that most theme parks are structured like video games—with their time warps, their multiple worlds of adventure, and their conversion of passive cinematic spectatorship into interactive play.[19] For example, when the young stars go behind the scenes of one of Universal's biggest attractions, "King Kong" (whose namesake not only is a veteran of two hit movies but also is featured in the current hit video game "Rampage"), they discover a secret passage that lets them warp ahead to the video game playoffs.

Like *Star Wars* and the "creative play" on "Muppet Babies" and "Garfield and Friends," *The Wizard* recycles past successes from various film genres. Against a backstory from a family melodrama like *Ordinary People*, it presents a road movie that works like a kiddie version of *Rain Man* and *The Color of Money*, but with a hero who is like the pinball wizard in *Tommy* and with a climax that comes out of classic gunfighter movies like *Shane* and Sergio Leone's spaghetti westerns. (In fact, the little wizard looks amazingly like a young Clint Eastwood, and at one point we even hear the Ennio Morricone musical theme from that Italian trilogy.) Yet these veteran structures are updated—with topical problems like runaways and broken families, current fads like "Super Mario Brothers" and the Power Glove, and postmodernist urban structures like video arcades, theme parks, and the decentered city of Los Angeles. Even though this marketing combination seems to have been made in a computerized heaven, the movie was a box office flop (for reasons we will consider in chapter 4).

Set in Nevada, *The Wizard* tells the story of a white middle-class ten-year-old boy named Jimmy (Luke Edwards), who was traumatized by the accidental drowning of his twin sister, an event that broke up his family. When his mother and stepfather institutionalize him (because he keeps trying to

Jimmy, Corey, and Haley are set against the warp zones of "Super Mario Brothers."

Jimmy, Corey, and Haley on the road, in a kiddie version of *Rain Man* and *The Color of Money.* ©1989 Universal.

run away to California), Jimmy is sprung by his thirteen-year-old half-brother, Corey (Fred Savage), who lives with his older brother (played by Christian Slater, who at the time was not yet known as the James Dean of the 1990s) and their father (played by Beau Bridges, fresh from his success in *The Fabulous Baker Boys*, which, incidentally, also draws on his real-life membership in a famous family starring father and brothers). On the road, Corey discovers that silent Jimmy is a wizard at video games; he also meets a thirteen-year-old Reno girl named Haley (Jenny Lewis), who advises him to take the kid to Universal Studio's theme park in L.A., where he can win $50,000 in the National Video Game Championships. Meanwhile, father and older brother go after the kids, improving their skill at video games along the way and playing demolition derby with a hateful bounty hunter, hired by the mother and stepfather to track Jimmy. They all

Jimmy at the video game championship playoff with previews of "Super Mario Brothers 3." ©1989 Nintendo and Universal.

come together in L.A. for the championships, where the finalists are confronted with "Super Mario Brothers 3" (a game no one's yet seen) and where Jimmy beats an older arch rival, a video fanatic named Lucas (an homage to George). Lucas is the proud owner of a Power Glove, which enhances not only his eye-hand coordination, but also his stature as an antagonist, by linking him both with Jack Palance's evil black-gloved gunfighter in *Shane* (whom little Alan Ladd defeats under a young boy's admiring gaze) and with the equally villainous animated Glove in *Yellow Submarine* (who terrorizes the Beatles on behalf of the Blue Meanies).

Jimmy's victory makes everyone see that he's not a crazy who belongs in an institution. Rather, by mastering new products and the alternative spaces and warp zones of video games, he proves that he (like Marty McFly in the successful *Back to the Future* series—which is also structured like a video

The video game championships help to bring daddy home and to reunite the dysfunctional family. ©1989 Universal.

game) is the consumerist hero of the future. Yet Jimmy is determined to settle with the past (for the filmmakers are determined to go for a tearful melodramatic ending and leave no popular genre untapped): he insists on burying a little box he's been carrying (which contains fetishized photos of his dead twin sister and of his unified family) in that famous desert dinosaur park somewhere between L.A. and Vegas. This site not only enables the filmmakers to cash in on the dinosaur craze, but also implies that the unified nuclear family is an extinct species—though, like the dinosaur, one that can be exploited commercially as an emotionally charged imaginary.

The Oedipalization of Home Video Games

The marketing of video games seems to be geared primarily to those with, potentially, the most intense fear of castration:

to game-boys like Jimmy who are still immersed in the oedi-pal phase, to incipient teenage mutants like Corey who are about to undergo the catastrophic changes of adolescence, and to powerless men like their father who would like to punch out Mike Tyson (or the villainous bounty hunter) and become superheroes. *Newsweek* describes the Nintendo craze as

> a madness that—like most—strikes hardest at adolescent boys and their young brothers; 60 percent of Nintendo players are males between 8 and 15. . . . Nintendo speaks to something primal and powerful in their bloody-minded little psyches, the warrior instinct that in another culture would have sent them out on the hunt or on the warpath . . . . [Yet] in Japan—where Nintendo games are . . . even more popular than in America—the story themes tend to-ward cuteness over heroics and gore.[20]

The oedipalization of video games, then, was not inevita-ble, but was partly determined by cultural coding and mar-keting decisions tailored specifically to the United States.[21] Several empirical studies have confirmed this strong male orientation in video games both in the arcade and the home—a bias that has helped make the games more popular with boys than with girls.[22] When I asked children whether the "Teenage Mutant Ninja Turtles" arcade game seemed to be made for both boys and girls or just boys, one seven-year-old male youngster replied emphatically: "Just boys . . . because boys like Turtles and girls don't, girls won't play them, they like Barbies . . . disgusting!" In a survey of close to two thousand students, from kindergartners through col-lege freshmen, one of the most comprehensive studies of the 1980s showed that "as early as kindergarten, boys and girls viewed videogames as more appropriate to boys."[23]

These findings are disturbing, particularly if the cognitive value of video games is accepted. For example, although Patricia Marks Greenfield acknowledges that gender may be a causal factor in video game skill (particularly after the age of ten or eleven, when boys generally demonstrate greater ability at iconic spatial representations than girls), she cites studies which demonstrate that video games can help girls catch up with boys in visual-spatial skills or help boys pull even farther ahead.[24] More significantly, she emphasizes the social danger of targeting these games exclusively to boys, since video entertainment is becoming a key "entry point into the world of computers for most children." Fearing that this imbalance "might contribute to the gendering of computers," she concludes: "There is an urgent need for widely available video games that make as firm contact with the fantasy life of the typical girl as with that of the typical boy."[25]

The same concern should also be extended to issues of race and class, for video games (and the movies about them, whose positive human characters are practically all Caucasian) seem targeted primarily for a white middle-class audience, who are also the primary market for personal computers. Although some might claim that video games, like "Sesame Street," are accessible to all classes (particularly in the arcade) and therefore help the economically disadvantaged youngster overcome the inequities of class difference, in practice they might actually increase the gap, for only those who can afford the Nintendo home system and its pricey software gain the full benefit of early training in computer confidence.

The fact that video games were introduced into the United States at a time when fewer households included a father may have contributed to their oedipalization. Video games provide an appealing surrogate against which a son can test his powers—not only do they let the game-boy defeat the missing patriarch, but they might even lure him back home for the playoffs (which is precisely the scenario in *The Wizard*). As one empirical study of twenty American families with new home video game sets suggests, "Video games have brought families together for shared play and interaction that they have not experienced since the appearance of TV."[26] Yet since the games are presently oriented almost exclusively toward male interests, they probably have the greatest effect on relations between fathers and sons.

Even in those homes (such as my own) where the father is present and nurturing, the games can help boys deal with their rebellious anger against patriarchal authority. For example, when I asked my son, Victor, whether he ever dreamed about video games, he told me that the previous night he had dreamed that he was sad because his daddy spanked him and he was crying, so he became Raphael (the most emotional and rebellious of the four Teenage Mutant Ninja Turtles) and went inside the video game (the way Garfield had gone inside the TV set) to save the other Turtles, who were being held captive by the villainous patriarch, Shredder. Even David Sheff, although he does not deal satisfactorily with the issue of gender, acknowledges and playfully exaggerates the oedipal rivalry in the Nintendo culture, advising fathers to use tips from Nintendo game master Howard Phillips "to humiliate our kids at Super Mario Brothers 3. . . . Enjoy your revenge. (Of course, you could also share these secrets with the kids, winning their respect forever.). . . [Or] you could blow your kid away first, then tell him how to do it himself. That would be satisfying, wouldn't it?"[27]

The oedipal dimension of video games accounts for certain choices within its system of intertextuality. One finds a heavy reliance on action genres (the epic, romance quest, and western) in which male heroes have traditionally grown into manhood and replaced father figures, and on myths (like David and Goliath, Jack and the Beanstalk, and its modern variant, *The Karate Kid*) in which little guys beat giants. This oedipal scenario also helps to explain the extraordinary appeal of the comedy *Home Alone* (the number one box office movie hit during the 1990 Christmas season), where a second-grader successfully defends his home against two adult burglars, maiming and burning them in the process (a plot that undoubtedly will soon be adapted to an equally successful video game). Among Nintendo's current hits, this oedipal pattern is most blatant in "Mike Tyson's Punch-out," where players identify with a tiny boxer named Little Mac-Little who challenges increasingly tougher opponents until he finally takes on Tyson; but it is also present in romances like "The Adventure of Link," where players identify with a short sixteen-year-old boy chosen to free the sleeping Princess Zelda and prevent the return of the powerful magician Ganon. Even the Super Mario Brothers were based on a *little* character from Nintendo's arcade game "Donkey Kong," whom its designer, Shigeru Miyamoto, describes as "a short, indomitable, mustached man in a red cap, . . . a kind of Everyman who rises to heroism in the face of adversity" and whose "insignificance . . . makes him so appealing."[28]

As in most oedipal narratives, women are usually marginal in video games, both as characters and as players. Yet according to Howard W. Moore, executive vice-president of Toys 'R' Us (the world's largest toy retailer and one of Nintendo's primary U.S. distributors), "[Nintendo] went from a core audience of boys from 7 to 14 and expanded in three directions: pre-schoolers, older adults, and girls."[29] By the end of 1990, there were media reports of two-year-old prodigies succeeding at video games, and Nintendo claimed that close to 50 percent of its players were over eighteen and 36 percent were female. Nintendo game master Howard Phil-

lips observed: "Video games are no longer considered toys.
... They are now an acceptable form of interactive entertainment for people of both sexes and of all ages."[30] Yet the
narrative content of the games still reveals a decidedly male
orientation.

Although a female does participate in the championship
playoffs in *The Wizard*, her powers clearly do not measure up
to those of the male players. Not only is she the first finalist
to be eliminated, but she is also ridiculed for her homeliness.
Like Jimmy's dead twin sister, the androgynous female is
quickly rejected as a site of identification for female spectators. Instead girls are led to identify with Corey's cute love
interest, Haley, who is supposedly a video game hustler but
is never seen playing the machines. Finding power in her
desirability to men, she·brags that she inherited her "great
legs" from her runaway showgirl mother and gamely foils
the villainous detective by falsely claiming that he touched
her breast.

In most video games, females are still figured as objects of
the male quest—the various sleeping beauties who wait to be
rescued by male winners. Even the few exceptions reinforce
gender stereotypes. For example, the arcade game "Ms. Pac-
Man" offers its female players little more than an oxymo-
ronic title and female masquerade; the voracious dot is
merely dressed up in traditional pink gender coding, long
eyelashes, and lipstick to create Pac-Man's female twin.

Some of the games structured as ongoing serial combat,
like "Renegade" and the popular "Double Dragon," include
formidable female opponents, but these characters are rarely as strong as their male counterparts. The latter game, in
which two players can fight each other, gives the option of
male and female subject positions—though both opponents
must identify with the same gender, if not necessarily the
same race (for example, one might have a white Linda in

blue against a white Linda in red, or a white Will in blue against a brown Will in white). The structuring of these options can be read in a variety of ways: not only as discouraging violence against women while reinforcing racial conflict, but also as acknowledging the equality of races rather than genders.

Another exception is "Metroid," which Sheff touts highly because the heroic Samus turns out to be a female in warrior drag—another androgynous twin. In this game, moreover, the main object of Samus's quest is to find and destroy the Mother Brain, a plot highly reminiscent of the movie *Aliens.* While some female players may feel more comfortable playing this game because of its female hero, they are nevertheless positioned to reject the monstrous maternal and to model themselves after the father—which can hardly be reassuring to feminists.

Cleverly designed for the expanded audience, "Super Mario Brothers 2" gives its players four options for identification: for the core audience of males between seven and fifteen, there are Mario and Luigi, veterans of the original "Super Mario Brothers," who have the greatest jumping power; for preschoolers, there's Toad, the tiniest figure, who has the least jumping power but the greatest carrying power; and for females, there's Princess Toadstool, who, despite her inferior jumping and carrying power, has the unique ability of floating for 1.5 seconds—a functional difference that frequently leads my son and his buddies to choose her over the others, even at the risk of transgender identification. Still, as in *The Wizard,* "Muppet Babies," and *Star Wars,* the female roles do not go beyond the conventional stereotypes of the female twin or, in this case, the spunky princess.

The expansion of the target audience is not continued, let alone furthered, in "Super Mario Brothers 3," the game featured in *The Wizard*. Here players can identify only with Mario, who may undergo many magical transformations, but none that transgresses boundaries of gender. Instead the game emphasizes animal masquerade as a reversible means of subject formation and phallic empowerment: the kings are transformed into animals when their phallic wands are stolen by the seven children of the patriarchal villain, Bowser, and Mario must disguise himself as a jumping frog, a flying racoon, or a tanooki (a badger who turns into an invincible statue) to win back the wands and restore the human kings to power. The action thus focuses on conflicts between fathers and sons, with little Toad and the Princess merely cheering Mario on.

The Super Mario Brothers on Television

Interestingly, the TV adaptations of this game seem to follow "Super Mario Brothers 2" in expanding the potential audience across borders of gender, age, and (even) race—perhaps because in this more established medium these issues are more closely monitored by parents groups and semiofficial agencies. In the most recent episode I saw of the syndicated "Super Mario Brothers Super Show" (aired on the Fox network at 6:30 A.M. on the weekday of October 11, 1990), the protagonists were all four characters from "Super Mario Brothers 2"—not only Mario and Luigi, but also little Toadstool and the Princess—and they were fighting against the villainous turtle Koopas from the game worlds of "Super Mario Brothers 1" and "3." Thus, there were more choices for spectator identification, and any child who owned or had played any one of the three games in the series would be sure to find several familiar characters in the animated TV cartoon. Moreover, unlike other television adaptations of video games I have seen, this series relies heavily on the soundtrack for its effects, using not only the distinctive music from the video games (which every parent with a Nintendo system would instantly recognize), but also, in this particular episode, Ray Charles's classic version of "Hit the Road, Jack." This song identifies the road movie genre to which this game narrative belongs (and that extends all the way back to epics like the *Odyssey* and *Gilgamesh*); it also reaches out specifically to a black audience, especially since the song proves to be a powerful weapon against the enemy.

As if to extend its intertextuality and broaden its appeal further, the cartoon appears in a show called "Club Mario" (perhaps anticipating yuppie pleasures to come at Club Med), which is cohosted by two dancing, rapping teens (one black, one white, and both evocative of MTV VJ's) who zap from one Nintendo game adaptation to another (for example, from "Super Mario Brothers" to "The Legend of Zelda"). The images are presented on a huge screen (which doubles as TV monitor and video game screen, as in the Nintendo system), and the screen in turn is positioned against an abstract background marked with colorful animated squiggles. Like the inset TV screens in the "Green Ranger" and "Lasagna Zone" episodes from "Muppet Babies" and "Garfield and Friends," this accentuated framing marks both the total constructedness of this "intermediate space of play" and the usefulness of postmodernist intertextuality in mapping and negotiating the terrain.

On the new NBC series "Captain N—The Game Master," the animated heroes are limited to Mario and Luigi, and the villains, spatial configurations, and music all come from "Super Mario Brothers 3." Yet an attempt is still made to reach out to a larger audience by positioning the world of the video game within other, more familiar contexts. Although the episodes usually begin in the ordinary world of animation (in the program that aired on October 20, 1990, for instance, the setting was identified as Brooklyn and called "the real world"), the heroes find a warp zone that enables them to enter the spatial world of the video game. This double reality is then put within a third spatial realm: a frame where a teenager (the spectator-player in the text) plays the video game in his living room and then enters the TV set (again like Garfield in "The Lasagna Zone"), which is *his* entry into the warp zone. This three-tiered structure literally dramatizes Greenfield's point that "video games build upon and utilize the visual-spatial skills developed by television."[31] Moreover, it demonstrates to all consumers that an ordinary TV set can become a point of entry into video games, into the super fantasy world of the Mario Brothers, and into the whole Nintendo Entertainment System. It will be interesting to see whether these complex spatial configurations and expansions of target audience are carried over into the Super Mario Brothers movies, the first of which is scheduled to be released by Disney later this year.

Short Circuits and Premature Deaths

Most video games also offer one of the traditional appeals of comedy: protean transformation and resilience as a means of overcoming death. These games position players in ongoing serial combat where they must constantly fight off death and try to acquire new powers that will periodically grant them more lives. In part, then, these games are modeled on life extension—increasing the length of a turn or, in consumerist terms, getting more for your quarter. As in Saturday morning television cartoons, the repetitive, segmented, serial nature of the narrative leads to a disavowal of obsolescence, castration, and death. This structure is apparent not only in games designed in the genre of romance, like the "Super Mario Brothers" and "Zelda" series, or of nonstop warfare, like "Teenage Mutant Ninja Turtles," "Contra," "Double Dragon," and "Renegade," but also in sporting games like "Skate or Die."

The narrative model proposed by Peter Brooks (based on the "master plot" from Freud's *Beyond the Pleasure Principle*) is thus relevant to video games as well. Before and after the game, when the screen is blank and the power turned off, the game world is literally in a state of quiescence, nonnarratability, and death. Between these two steady states, the players are constantly threatened by short circuiting and premature deaths (which indeed are called "deaths"), while their compulsive repetitions are rewarded (for this is the only means of advancing in the game). Spatialized as detours and warp zones, the narrative elaborations serve to postpone and intensify the final gratification: mastering the game. After experiencing the closure of the endgame, the player frequently abandons the cassette and turns to another narrative for new postponements. Yet the hyperserialization both within and across these road games enables the play to be extended over weeks, months, and even years, as players improve their skill and advance from one "level" or "world" or "game" to another. Such a structure is bound to lead to cognitive development, for, like drinking milk or doing daily aerobics, the compulsive consumption of video games appears to accelerate growth.

A Cognitive Perspective on Video Games and Their Commodification

In playing video games where constant practice is essential, little kids like Jimmy (in *The Wizard*) or my son, Victor, frequently triumph over older siblings and parents—partly because they have more play time, partly because they are less fearful of making a mistake when others are watching,[32] but primarily because they are experiencing a major break-through in cognitive development. Although a few research-ers have reported that video games can trigger seizures in epileptic children (a finding that was greatly exaggerated in the mass media), most empirical studies have demonstrated that the games have considerable educational and therapeu-tic value for a diverse range of groups—including adoles-cents, athletes, would-be pilots, the elderly in old-age homes, cancer patients undergoing chemotherapy, stroke victims, quadriplegics, and young children suffering from palsy, brain damage, and Down's syndrome. Moreover, most re-searchers agree that youngsters seem to be the most skillful players. Patricia Marks Greenfield, who has written one of the best books on the subject, acknowledges:

> When I played Pac-Man for the first time, I had watched it played quite a number of times, and I assumed I would be able to play it myself, even if not with consummate skill. But when I started, I found I could not even distinguish Pac-Man, whom I was supposed to control, from the other blobs on the screen! A little girl of about five had to ex-plain the game to me. . . . I think that, as a person social-ized into the world of static visual information, I made the unconscious assumption that Pac-Man would not change visual form. My hypothesis is that children socialized with television and film are more used to dealing with dynamic visual change and are less likely to make such a limiting assumption.[33]

This generational gap is the central irony in the popular "Inspector Gadget" TV series (currently in syndication on Nickelodeon): although the adult inspector (like a parodic James Bond) is equipped with all the latest macho hardware, the true winning player in this game of spies is his little niece Penny (together with her underdog, Brain), largely because of her superior skill with computers. It is probably difficult for most adults to learn how to play these computer video games rapidly for the same reason that it is difficult for us to learn a second language: because our deep structure for language acquisition and for the interlocking systems of various modes of representation is already fixed.[34] Young children, in contrast, are still in the process of creating the necessary circuitry for this new restructuring. While there are video game prodigies as young as two years old (like little Adam Knoedler, who recently received so much media attention), seven to twelve seems to be an optimum age for players.

Piaget's theory of genetic epistemology helps to explain why the core group for video games starts around age seven or eight: namely, "it is precisely at this age that we can place the first period of reflection and logical unification, as well as the first attempts to avoid contradiction."[35] According to Piaget, at this stage the child begins to organize "operational groupings of thought concerning objects that can be manipulated or known through the senses"—a patterning on which the structure of memory is partly dependent.[36] The seven-year-old child also begins to perceive the social need to verify thought, and as a consequence thinking becomes less egocentric and more subject to logical argument and proof. The child's thinking becomes capable of "transitive combinativity, reversibility, associativity and identity . . . all of which characterize logical 'groupings' or arithmetical 'groups.' "[37] Becoming capable of various forms of conservation and categorization, the child is freed from total dependence on immediate perceptions and is able mentally to move fluidly backward and forward in space and time. Perhaps most important for video games, "Before 7 years, one can find only reproductive images, and all of them are quite static. . . . After 7 to 8 years, anticipatory images appear, but they are not only applied to new combinations. They also seem to be necessary for the representation of any transformation even if it is known, as if such representations always entailed a new anticipation."[38]

Significantly, in Catholicism seven is also the age of First Communion, when the child learns the catechism and Ten Commandments and becomes accountable for his or her sins. It is as if this cognitive ability to imagine and anticipate hell's punishments is essential to the subject's candidacy for both salvation and eternal damnation. Seven is also the precise age in the original "Teenage Mutant Ninja Turtles" comic book when Oroku Saki, traumatized by his brother's murder, begins to be transformed into the villainous Shredder. In both moral systems, then, at seven one apparently develops the ability to make an informed moral choice.

Applebee discusses the impact of this cognitive shift on the child's concept of story in some depth; nevertheless, he acknowledges a major omission in his study: he does not look at "the *limits* of a child's comprehension and understanding at each age, to find either the level at which frustration ensues, or the performance that can be obtained when the child works in conjunction with a teacher or peer," reminding us that "effective teaching is aimed not so much at the ripe as at the ripening functions."[39]

This ripening process is precisely the area explored by Vygotsky, who departs from Piaget's model of genetic epistemology by introducing a "zone of proximal development," which expands the role of learning in child development and leads him to conclude that "the only 'good learning' is that which is in advance of development." Vygotsky claims that "play creates a zone of proximal development of the child. In play a child always behaves beyond his average age, above his daily behavior; in play it is as though he were a head taller than himself. As in the focus of a magnifying

glass, play contains all developmental tendencies in a con-
densed form and is itself a major source of development."
Thus, he maintains, "the state of a child's mental development can be determined only by clarifying its two levels[:]
... the actual development level as determined by independent problem solving and the level of potential development
as determined through problem solving under adult guidance or in collaboration with more capable peers."[40]

The playing of video games, I suggest, provides a similar
kind of guidance, accelerating the child's movement between
these two levels—that is, across the "zone of proximal development." Critics sometimes charge that video games isolate children from their peers; yet when my son and one or
two friends (or his father) play video games together, the
players often help each other in just this way. Instead of
choosing to play against each other or just to take turns, they
may agree to let the one who is most advanced in a particular game do most of the playing so the others can watch
and learn new moves, or else they will let the novice do most
of the playing while the more advanced player coaches.

Perhaps even more importantly, as investigators such as
Greenfield have noted, the very structure of video games
contributes to this ripening process as well—by fostering
equilibration, by demanding shifting identifications with a
wide range of subjects and objects, by forcing children to use
the inductive process, by providing an immediate means of
verifying hypotheses, by requiring sensorimotor eye-hand
coordination and processing of visual information from multiple perspectives, and by developing skills in iconic-spatial
representation once restricted to elite technical occupations
(such as pilots and engineers).[41] In fact, I have noticed that
the better Victor becomes at video games, the more interested and skillful he is at drawing cartoons. As Papert observes, "Learning a physical skill has much in common with

building a scientific theory," and this formal analogy is particularly apparent when the skill is playing video games.[42] Piaget claims that the "actualization" of cognitive development possibilities depends on exercise (that is, self-regulated hands-on experience), interactive problem solving, and the influence of the social environment[43]—a combination that is offered by video games, particularly when validated by a wider superentertainment system built on transmedia intertextuality. His model, however, does not acknowledge the possibility of acceleration, as does Vygotsky's.

Vygotsky's concept of cognitive acceleration through play has been applied to Emily's presleep monologues by Dore (as seen in chapter 1), to television and video games by Greenfield and associates (who argue that both media "augment" skill "in reading visual images as representations of three-dimensional space"),[44] and to computers by Papert. Papert rejects Piaget's assumption about the invariability of cognitive development (that the "concrete operations" of conservation are *always* acquired around age seven and the "formal operations" of combinatorial tasks around age eleven or twelve), but claims: "If computers and programming become a part of the daily life of children, the conservation-combinatorial gap will surely close and could conceivably be reversed: Children may learn to be systematic before they learn to be quantitative!" Admitting that he is "essentially optimistic—some might even say utopian—about the effect of computers on society," Papert unfortunately extends this optimism even to the consumerist aspects of our developing computer culture (revealing an unlimited trust in the marketplace):

Increasingly, the computers of the very near future will be the private property of individuals, and this will gradually return to the individual the power to determine patterns of education. Education will become more of a private act, and people with good ideas, different ideas, exciting ideas will no longer be faced with a dilemma where they either have to "sell" their ideas to a conservative bureaucracy or shelve them. They will be able to offer them in an open marketplace directly to consumers.[45]

Nevertheless, despite (or perhaps partly because of) this utopian view of consumerism, Nintendo recently gave Papert's MIT laboratory a $3 million grant to explore the educational value of video games.[46]

Although Greenfield agrees with Papert about the transformative potential of computers, arguing that "video games are the first example of a computer technology that is having a socializing effect on the next generation on a mass scale, and even on a world-wide basis," she does not share his optimism about their consumerist context.[47] Even if video games and television/toy tie-ins help to accelerate cognitive development at certain ages (as her studies have shown), the way they are marketed can still have questionable effects. As she observes in her analysis of tie-ins, for example:

> All indications from previous research are that product-based television is a potent selling tool to a particularly vulnerable audience . . . [which] applies, in principle, as much to *Sesame Street* as it does to *Smurfs* and *Teenage Mutant Ninja Turtles*. Although one program is on public television and has an overt educational purpose, while the others are on commercial television and have the overt goal of entertaining, both seem, for better or for worse, to be socializing very young children to participate in a commercial, consumer-oriented society.[48]

Clearly, the acceleration of the child's ripening process has implications for marketing, for with a wider age range certain entertainment products can become more versatile.

Based on the expanding appeal of video games (which "are more sophisticated than male action figures or trucks, but are enjoyed by children as well as teens"), for instance, Standard and Poor advises toy manufacturers: "There is no longer any reason why certain manufacturers should limit themselves to rigidly defined markets such as the under-12 segment or adult novelty products and board games. A blurring of the distinctions among children, teens, and young adults has taken place as children become increasingly more sophisticated and mature in their choice of entertainment."[49] This kind of statement lends support to Susan Willis's argument that "commodities offer the young child a means to articulate his or her notions about the transition to adolescence."[50] Nintendo seems to be well aware of this dynamic, which is why they are developing games and marketing strategies for adults (who now represent almost 50 percent of the market), to make sure that players do not outgrow the games. According to Peter Main, Nintendo's vice-president in charge of marketing: "Our object from Day One was to move beyond the narrow base of the historic video game user—boys 8 to 13—because the 13-year old boy will turn 14 years old, and by that very chemistry passes from our grip."[51]

These marketing implications should not keep us from acknowledging the educational value of video games, however. In contrast to C. Everett Koop, who as U.S. surgeon general attacked video games for creating "aberrations in childhood behavior," the majority of the psychological studies and both of the books published thus far on this subject (Greenfield's *Mind and Media* and Loftus and Loftus's *Mind at Play*) deny that the games are addictive or that they foster aggression and social isolation. As Greenfield observes of the violent content, "The impact of playing a violent video game alone is exactly the same as watching a violent cartoon."[52]

Instead, most of the research emphasizes the value of the games for cognitive development and their potential usefulness for psychological testing.[53]

Most parents who buy a Nintendo system probably assume (or at least hope) that the games will improve their children's visual memory and eye-hand coordination and teach them how to use time and concentration to master a skill. Just as I have linked Victor's video game playing to his passion for drawing cartoons, other parents probably tell themselves that their children will use these cognitive abilities later in playing a musical instrument, excelling in a sport, or succeeding academically. But it is equally possible that these games will lead youngsters to lose sight of certain important distinctions, by reconceptualizing those other activities as merely part of the same superentertainment system—concluding, for instance, that athletes who win gold medals in the Olympics, or writers and scientists who win the Nobel Prize, are performing tasks that are no more important or difficult than winning at video games—a perspective compatible with the postmodernist erasure of boundaries between high art and mass culture.

In this chapter I have argued that, because of the ideological assumptions implicit in the software and marketing of cartridges, video games not only accelerate cognitive development but at the same time encourage an early accommodation to consumerist values and masculine dominance. A similar dual effect is achieved in the Teenage Mutant Ninja Turtle myth, where "glowing ooze" accelerates the physical growth and cognitive development of Splinter the rat and the four baby Turtles and simultaneously bonds them as father and sons, master and disciples, in a male clan of pizza-loving ninjas.

In the case of the superentertainment system, transmedia intertextuality works to position consumers as powerful players while disavowing commercial manipulation. It levels all ideological conflict within the single narrative of an all-encompassing game. And it valorizes superprotean flexibility as a substitute for the imaginary uniqueness of the unified subject. Nowhere are these dynamics more powerfully demonstrated than in the system of intertextuality constructed around those ultimate sliding signifiers, Teenage Mutant Ninja Turtles—a commercial network that rivals the popularity even of the Nintendo Entertainment System. According to Standard and Poor's 1989 survey of the toy industry, the two biggest hits that Christmas were Nintendo home video games and the plastic Turtle figures produced by Playmates (a success that was repeated in the 1990 Christmas season). Their merger in a video game was bound to be a hot seller; far less certain was which system would assimilate the other.

4

Teenage Mutant Ninja Turtles:
The Supersystem and the Video Game
Movie Genre

There's never been a success story quite like it in the
annals of comic book fandom. About four years ago,
Peter Laird and Kevin Eastman . . . sketched out four of
the most unlikely heroes in the history of comics. Take a
quartet of genetically altered turtles, name them after
Italian Renaissance artists, add a diet of pizza, throw in
a little martial arts action, and you've got *Teenage Mutant
Ninja Turtles.*

The first *TMNT* comic book [1984] was in grungy
black and white and was limited to a press of two or
three thousand copies. . . . Now *TMNT* are part of a
larger industry. There are t-shirts, toy action figures,
Saturday morning cartoons . . . the list goes on. Could
a Nintendo game be far behind? You bet your
nunchucks."

*Game Player's Buyer's Guide
to Nintendo Games* 2, no. 5 (1989)

Since this minihistory was written, not only have two successful TMNT Nintendo home video games and a spinoff
for Game Boy called "The Fall of the Foot Clan" been developed, but also a popular arcade game, a blockbuster
movie with a sequel, a top-selling original soundtrack album,
a rock group that performs live in concerts, a network television series (also in syndication), a collection of popular

home videos of both the live-action movie and the animated TV series, a new syndicated comic strip by Eastman and Laird, a dramatic increase in kiddie enrollments in martial arts classes (one ad in the Los Angeles yellow pages reads, "Tiny Tot Ninja Turtle classes—3 years & up"), and a dazzling proliferation of over one thousand Turtle products— all of which has generated a media blitz on "Turtlemania." The December 1989 issue of *Playthings* reports that

> in 1987, despite a downturn in the sales of boys' action figures, Playmates introduced Teenage Mutant Ninja Turtles. Twenty-three million dollars worth of action figures and $20 million worth of Turtle-related products have been sold since June 1988. Aside from action figures, Playmates offers dozens of Turtle playsets and accessories, including the popular Turtle Party Wagon and Turtle Blimp, and even cuddly Turtle plush. By the end of the year, 55 licensed manufacturers will have produced a wide variety of "turtilized" products, from lunch boxes and bubble bath to a talking Turtle toothbrush.[1]

By the 1990 Christmas season forty-four of these Playmates TMNT action figures were on the market—most of which were sold out in Toys 'R' Us and other popular retail outlets, despite the overall decline in Christmas toy sales. Such statistics clearly demonstrate that these amphibious media stars now form the nucleus of a commercial supersystem.

Growing into a Supersystem

A supersystem is a network of intertextuality constructed around a figure or group of figures from pop culture who are either fictional (like TMNT, the characters from *Star Wars*, the Super Mario Brothers, the Simpsons, the Muppets, Batman, and Dick Tracy) or "real" (like PeeWee Herman, Elvis Presley, Marilyn Monroe, Madonna, Michael Jackson, the Beatles, and, most recently, the New Kids on the Block).[2] In order to be a supersystem, the network must cut across several modes of image production; must appeal to diverse generations, classes, and ethnic subcultures, who in turn are targeted with diverse strategies; must foster "collectability" through a proliferation of related products; and must undergo a sudden increase in commodification, the success of which reflexively becomes a "media event" that dramatically accelerates the growth curve of the system's commercial success.

Even though most of the children I interviewed at the video arcade (see appendix 2) were terribly naive about money and the capitalist system, they seemed keenly aware of the dynamics of consumerist desire. They knew from their own experience that the reported popularity of a commodity and its promotion through commercial tie-ins greatly intensify its desirability to consumers. For example, when asked why they thought Teenage Mutant Ninja Turtles were so popular, one eight-year-old Caucasian boy responded, "Because everybody knows about them and they have lots of stuff," and a ten-year-old Latino boy replied, "They are selling a lot of stuff in stores and usually I buy things like that." Susan Willis claims that "children have difficulty conceiving of their toys as having been made, . . . [since] commodity fetishism erases production and presents the toy store (or TV commercial) as the toy's point of origin." Nevertheless, "children learn and want to be consumers at an even earlier age"—that is, they want to buy into the system.[3]

The stunning success of the TMNT supersystem was particularly extraordinary because to most adults it was so baffling and yet to most children so immediately appealing and accessible. American youngsters of all ages, classes, and economic backgrounds were able to participate in the system to varying degrees, for almost everyone could afford a quarter to play the arcade game (even though a quarter buys little play time) or slightly more to buy the comic book or cookies, and practically no one was too young to wear the t-shirt. Thus, even the usually marginalized categories of the infantile and the poor were being actively hailed (or, in Althusser's terms, interpellated) as members of a highly socialized commercial network: that is, they were being integrated as consuming subjects along with those whom they perceived as more empowered. Paradoxically, though, membership in this system also authorized these individuals to engage in the socially disapproved behavior of fighting, which is one reason why Turtle toys, clothes, and jargon have reportedly been banned at several day-care centers and elementary schools.[4]

I first witnessed this phenomenon at the birthday party of my three-year-old nephew, where a man dressed as a Ninja Turtle came to entertain the youngsters. He was immediately recognized, even by the two-year-olds—who were proudly wearing the t-shirts, who already knew the language and ninja moves, and who were immediately caught up in the fantasy of belonging to the cult. One five-year-old was actually convinced that a villainous Foot soldier was hiding in a bush, and to dispel the child's anxiety the visiting Turtle finally had to go outside and pretend to chase away the phantom killer. I have also noticed that one of my son's three-year-old friends (the brother of a seven-year-old girl) frequently brings all of his Turtle paraphernalia and wears his Turtle shirt and shoes when he comes to our house, as if to demonstrate to my son, Victor, and to his older sister that he is not too young to belong to the Turtle network. Although he does not yet play the home video game with the older children and has not yet seen the movie, he can already perform the ninja moves. Even these two- and three-year-olds derive pleasure from identifying with the Turtles, who love to "fight"—an activity ordinarily condemned by their parents. It is a pleasure similar to that which children of all ages derive from identifying with mischievous animals like Garfield and Heathcliff (who also love to fight), or unsocialized creatures like Animal, Slimer, and Cookie Monster, or a renegade family like the Simpsons—identifications that are rendered safe by the distancing techniques of animation and animal masquerade. (For more empirical information about how young children enter the TMNT supersystem, see appendixes.)

The supersystem coordinates the growth curves both of its marketable components and of its consumers, assuring young customers that they themselves form the nucleus of their own personal entertainment system, which in turn is positioned within a larger network of popular culture. As the live appearance of men dressed in Turtle costumes at birthday parties and public events grows into a live musical performance or rock concert, kiddies are simultaneously being prepared for their entry into teenage pop culture.

Turtle Growth on TV

This coordination of the growth curve is highlighted in the new hour-long TMNT animated television show, which premiered in the fall of 1990 on CBS in the 8:00–9:00 A.M. time slot and quickly became that network's top-rated Saturday morning program. The show's entry into the Saturday morning field forced "Muppet Babies" and "Garfield and Friends" to move back a half-hour, to the 7:00–8:00 and 9:00–10:00 slots, respectively, and "PeeWee's Playhouse" to move forward, to the 10:30–11:00 slot, where presumably it could attract older viewers and retain former fans as they matured (and came to appreciate sleeping in on Saturday mornings). Because these later Saturday morning network shows are frequently preempted by sports on the West Coast, however, the higher rated "TMNT" program was soon reversed with "Garfield and Friends"—but only on the West Coast.

Like the previous half-hour syndicated TMNT television series, the new network Turtles show continues to feature the protean malleability and reflexive transmedia intertextuality of its amphibious heroes. In practically every plot one of the Turtles and at least one of their friends are transformed into some undesirable regressive form by an advanced technological gadget—either one of Donatello's inventions gone awry or a scientific apparatus created or appropriated by a villain. For example, in an episode broadcast on Saturday, October 6, 1990, first one of the Turtles (Michelangelo) and then TV reporter April O'Neil are "miniaturized" by a "short" scientist who harbors Napoleonic ambitions, in a plot that recycles both the adult classic *The Incredible Shrinking Man* and Disney's kiddie version, *Honey, I Shrunk the Kids.* Calling himself "a big shrinker," this little patriarchal villain evokes not only the historic figure of Napoleon through the "sizing" of his ambition, but also Captain Bly (from the adult narrative *Mutiny on the Bounty*), through his British accent, naval costume, and obsession with ships, and Inspector Gadget's archenemy, Dr. Claw (from the popular animated children's series now in syndication on Nickelodeon), through his scary cat, Claude, and his high-tech hardware.

Like "Muppet Babies," then, this episode is blatant in connecting protean transformation and intertextuality with cognitive, physical, and emotional growth and with the various anxieties aroused by such growth. The giant rat guru, Master Splinter, explicitly states the moral in terms of the relativity of size—"Bigger is not always better"—which Michelangelo (now restored to his former mutant gigantism) retranslates as, "Small is cool with me." These aphorisms become more resonant in light of the episode's central irony: when Michelangelo is miniaturized, he is actually restored to the "normal" size of a turtle, implying that even so-called physical and perceptual norms (like big and small, advanced and regressive) are merely relativistic social constructs.[5] Although this theme is pointedly dramatized when Michelangelo is momentarily frightened by the huge shadow of a tiny kitten, its implications are more significant when we see the supposedly full-sized April O'Neil already miniaturized on a TV monitor or computer screen *before* the villain pushes his power buttons.

In the context of this growth narrative, such size reductions seem to imply that high-tech mass media like television and computers are replacing the Lacanian mirror in subject formation. They are creating an imaginary signifier that is not static or stable, but dynamic and processual, a signifier that is constantly moving backward and forward in time and constantly shrinking and growing—like *Alice in Wonderland* or *Through the Looking-Glass*, like the growing kids and their magic mirror images in the milk commercials, like the Muppet babies in their hybrid world of animation and live action, like Garfield in the Lasagna Zone and his friend Sheldon half out of the shell, and like the Super Mario Brothers in the complex warp zones of their video games and TV series.

Since every supersystem has its own unique history and its own pattern of growth, adaptations can move in any direction; the specific sequencing is merely a combination designed for peak marketability. It can start with a movie (like *Star Wars*), a TV series (like the Muppets), a video game (like Super Mario Brothers), or a comic book (like TMNT). Yet as Sheila Benson, film critic for the *Los Angeles Times*, has pointed out, the boundaries between comics and movies are becoming especially permeable:

> Visually, the comics and the movies had fed off each other for decades. . . . [But] the gap between the style of comics and movies is getting smaller every summer. Just like the best comics, the most popular movies of the last 15 years are studded with characters who are already larger than life: *Raiders of the Lost Ark*, *Rocky*, *Jaws*, *Star Wars*. It's not hard to imagine an artist's hand drawing *Back to the Future*: it's no surprise that *Robocop* is already between the pages of a comic book.[6]

Roland Barthes observed: "The one text is not an (inductive) access to a Model, but entrance into a network with a thousand entrances."[7] Despite the prior success of the TMNT comic books, toy figures, video games, and TV series, most American adults entered the Ninja Turtle network by becoming aware of the movie.

TMNT *and the Video Game Movie Genre*

Making over $25 million its opening weekend alone (one of the biggest-grossing three-day openings of all time), the film *Teenage Mutant Ninja Turtles* has since gone on to become the highest-grossing independently released film in movie history, thereby validating the name of its producer, Golden Harvest. After 178 days in the theaters, it had taken in over $133 million, more than doubling the $54 million made by the former record holder, *Dirty Dancing*. In the May 30 issue of the *Hollywood Reporter* (right before the big summer movies for 1990 opened), *TMNT* held second place (only $2 million behind *Pretty Woman*) in the "Year's Boxoffice Top 10." These figures are all the more remarkable when one considers that the film has no recognizable stars, that it cost only $12 million to make (modest by Hollywood's current stan-

dards), and that nearly half its audience was between the
ages of five and twelve, whose tickets cost half the price of
adult admissions.

The box office success of *TMNT* is now being repeated
in home video rentals, which (according to the October
15, 1990, issue of *Variety*) have already brought in an additional $65 million. In *Variety*'s list of "All-Time Film Rental
Champs," *TMNT* is ranked in fifth place for movies released
on video in 1990—behind the adult films *Ghost* ($90 million),
Pretty Woman ($85 million), *Total Recall* ($70 million), and *Die
Hard 2* ($68 million) but well ahead of *Dick Tracy* ($60 million), *Back to the Future III* ($47 million), and *Gremlins 2* ($22
million). Perhaps even more impressive, *TMNT* is already in
thirty-ninth place for top video rentals of all time, where it
is tied with *Back to the Future II* (released on video in 1989)
and *Coming to America* (1988) and far ahead of all Disney's
animated classics.

Why did *TMNT* do so much better at the box office and
in home video rentals than *The Wizard* (which flopped in the
theaters at $9 million and took in only another $6 million in
rentals) and earlier video game films like Disney's *Tron*
(which took in $27 million at the box office and $17 million
in rentals) and *The Last Starfighter* ($22 million in theater
receipts and $13 million in rentals)? I think the answers are
primarily related to marketing strategies and their aesthetic
consequences.

Positioned respectively at the peak and crash of the first
home video game boom, *Tron* (1982) and *The Last Starfighter*
(1984) were aimed at an older audience than *The Wizard* and
TMNT—at young adults with personal computers and at
teenage patrons of arcades (which survived the crash and
always accounted for a higher percentage of the video game
market). Both are science-fiction films featuring the fast-
paced action and fantasy one ordinarily finds in arcade

games. Both incorporate video game imagery (it is particularly dazzling in *Tron*) and are specifically linked to an actual arcade game. Both feature oedipal heroes, who are grounded in a domestic melodrama with economic overtones (business rivalries and program piracy in *Tron*, and college tuition blues in *Starfighter*). As a talented "cyberspace cowboy," *Tron*'s Flynn doubles as user and program and excels in both science and the arcade; as a fatherless teen in transition, Alex is recruited from his trailer park by an alien air force to be the Last Starfighter and is doubled by a simuloid. Because of their malleability as sliding signifiers, both heroes find a lucrative future in the fantasy warp zones of video games.

Positioned within the second video game craze, *The Wizard* and *TMNT* were geared more to the home video game market. The producers of *The Wizard* probably miscalculated by relying so heavily on star power—on young Fred Savage for kiddies, Christian Slater for teens, and Beau Bridges for adults. Young spectators may well be more readily presold on characters than on actors. When I asked my son, Victor, which of these two films he liked better, he said, "I like both because *The Wizard* has Nintendo and *TMNT* has my heroes." When I asked him whom he identified with in the movies, he replied, "With Jimmy in *The Wizard* and with Michelangelo in *TMNT*." Thus, in contrast to *TMNT*, while watching *The Wizard* he experienced a split between his object of desire and his object of identification. This gap may explain why some young spectators grew bored, complaining that they would rather be home playing the video game themselves rather than sitting in the theater passively watching it being played by the actors. Although *The Wizard* featured "Super Mario Brothers 3" and the Power Glove, the game was not yet available in the stores and the glove was used very minimally on screen. Viewers merely got glimpses of these products in action, without any interactive relation; they were restricted to traditional cinematic suture, identifying with kids who were playing with the new products in the film. Moreover, despite his so-called wizardry, the young hero Jimmy does not function as a sliding signifier like the heroes of the other films in the genre. Perhaps even more significantly, the story remains totally immersed in low-mimetic domestic melodrama (with few flights into fantasy) and contains almost no violent action (except for the demolition derby between father and bounty hunter). These differences may partly explain why the film failed to draw the home video game audience, and why it was relegated to the subordinate role of simply promoting the Nintendo system.

TMNT provides a much more effective model for a lucrative movie–video game tie-in. It is the first film in the genre to use an accelerating intensification of intertextuality to make the moviegoing experience a "unique" component of an existing network rather than a discrete event. This participation in a preexisting system may also help to explain why *Batman* did so much better in its opening weekend at the box office than *Dick Tracy*. Even though both were based on comics and both relied on a highly stylized look and a brilliant villainous performance to gain critical praise, only *Batman* (like the *Superman* series before it) was part of an elaborate ongoing network that included not only the original comic and the current media hype, but also numerous radio and TV series, parodies, and spinoffs. Thus it was the Batman character and perhaps the stunning visual logo, rather than the stars, that drew spectators to the theater. *Dick Tracy*, in contrast, in trying to adapt a classic comic strip, had to rely solely on media hype and the star power of the Madonna-Beatty romance.

Like *Batman* and the *Star Wars* sequels, the TMNT film was eagerly awaited by young fans who had already been recruited into the TMNT network by means of other "unique" consumerist experiences—exposure to the original black-and-white parodic comic book and the successful series of sequels, reprints, and toys that it spawned; play with Nintendo's home video game, which sold out at most stores by Christmas; and experience with Konami's new arcade game, which quadrupled in popularity and profit by letting four players play (and feed the machine quarters) at the same time (thereby addressing the charge that video games isolate players and decrease social interaction with other children). The children's consumerist desire was further inflamed by months of advance advertising in movie theaters and on TV, which made many demand that their parents take them to see the movie as soon as it appeared. The strategy of independent distributor New Line Cinema was to have its "giant promotional campaign" peak on the day of the film's nationwide release. When the movie finally opened on March 30, 1990, it had immediate mass penetration in theaters "everywhere," as did its novelization by Dell, one million copies of which appeared in the stores that same week. There were also immediate successful marketing tie-ins with Burger King (who first gave away toys and then sold video tapes) and Toys 'R' Us (which created separate TMNT sections in all their stores). Interviews revealed that movie sequels were already in the works, and Dell announced plans to publish four more novelized adventures and to sell a boxed set of five the next Christmas. Thus, like the strange "glowing goo" that caused the Turtles to mutate, the movie accelerated the growth curve of the TMNT network, transforming it into a supersystem. Appropriately, the first movie sequel is called *Teenage Mutant Ninja Turtles II: The Secret of the Ooze*.

Consistent with Standard and Poor's advice to toy manufacturers for the 1990s, the producers of the original TMNT movie took the young core audience for granted and tried to appeal as well to parents and teens (who were probably the readers of the original comic book)—and so they went for a PG rating rather than a G. As Tom Gray, the Los Angeles–based executive in charge of the production company, Golden Harvest, claimed before the film's release: "We purposely skewed this movie for an *older* audience. We know that the kids would come, but we really wanted to make it for the teenage and university level. The script is very, very hip and very timely. We will probably end up with a PG-13 or a PG. . . . A G-rating would kill us."[8]

One way of reaching this expanded audience was to stress the creative connections with television, with which all three generations would be familiar. Jim Henson of Muppet fame designed electronically controlled "animatronic" puppet costumes for the Turtles; Bobby Herbeck, who has written for "Different Strokes," "The Jeffersons," and "Small Wonder," did the screenplay; Todd W. Langen of "The Wonder Years" rewrote the script; and Steve Barron, who has done over 250 music videos, including Michael Jackson's "Billie Jean" and "Money for Nothing" by Dire Straits, directed. As in the animated TV series, April was changed from a computer programmer to a TV investigative reporter; Shredder was introduced while watching TV; and the Turtles are seen watching not only April's newscasts, but also a cartoon of the Tortoise and the Hare. The film also includes many verbal allusions to TV programs and commercials. For example, when two of the Turtles embrace, Donatello quips: "It's a Kodak moment." And when April and her love interest, Casey Jones, are bickering, Donatello remarks: "Gosh, it's kind of like 'Moonlighting.' "

The success of the film may be due in part to the reassurance offered by the optimistic TMNT myth, for, like the resilient comic figures of animated cartoons, these protean heroes are able to survive every violence and calamity—

especially those that are most terrifying to today's young-sters. Far from being poisoned, corrupted, or disillusioned by toxic waste, junk food, substance abuse, urban decay, dys-functional families, parental abandonment, homelessness, gang violence, or teenage traumas, these happy mutants ac-tually thrive in the urban sewer and are strengthened by such postmodern threats. Like milk (in those TV commer-cials where "milk does a body good"), the mysterious radio-active ooze magically accelerates the growth of the Turtles, turning them into superheroes who are super good, super big, and super powerful. The myth implies that the way to fight current dangers is by entering a supersystem where (as the devouring Octopus Ursula tells Ariel, the title character of Disney's *Little Mermaid*) "you can become a [mutant] yourself"—that is, by a total immersion in consumerist mass culture, an area in which the United States still reigns su-preme.

The extraordinary success of the film owes a great deal to the Turtles themselves, whose presold identity as sliding sig-nifiers was far more appealing to the kids than any human stars from movies or television would have been. Undaunted by the spectacular commercial failure of *Howard the Duck*, the producers of *TMNT* decided to rely primarily on their live-action animal protagonists and to forget about human stars. Tom Gray claims: "All along, my concept was the Turtles are the stars. . . . I want to sell *the Turtles*. I believe in the Turtle concept and I don't want to have people say, 'Hey, wasn't Chevy good as Donatello?' "[9]

What distinguishes the Turtles is their amazing powers of assimilation and accommodation. Their passion for pizza not only sets up the marketing tie-in with Domino's Pizza (which is prominently featured in the film), but also marks them as avid consumers like Garfield and Pac-Man. When this penchant for consumption is combined with their talent for imitation (which they learn from their Japanese ninja master), the Turtles emerge as powerful assimilators. According to Piaget, the collaborative combination of assimilation and imitation is an essential condition for reversible mental operations, one of the key traits characterizing the operational thought of the seven- or eight-year-old.[10]

Evoking the comic prototype of Proteus (the Greek sea god who fluidly changes shape), the Turtles' powers of accommodation are even more formidable than their powers of assimilation. Their status as amphibians, teenagers, mutants, and American ninjas with Italian names and California surfer jargon quadruples their capacity as transformers, making them the ultimate sliding signifiers: they can easily move from an animated TV series into a live-action movie, and they can transgress borders of species, race, ethnicity, generation, and media. While such cross-cultural malleability might help construct subjects who are less prejudiced against alien Others, the changes promoted are far from revolutionary. Susan Willis's analysis of the Transformer toy genre is also relevant to the kind of changes we find in the Ninja Turtles (and to a lesser degree in video games):

> Everything transforms but nothing changes. This is a fitting motto for late-twentieth-century capitalism, particularly as it is embodied in the mass toy market. . . . Often the complicated series of manipulations required to produce the transformation from car to robot and back to car again baffle the adult left reading the toy's instructions, while the four-year-old child, using fingers and intuition, performs the transformation unaided. What's interesting about the Transformers is the way the notion of transformation suggests spontaneity and change, while the reality of the toy teaches program and preprogrammed outcome. . . . Such toys weld transformation to consumption and offer a programmed notion of change to supplant con-

The Teenage Mutant Ninja Turtles stand by their motto in their fight for "Truth, justice, and the American Way!" ©1990 Northshore Investments Limited. All Rights Reserved. Photo by Timothy White.

ceptualizing change in any other way and to compensate for the absence of meaningful social and historical change. The fascination with transforming toys may well reside in the utopian yearning for change which the toys themselves, then, manage and control.[11]

This absence of meaningful social change is particularly apparent on the register of gender, for despite all the boundaries that the Turtles cross, the Manichaean lines between good and evil and between male and female hold firm. Unlike their archetype, Proteus, and their favorite fan, April O'Neil, the transforming Turtles never adopt androgyny as part of their identity, even though their gender is acknowledged to be a social construct. Even in the TMNT home video games, where players can switch identification from one Turtle to another at any moment, or even in the arcade game where four people can play at the same time, all of the player positions are exclusively male.

April O'Neil is the only female character who appears throughout the network, yet, except on the register of gender, she has much less fluidity than the Turtles. In many episodes of the CBS television series, April's courageous behavior is played off against the cowardice of her coworkers—the conventionally "feminine" Irma, who frequently faints, and the effeminate (possibly gay) cameraman Vernon, who constantly "chickens out" and whom the Turtles call a "wimpazoid." Though the Turtles find April quite "foxy," the film avoids any trace of transspecies romance by pairing April with Casey Jones, a self-appointed streetwise vigilante who fights alongside the Turtles. Not only is Casey human, but he even shares April's Irish-American ethnicity. As a spunky TV news reporter and "the Turtles' greatest fan!" April plays Lois Lane to their Supermen. This role authorizes her access to the word and to control over the

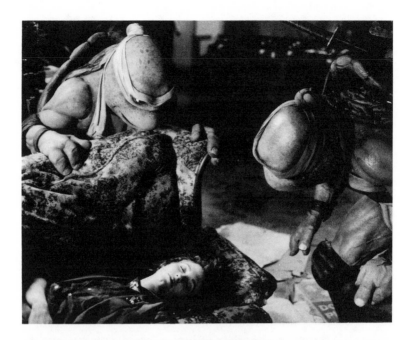

The Turtles find April O'Neil quite foxy, but she has less fluidity than her amphibious friends. Photos by Alan Markfield.

gaze, and it empowers her to confront corrupt patriarchs like Police Chief Sterns and even to throw a few punches at the Foot soldiers. Like Haley in *The Wizard*, April is portrayed as a spirited, red-headed, freckle-faced tomboy and daddy's girl, a Howard Hawks–ian woman who is attracted to male bonding. In fact, she is so deeply connected to her dead father that she preserves his antique shop, fetishizing her patrimonial legacy.

Like so many films and video games of the 1980s, *TMNT* is primarily a discourse on fathers and sons, addressing the *actual* absence of the father from so many American homes. Although this dimension is also present in the other three films in the video game genre and in the other versions of the Turtles' tale, it is greatly intensified in the TMNT movie. The main dramatic conflict centers not on the Turtles (who are always good), but on a wayward boy named Danny Pennington who rebels against his father (who is also April's boss) because he thinks his dad doesn't love him. After running away and becoming a Foot soldier, Danny betrays April and the Turtles but is redeemed by Splinter, who assures him that "all fathers care for their sons." Like "the Kid" in *Dick Tracy*, Danny has been included in the story to insure that *all* young boys have someone with whom they can firmly identify—just in case they are unable to cross borders of gender, generation, or species to identify with April, Casey, or the Turtles. As in *The Wizard*, *TMNT* grounds its slim plot in contemporary social problems—the millions of teenage runaway and throwaway dropouts who are neglected by their single-parent families and who are on the verge of becoming hardcore criminals in a decaying urban America, which is policed by incompetent patriarchs like Chief Sterns.

The ideal patriarch is Splinter, the Japanese-American rat guru, whereas Tatsu, Shredder's second-in-command, is an abusive father to his Foot soldiers. Photos by Alan Markfield.

Thus, the film's primary moral conflict is a choice between good and bad fathers. The evil patriarch is Shredder, whose headquarters the press kit describes as "a cross between Pinocchio's 'Pleasure Island' and a ninja 'Fagin's Lair.' " Like the head of a modern terrorist organization, he recruits young delinquents, molding them into a disciplined army of criminals, telling them: "This is your family, I am your father." Shredder's evil is fully exposed when Tatsu, his ninja instructor and second in command, becomes the abusive father, callously killing one of their sons.

The ideal patriarch is Splinter, the Japanese-American mutant rat who learned to be a ninja in the old country by imitating in his cage the moves of his master. We learn in a flashback that one day in a New York sewer he discovered the four mutant Turtles, who, like Oedipus and Moses, were abandoned in infancy. Splinter adopts, names, and trains them in the ninja arts and lovingly calls them "my sons." These mutants enjoy the same master-disciple, father-son relations that proved so commercially successful in *Star Wars* and *The Karate Kid*. Significantly, the names of both the villainous and the ideal patriarchs—Shredder and Splinter— suggest divisiveness, yet the latter also evokes an apparatus (a splint) that helps to repair ruptures. It may well be that the idealized father-son bonding between Splinter and the Turtles reassures its young spectators that those disturbing oedipal tensions and castration anxieties can be overcome. That is part of the myth's great appeal.

In this world of glorified father-son bonding, the maternal is more invisible than ninjas. No mothers are seen or mentioned; April, Danny, and the Turtles are all pointedly motherless. This is not the case in the novel, where Danny thinks about his mother, or in the original comic book, where April works as a computer programmer for a villainous black scientist who creates an army of robot "mousers" run by a larger central "mother computer" (as in *Alien*). Besides April, the only other females (or potential mothers) in the movie are victims: an anonymous old woman has her purse snatched by Foot soldiers, and the bride of Splinter's master is murdered by Shredder in a flashback. One exception is the sexy young girl seen among the many male "punks" in Shredder's warehouse, where (as in Pinocchio's "Pleasure Island") delinquents are encouraged to do whatever they want—smoke, drink, gamble, draw graffiti, and (most significantly) play video games. Presumably the girl's singular presence is meant to suggest forbidden sexual pleasure, which is otherwise discreetly omitted from this PG-rated movie. As with the oedipalization of video games, the film attempts to make postmodernist flexibility compatible with a patriarchal orthodoxy that demands the total repression of the maternal and a rigid rechanneling of erotic desire.[12]

Yet the Turtle network does create some ironic distance around the issue of gender, primarily through masquerade. The opening line of the original parodic comic book is "Stupid Turtle costumes!" which immediately marks the Turtles' amphibious slippage between human and animal identities as the masquerade of subject formation. This dimension is elaborated with additional irony in the movie, where the Turtles are cybernetic animals (like Papert's computer-controlled Turtle that moves within the cognitive minicultures of the "LOGO environment" and that the kids in his experiments use as a "computational object-to-think-with").[13] But here humans are both controlling and wearing heavy electronically controlled puppet costumes (the precise combination of puppetry, electronics, and humanity is a closely guarded secret). Nowhere is this masquerade more blatantly linked with gender than in "April Foolish," one of the four TV episodes from the animated syndicated series that were sold at Burger King.

Female Masquerade in "April Foolish"

As an adaptation of "The Prince and the Pauper," this TV episode teaches young spectators how to use masquerade to function more effectively as consumers. The central setting is an embassy masquerade party, where the Turtles are mistaken for humans in amphibian drag and awarded a prize for most ridiculous costume, and where April is mistaken for Princess Mallory (when she exchanges her androgynous yellow jumpsuit for a hyperfeminine royal gown). She is then inadvertently kidnapped and held for ransom by Shredder, who hopes to obtain the emperor's lidium 90, "the most valuable element on earth" (for more plot summary, see appendix 1). Most interesting in the episode is the way gender is positioned along with other valuable commodities like diamonds, pizza, and amphibious media stars (minerals, vegetables, and animals) as a cultural construct whose meaning and value are as "unstable" as the lidium 90, which deconstructs when exposed to the atmosphere.

The gender switching begins when April's sound technician, Irma, tells her she can't wear her jumpsuit to the party, advising her to become "a new woman" so as to find "a new man." April's transformation is specularized when she goes to the sewer, where Splinter and the Turtles are eating. Defending his choice of sushi, Splinter pronounces his transformative credo: "A wise person embraces as many new experiences as possible"; but then, when he is offered marshmallow-pepperoni pizza, he qualifies his thesis: "Some things are more embraceable than others." Just then April enters, and one of the Turtles quips, "Talk about embraceable!"—establishing her as a consumable like pizza. (This connection is later reinforced at the party when Leonardo asks, "Do you see April?" and Michelangelo responds, "No, something better, it's pizza!") Applying the sliding signifier explicitly to gender and class, Donatello exclaims: "Gosh, April, you look just like . . . a girl," and Raphael adds: "Yes, you clean up real good," echoing a line from *Pretty Woman* (the blockbuster Cinderella movie that was *TMNT*'s toughest competition at the box office, probably because it promises that class differences can be easily erased by cross-dressing and compulsive shopping).

April's feminization arouses in the Turtles the dual masculine desire both to protect and to ogle ("We better keep an eye on her . . . maybe two"), which, in the very next scene, is unified in the male gaze and explicitly linked to patriarchal power. Here April's double, the "real" Princess Mallory, accuses her father of "looking after her like a child," complaining: "I hate masquerades . . . you always make me go as a princess." As soon as she dons plebeian drag, Mallory becomes the active subject rather than the object of the gaze, especially when watching April's princess impersonation on TV.

Upon arrival at the party, April, like Cinderella, is immediately mistaken for a princess, for the servants hail her as "Your Highness." Like the hooker heroine of *Pretty Woman*, April admits that this is an interpellation she "could get to like," and presumably, so could most young female spectators. (When I showed this tape to a group of youngsters, all the girls preferred April in her princess masquerade, and some said that if they were invited to a costume party they would also like to dress as a princess; see appendix 1.) This princess drag proves particularly effective in fooling the lower classes, for even Shredder's retainer Rock Steady admits: "All those princesses look alike to me"—a remark with racist overtones, which undoubtedly applies to the entire female gender, especially as represented in fairy tales and video games.

These differences in gender, species, and class may be merely social constructs, but the episode implies that they are still essential to successful narrative. Thus, at the end of the episode April claims she has learned "that a disguise is a great way to get a story." Donning a bald wig, she tells the Turtles that next week she will disguise herself as a bald-headed diplomat, whereupon a Turtle remarks: "Paint that thing green and you can pass as one of us." This ending reminds us that both females like April and superheroes like the Turtles are similarly constructed by masquerade. Yet this ending also encourages young spectators of both genders to go out and buy the necessary paraphernalia that will facilitate their own empowering identification with these awesome sliding signifiers.

Masculine Masquerade in the Movie

In the TMNT movie, masquerade is focused not on April's femininity, but on the masculinity of Casey Jones and the Turtles, all of whom are presented as male impersonators. With their minds and bodies still in flux, they are still on that "long forced march" toward becoming a gendered adult— or, more specifically, a fully empowered phallic subject. When Raphael goes out on the streets, for example, he masquerades as "Bogey" with trench coat and fedora, and Michelangelo does imitations of Cagney and Rocky. The Turtles reach the final stage of their development when they put their bald green heads together to meditate and miraculously bring forth the spirit of their captive master, who tells them that the source of their new power is "a father's love for his sons." In other words, a boy becomes a man by masquerading as his father—a point that is made literal in the scene where Shredder costumes his Foot soldier in the head-band that carries his own insignia: the Name-of-the-Father. In Danny's case, the rite of passage is identified with the Naming-by-the-Father; he becomes a man when his dad agrees to call him Dan.

Yet it is Casey Jones, the all-American bricoleur jock, who adopts the most disguises—not only the uniform of the Foot clan, but also the array of phallic sporting equipment that he uses as weaponry (hockey stick, baseball bat, and golf club). Even his name evokes earlier American folk heroes, who represented, according to Willis, "the centered, very solid construction of masculinity," particularly in contrast to twentieth-century transformative superheroes (like Super-man and Batman). Because these twentieth-century super-heroes "are locked on the perpetual articulation of the mo-ment of transformation," their "masculinity is constructed as a duality"—sometimes strong and hypermasculine, and other times weak, bumbling, and even nurturing.[14] As a slightly older, more traditional loner hero who fights along-side the Turtles without really being one of them, Casey Jones manages to conflate these two models. Although he is verbally compared with "Wayne Gretsky on steroids" and visually (especially in his undershirt) reminds one of the young Brando in *A Streetcar Named Desire*, his macho status is destabilized when April refers to him as "a nine-year-old trapped in a man's body," as well as when a Turtle accuses him of claustrophobia and he defensively responds: "I never even looked at a guy before!" The androgyny of this long-hair makes him a better match for April, to whom he con-fides with affection, "I love it when you're pushy!"

Despite the focus on father-son relations and the exclu-sion of the maternal, this flexibility in masquerade implies that gender is a cultural construct and that one has the power to exaggerate, change, or possibly even to choose one's own gender identification. In the case of spunky April O'Neil, her unisex jumpsuit suggests her choice of androgyny—an identification that presumably qualifies her to be the Turtles' best buddy. In "April Foolish" when she masquerades as a hyperfeminine princess, her costume immediately marks her as a target for victimization. At the end of the episode, when she dons a bald wig, she exaggerates the other side of androgyny and moves (visually and narratively) toward phallic empowerment—both in politics (disguised as a diplomat at the conference she plans to crash) and in battle ("Paint that thing green and you can pass as one of us").

This malleability is much greater with the Turtles, a species whose gender is not immediately apparent (at least to most human observers). Thus, unlike most superheroes, their gender appears to be totally "constructed" by their costuming, weaponry, behavior, and names, which are bestowed on them by their patriarchal master, that is, by the symbolic order—and that means that these accoutrements of masculinity can also be obtained by the young spectators who buy into the TMNT supersystem.

As a valorizing category within the TMNT myth, masculinity therefore proves to be not biologically determined, but culturally constructed—a role that can be chosen, learned, or acquired, even by aspiring members of so-called inferior species like rats, turtles, females, kiddies, and teens. Yet in order to succeed on this quest for empowerment, one must undergo one or more kinds of transformation: martial arts training (Splinter), mutation (the Turtles), masquerade (April in her jumpsuit), moral conversion (Danny), membership in the TMNT system (kiddie spectators). While this conception of masculinity might offer more flexibility than biological determinism, it can hardly be consoling to feminists, for the maternal is totally suppressed and power is restricted solely to the male sphere. The only way for a female to be empowered within this mythic world is to become, not a Barbie-like princess (as Irma advises), but an androgynous daddy's girl like April—that is, one of the boys.

In presenting masculinity as a cultural construct, the movie allows male bonding and martial arts to function as the primary spectacle, which can be watched, documented, and transformed into pop culture by an empowered tomboy like April. She covers their story not only on TV, but also in her cartoon drawings. At the end of the novel (and probably in an earlier version of the screenplay), she and Danny take her drawings to a comic book publisher, who rejects them as "too farfetched." Even in the movie, April and Danny are models of how human consumers (both girls and boys) can interact with protean superheroes like the Turtles: as in the "Green Ranger" episode of "Muppet Babies," it is a matter of being morally converted, like Danny, and of making them the basis of one's own creative invention, like April.

One of the most unusual and original features of *TMNT* is the way it elicits an interactive response from its young spectators, which helps to compensate for the deliberate omission of video game action from the movie. (This omission is made quite pointed when one of the Turtles uses the phrase "shell shock"—a term from the video game—and another rejects it as "too derivative.") The interactive response centers not on solving the riddles of the plot, but on the cognitive task of distinguishing among the four Turtles who, despite their illustrious Italian names and color and weapon coding, look exactly alike. When I saw the movie, I was surrounded by kiddie spectators who kept saying aloud, "That's Michelangelo," or "There's Leonardo," as if identifying the Turtles and demonstrating their knowledge of these iconographic codes was the most enjoyable part of the moviegoing experience. (It reminded me of Victor's experience watching his first movie, *The Empire Strikes Back*, and the pleasure he took in recognizing the characters.) Although the color iconography was not in the original comic book, a similar color coding is operative in Pac-Man (to mark an enemy's death) and in *Tron* (both the movie and arcade game). In the case of *TMNT*, however, the color and weapon coding works across the system of intertextuality.

I remember the mixture of pleasure and discomfort that Victor once displayed when he recognized a "mistake" on a TMNT t-shirt, where the color and weapon coding were in conflict—pleasure in his own powers of discrimination, yet discomfort in finding inconsistencies in a logical system. Another instance occurred on Halloween, when, instead of carrying his nunchucks (a favorite toy, which gave him great pleasure and which was purchased specifically to go with his Ninja Turtle costume), at the last minute Victor decided to carry an old stick because, unlike the nunchucks, it did not conflict with the purple color coding of his headband. On a third occasion the discomfort clearly outweighed the pleasure when Victor vehemently rejected a TMNT folder, on which the Turtles (with menacing facial expressions) were arranged in an Escher-esque design with two Turtles on the bottom and the other two upside down at the top (so that it was impossible to see all four right side up at the same time). While one could argue that Victor was reacting against the violent expressions of his beloved heroes, this aspect was no more extreme than in many other images he had enthusiastically approved. I am convinced that his disturbance arose because it was very difficult for him to assimilate the image within his mental spatial models either of reality or of the TMNT supersystem. His negative reaction was so strong that not only did he refuse to use the folder, but he actually demanded that it be thrown away so he would never have to see it again. According to Papert, one of "the fundamental fact[s] about learning" is that "anything is easy if you can assimilate it to your collection of models. If you can't, anything can be *painfully* difficult" (italics are mine).[15]

For the uninitiated moviegoer, the TMNT film foregrounds the cognitive task of recognition in a long reflexive sequence that ruptures the narrative. April sketches the Turtles and in a voice-over (as if she were reading from a diary) explicitly distinguishes them as dramatic characters by explaining how differently each one reacted to their first defeat. These distinctions are "supported" by having each drawing dissolve into a live-action illustrative scene, a technique reminiscent of "Muppet Babies." Yet ironically, all these "different" reactions focus on male bonding.

Even though the Turtles are barely distinguishable visually, they carry unique "designer" labels. From a humanist perspective, the naming of the Turtles after Michelangelo, Donatello, Raphael, and Leonardo can be read either positively, as an attempt to familiarize youngsters with these important names (which they will later encounter in a more lofty or different class context), or negatively, as a vulgar co-optation of the Old Masters (contradictory readings that can also be applied to the use of Fellini on Saturday morning television). From a postmodernist perspective, however, these icons of uniqueness are merely being refigured as surviving players in a larger system of mass entertainment.

As we saw in the case of Garfield, this paradox of uniqueness is central to advertising discourse, where the false promise of distinctiveness is granted by legally protected brand names and extended to spectators who consume products designed for mass tastes. Thus, one takes pride in belonging to a cult that appreciates a supposedly unique product with ever-expanding popularity (once the TMNT movie became a big success, some of its newspaper ads were headlined, "Give in to the TURTLE URGE! [Everyone Else

Has]"—but the more popular the product becomes, the less prestigious the cult.

Interestingly, the TMNT movie does not emphasize the Italian names of the Turtles, but uses instead their Americanized nicknames—Raph, Don, Mikey, and Leo. The film highlights not the uniqueness of individual Turtles, but their bonding as a foursome, a distinction that children seem to absorb. For example, when I asked Victor why he chose to identify with Michelangelo rather than with the other Turtles, he replied: "Because Leonardo argued with Raphael, and Raphael got beat up, and Donatello said things that weren't nice about Raphael." This emphasis on bonding also conveniently quadruples the selling power of the Turtles by fostering "collectability," since most young consumers desire the complete set of ancillary products: all four flavors of cookies, all four videotapes at Burger King, all the Playmates action figures at Toys 'R' Us, and the TMNT Collectors Case, which safely stores at least twelve statuettes.

The conflict between uniqueness and bonding is centered on Raphael, the most emotional of the four Turtles and the one who is almost killed by the Foot clan. At one point Splinter tells him: "You are *unique* among your brothers in that you choose to face this enemy [anger] alone!" The Turtles' primary mission is to become stronger as a foursome with the aid of paternal love. Thus, rather than being identified exclusively with the Old European Masters and their cult of uniqueness, the Turtles are vividly linked with the team spirit of their Asian Ninja Masters, who apparently have far greater popular appeal with American moviegoers of all ages, particularly at this moment in cultural history.

TMNT is the only film in the video game genre that makes strong use of the Asian connection—with its Japanese samurai backstory and a producer like David Chang, vice-president of international production for the Golden Harvest Group in Hong Kong, which specializes in the martial arts genre and even produced a documentary on Bruce Lee. Instead of including inset video game references like the other three films in the genre, the entire narrative of *TMNT* simulates the nonstop combat structure of most video games, a strategy that must have contributed to the film's success. Moreover, as in the games (but not the original comic book), the violence is stylized and bloodless,[16] and it is figuratively extended to the economic arena: when April is being mugged by ninja Foot soldiers in the subway, she sneers, "Am I behind on my Sony payments again?"

This joke reveals the "other scene" of global economics, where the struggle for power is not illusory (as it is in the Turtles movie and video games) and where the Japanese have proven to be formidable players. Part of the film's timeliness comes from reflexive allusions to the Japanese invasion of American markets, which make the film's references to the wave of Japanese-style "silent" crimes more resonant. Adopting a strategy similar to that used by Eastman and Laird in the original comic book, the movie imitates the Japanese technique of assimilating successful models of old foreign masters. It adapts the samurai and kung fu conventions the way Japanese filmmakers like Kurosawa earlier absorbed and transformed the western in the post–World War II era, or the way Eiji Tsuburaya built on *King Kong* to create his popular series of Godzilla movies with their fantastic elaborations in the mid-1950s.[17] Thus the TMNT movie breaks with the traditional conception of orientalism, where one is defined strictly in opposition to the alien Other, and instead adopts a postmodernist form of intertextuality and accommodation, fluidly consuming and becoming the Other—a strategy now being used not only by Teenage Mutant Ninja Turtles, but also by Japanese multinational corporations in their acquisition of American properties. As Akio Morita, the founding chairman of Sony, said shortly after his company's 1989 purchase of Columbia Pictures (for $3.4 billion): "We are more willing to act in the U.S. like a U.S. company, in Europe like a European company, and in Japan like a Japanese company. That's the only way a global company like Sony can truly become a significant player in each of the world's major markets."[18]

5

Postplay in Global Networks: An Afterword

> The most crucial and decisive battle of World War II is
> about to be fought . . . by you! . . . As the top gun of
> the Navy's most elite crew of fighter pilots, you must
> pilot your specially-outfitted P-38 into the very midst of
> the enemy squadron. . . . The outcome of history's most
> fateful air/sea battle rests in your hands! Can you avenge
> Pearl Harbor?
>
> Cartridge cover of the Nintendo video game
> *1943: The Battle of Midway*

My friend Kenneth Newell has noted the irony of a Japanese video game being sold in the United States that reenacts the historic battle that was a crucial turning point in World War II, leading to Japan's defeat and America's emergence as a major world power. In making this game part of their victorious new superentertainment system and marketing it so successfully in the United States, perhaps Nintendo is demonstrating that World War II was only one phase of a larger global sporting event that is still in progress. This reading is supported by similar ironies, such as Hiroshima's football team being called "The Bombers." The case of Matsushita, however, is even more directly related to the game in question. In order to minimize anti-Japanese reactions to its recent purchase of MCA/Universal for $6.59 billion (the largest takeover to date of an American company by a Japanese

154

firm), Matsushita reportedly strove to close and publicize the deal well *before* December 7, the anniversary of the attack on Pearl Harbor. Apparently Japanese corporations like Matsushita, Sony, and Nintendo are well aware that their stunning economic success can be read as an ironic reversal of the Battle of Midway.

Within this game of global economics, where the growing power of synergy is becoming increasingly apparent, the assimilative Pac-Man–like strategy of erasing opposition by absorbing former opponents (their markets, properties, and distinguishing characteristics) is by no means limited to Nintendo, Sony, and Matsushita. A recent front-page *Los Angeles Times* story on Dentsu, the largest advertising company in the world, reported:

> Dentsu represents almost every major Japanese corporation, even competing ones, under its banner of "total communication service.". . . [It] is renowned as the hand behind the conservative Liberal Democratic Party, perennially the ruling party. . . . The cozy web of relationships extends to the opposite end of the political spectrum as well. . . . Dentsu is tied closely to the two Japanese news agencies, Kyodo and Jiji, in a cross-shareholding arrangement that results from their once having been merged as the Domei news agency, which disseminated government propaganda in the dark decade through the end of World War II. . . . Domestically oriented Dentsu plans to expand its global network dramatically and is shopping overseas for acquisitions.[1]

In no way do I intend these statements as "Japan-bashing," which is unfortunately pervasive right now in the United States; rather, I am merely trying to suggest the scope of the game in which we are competing and the many interpenetrating levels of intertextuality on which it is being played. Since closure to my project would contradict its line of argument, in this brief epilogue I will merely attempt to reposition my discussion within a larger context: that of global political economics. To develop this aspect in depth would of course require another book, so I will limit myself to indicating a few directions that such an argument might follow—directions apparent to anyone who has even casually followed the news over the past year in any major urban newspaper, such as my own hometown daily, the *Los Angeles Times*.

Ninjas and Networks

On the new economic battleground of the 1990s, successful Japanese corporations like Nintendo, Sony, Matsushita, and Dentsu are emerging as the powerful Mutant Ninjas who use assimilation and accommodation to master and transform the game of multinational consumer capitalism. In this battle for world markets, one of Japan's major rivals is still the United States. With their respective ideological emphases on team spirit and individualism, both nations (like the Turtle and Nintendo networks) are vying to absorb the other within its own system. At the moment Japan clearly has the edge: in 1989, the U.S. trade deficit stood at $108 billion, 45 percent of which was with Japan, making the United States the world's largest debtor nation and Japan the world's largest lender. In the American press, this edge is also being dramatized by narratives featuring individualized Japanese characters and companies, who have been able to convert their old-style imitation into a postmodern form of creative transformation, as in the following story that also appeared recently on the front page of the *Los Angeles Times*.

> As a young Toshiba engineer in 1950, Sakae Shimizu was assigned to develop a power transformer. Surveying the

field, he concluded that U.S. technology was best and arranged a licensing deal with General Electric Co. Today ... Shimizu could no longer purchase, imitate or expropriate from the United States the transformer know-how that Japan requires. Toshiba and others in Japan have surpassed U.S. firms in key areas of transformer technology.... [They] are part of a new Japan—one that aims to invent, not imitate.... As the United States is exhorted to become more like Japan, some Japanese firms see their future in employees who are more like Americans—inventive, individualist, free-thinking.[2]

One area in which the Japanese have proved their inventiveness is scientific research, where they demonstrate a very different combination of team play, competition, and individualism than are found in the United States. As with land and other natural resources, Japan has a much smaller supply of scientific researchers than the United States, yet the Japanese have developed effective cooperative strategies for maximizing use of these resources and for devoting them almost exclusively to economic survival. For example, although Japan has only one-tenth the number of researchers working in robotics as the United States, the two countries' level of development in this area is about the same. This finding was reported by Jet Propulsion Laboratory's Stephen Peters, the first foreign scientist allowed to participate in a planning session at Japan's largest government lab, the Electrotechnical Laboratory in Tsukuba.[3] Peters claims that in order to use their limited number of scientists more efficiently, the Japanese divide up research tasks and share their findings, thus avoiding duplication of efforts and displacing the competition to a later stage of R&D: application of the research to the development of consumer goods. This same strategy is also operative in private research labs, which in 1988 accounted for 80 percent of Japanese research (in contrast to the United States, where only 60 percent of scientific investigation is privately funded and where much of the remaining 40 percent is linked to military projects). According to Stanley Krueger, president of the Japanese office of United Technologies, "In the end everybody has the same nugget of technology. Then the question is, who gets to the market first."[4]

Ironically, one of Japan's major postwar accomplishments was to ideologically reinscribe postindustrial capitalism by proving that individualism was not an essential element, as our own ideology would have us believe. At first the Japanese subverted the aura of "uniqueness" through an intertextuality of cheap imitations, which soon became a sophisticated, invasive postmodernist simulacrum superior to the original. In cinema, the most immediate example is Akira Kurosawa's reinscription of the western genre in films like *Seven Samurai* and *Yojimbo.* Noël Burch, who noted Kurosawa's ability to improve on the Western cinematic models he borrowed, feared that such appropriations of individualism would subvert traditional Japanese values.[5] Hollywood's domination over world markets seemed so entrenched, Burch never considered that the American conventions themselves were also subject to subversion (if he had, he would have welcomed such a development). Yet as we are seeing right now, the Japanese are transforming those Western conventions they borrowed both from cinema and capitalism, helping to decenter both in the process.

Decentering the Oscar

The 1990 Academy Awards celebration officially acknowledged Hollywood's international decentering by having several of its awards announced in foreign settings—Buenos Aires, Moscow, Geneva, London, and most significantly Sydney, since 20th Century Fox had recently been purchased by Australia's News Corporation. Even so, few members of the global audience for that event would have believed that by the end of the year four of Hollywood's major studios would be owned by foreign companies—not only 20th and Columbia, but also MGM/UA (which was bought by the European conglomerate Pathe) and Universal (taken over by Matsushita). Now only Warner Brothers, Paramount, and Disney studios remain as domestic targets for foreign acquisition, and will undoubtedly be pressured to seek out mergers in order to compete with their multinational rivals.

On the night of the Oscars, as if to single out Japan's dramatic entry into Hollywood with its 1989 purchase of Columbia Pictures (and perhaps to atone for the Academy's embarrassing 1987 preference of director Sydney Pollack for *Out of Africa* over Kurosawa for *Ran*), the centerpiece of the ceremonies was the special lifetime achievement award to Akira Kurosawa on his eightieth birthday, presented by Hollywood's all-American "wonder kids" George Lucas and Steven Spielberg (who, we were reminded, are personally responsible for eight of the top ten box office successes of all time). Accompanying the award was a montage of clips from Kurosawa's canon; spanning three decades of the postwar era, this selection demonstrated the director's status as a multinational icon, for it included his great adaptations of Western Shakespearean classics (like *Throne of Blood* and *Ran*) as well as works later adapted by the West (like *Rashomon*, *Seven Samurai*, and *Yojimbo*). (Two significant omissions were *The Hidden Fortress*, the primary source for the plot of *Star Wars*, and *Dersu Uzala*, the Soviet-Japanese co-production made in Siberia that won an Oscar for best foreign film of 1976.)

The staging of the award seemed designed to underscore the irony that the genius and influence of this Japanese master are more appreciated by commercial Hollywood auteurs like Lucas and Spielberg than by the Japanese film industry, which will no longer finance his projects. As film critic Charles Champlin reported the following morning: " 'Kurosawa can't get a job in Japan,' Spielberg remarked to a friend not long ago, in a mixture of indignation and astonishment. Indeed, George Lucas was instrumental in helping Kurosawa find financing for *Ran* and Spielberg himself used his own powers of persuasion to get Warner Bros. to back Kurosawa's latest film *Dreams*."[6]

The Decline of Japanese Software

Kurosawa's problems with financing are closely tied to the overall decline of the Japanese film industry. By 1989, movie ticket sales in Japan were down to 143.5 million (a mere 13 percent of the all-time 1958 peak of 1.3 billion), and only 1,912 movie theaters were still doing business.[7] This decline was apparent even in the United States, where Japanese-language movie theaters, which had been going strong for at least eighty years, were now disappearing. On October 31, 1990, film critic Kevin Thomas observed: "Ironically, at a time when Japanese companies are investing heavily in the American film industry and the Japanese-speaking community is growing, the last of those theaters [in Los Angeles] is going out of business."[8]

Largely because of this sharp decline in the Japanese film industry, Japanese movie studios have been reluctant to back venturesome movies; instead they are increasingly investing in other leisure activities, such as video porn, bowling alleys, bicycle races, and amusement parks. Even in the purchase of MCA/Universal, it was reported, "a key factor appears to have been MCA's theme parks in which Matsushita was deeply interested";[9] and after acquiring Columbia Pictures,

Sony announced its intention of opening a chain of international amusement parks called "Sonyland," which would soon display the company's latest cutting-edge soft- and hardware and make Disneyland look obsolete. The Japanese films that are doing well at the box office these days are *not* (for the most part) art films in the tradition of Kurosawa, but primarily commercial fare. For example, the biggest success in 1989 ($35 million in ticket sales) was *Kiki's Delivery Service,* an animated film about a young witch who makes deliveries on her broomstick—a premise no sillier than that of *Teenage Mutant Ninja Turtles.*

As the world becomes ever more "multinational," tastes in mass media become increasingly uniform worldwide, and business interests, regardless of nationality, seek software with a track record of global appeal. With the Japanese film industry at its nadir and with current Japanese films proving limited in international marketability, successful electronics giants like Sony and Matsushita (which sells its products under the more familiar brand names Panasonic, JVC, Quasar, National, and Technics) are investing in Hollywood in order to acquire American software that can match and extend the power of their own hardware. As Elaine Dutka and Nina J. Easton put it:

> Experts say that, with the coming entertainment revolution, the values of studio libraries will skyrocket, making the MCA and Columbia deals look like bargains in retrospect. . . . The value of the movies themselves will skyrocket given the privatization of European broadcast stations, greater at-home access and the possibility of packing more and more programming on satellites through digital compression.

They quote Andrew Lippman, associate director of MIT's Media Laboratory, as saying: "It's 'old-think' to have a U.S.

vs. Japan attitude. . . . Without international cooperation, it will be impossible to distribute a program worldwide."[10] In this process of radical restructuring, then, not only hardware and software are being transformed, but also nations and industries.

In the 1970s and 1980s, partly because of Japan's technological innovations in and growing domination over electronics hardware (television sets, compact disc players, and video cassette recorders), American movies have been increasingly domesticated as part of an ever-expanding home entertainment system, which, in the global context of multinational consumer capitalism, has redefined our conception not only of "movies," but also of "home." When Sony took over first CBS Records and then Columbia Pictures, it also raided Warner Communication (one of its big American rivals) to recruit the producing team of Peter Guber and Jon Peters, those Super Mario Brothers of Hollywood, to run the studio. Because both this deal and Matsushita's later takeover of MCA/Universal were "brokered" by "superagent" Michael Ovitz, chairman of the Creative Artists Agency (which represents superstars like Steven Spielberg, Robert Redford, and Tom Cruise), the definitions of Hollywood agent and superstar also underwent transformation.

Now that it controls a major movie studio, Sony will probably help pioneer Hollywood's conversion to high-definition television (HDTV) technology, thereby erasing a functional difference between the two modes of formerly competing image production (as well as between two competing nations) and cashing in on its former mastery of video hardware. Robert Epstein reports that "when Sony paid $3.4 billion for Columbia and moved it to the Culver City lot, it also budgeted another $10 million for its 2-year old HD team. Right now, the Sony people say their main interest in Culver City is to demonstrate their equipment in a studio setting."[11]

And if Sony/Columbia is pursuing this course, can Matsushita/Universal be far behind?

The Compositing Power of HDTV

In contrast to film and video, the new HDTV medium has an enormous capacity for increasing the compositing power both of images and of international markets. With its digital picture and sound and its video luminance of 1,920 pixels per line, HDTV can composite up to twenty-seven generations without significant loss of resolution. Undoubtedly, it has the potential to enhance the clarity, realism, and involvement of any visual/auditory representation. Yet what has seemed most compelling, at least during the first five years of application, is its capacity for surrealism and special effects—that is, its ability to make obvious simulations look "realistic." This paradox may be explained by the extraordinary technical compositing power of the medium; or by the postmodernist cultural context in which this new technology is being developed; or by the current popularity of music videos, which have appropriated and commercialized the surrealist aesthetic; or by the economic consideration that special effects is the only area where the medium is presently commercially competitive—or by a combination of all these factors. Such use has not been restricted to music videos and commercials, but has also occurred in the feature film *Julia and Julia* and in sequences from big-budget movies like *Back to the Future*, *The Abyss*, and *The Hunt for Red October*. Despite its poor showing at the box office, Kurosawa's American-financed *Dreams* (1990) made one of the most visionary uses of this new technology to date, particularly in the episode (shot in Sony HDTV and later transferred to film) where the dreamer enters the paintings of Vincent van Gogh (played by Martin Scorsese). The sequence creates a stunning "composite" vision of Japanese/European/Italian-American artistry in the combined visual media of dream/painting/cinema/HDTV—a highbrow analogue to the kind of pop fluid assimilations we found in *Teenage Mutant Ninja Turtles*.

The "compositing" power of HDTV is especially controversial in the economic sphere. With three different standards of television signals currently in operation (NTSC, the technically inferior system used by North America and Japan for broadcasting to over 40 percent of the world's TV sets; PAL, used in Australia and most of Western Europe; and SECAM, used in France, Eastern Europe, and the USSR), many feel that the choice of a new standard for HDTV represents "an opportunity to establish a . . . compatible standard for universal international signals . . . that would streamline signal transmission and interpretation."[12] Europe, however, is doggedly resisting such global unification in order to retard the expansion of Hollywood software (whether controlled economically by the United States or Japan) in European markets, which are rapidly being restructured into a new economic supersystem that will be larger than Japan and the United States combined.

The current shakiness of U.S. domination over global mass media is nowhere more apparent than in the plans for HDTV, which is already being used for some regular broadcasts in Japan and which promises eventually to affect the whole superentertainment system—movies, electronic cinema, terrestrial and satellite broadcasting, video software (including video games), databases, and other scientific and educational uses of video. Robert Epstein reports:

Last week Sony introduced three HD products for sale in Japan only: a 36-inch commercial HD monitor, a commercial HD decoder and a $17,000, 36-inch-wide television set capable of HD pictures once a consumer decoder is implanted in it. . . . Now [Sony] and other consumer product manufacturers are getting ready to sell HD sets, once the FCC next year and the rest of the world two years later agree on how many lines make for high definition. What follows will be HD video recorders, players and cameras.[13]

The Japanese television network NHK is also doing HD production in New York (at the Kaufman Astoria Studios) and Los Angeles (at KSCI), and is sponsoring workshops on HDTV and experimental productions in some of America's leading film schools, including the University of Southern California School of Cinema-Television. Yet America's role in this new technology is still quite indefinite. As Dutka and Easton report, "While the HDTV debate continues in Congress, the Federal Communications Commission is going forward with a testing program and says it will adopt an American HDTV standard in 1993, creating in all probability, three different standards worldwide—ours, Japan's and Europe's."[14] Despite such reassurances, A. G. Hawn warns that the United States still lags far behind:

With the European and Japanese investment in R&D already exceeding $1 billion and the yearly market projected at $20 billion by the mid 1990s, it becomes increasingly important that some major decisions be made as to the role of the United States in the marketplace. . . . But while the Japanese will have a system on-line sometime early this year and the Europeans are expecting to be in operation by 1992, the United States has made little progress toward the development of a signal standard or distribution program that would enable the consumer to utilize the system."[15]

The Theatrical Realm of Global Politics

Similar warnings were expressed by Congressman Edward J. Markey, chairman of the House Telecommunications and Finance Subcommittee, in reaction to the first public announcement (on September 25, 1990, in the *Wall Street Journal*) of Matsushita's negotiations to purchase MCA, whose holdings include Universal Studios (the producers of serial blockbusters like *ET*, *Jaws*, and *Back to the Future*); the Universal Studio tours in Los Angeles and Orlando, Florida; 49 percent of the Cineplex Odeon theater chain; Geffen Records; and Putnam Publishing. Strongly opposing the takeover, Markey declared: "When Matsushita melds its vast hardware empire with MCA's huge video software library, it will be in a position to dominate the global communications marketplace and squeeze American companies out of key markets. . . . The Japanese and the Europeans are in the seventh inning of the global technology game, and the U.S. is arguing over how to get to the ballpark."[16]

The MCA deal was not seriously threatened by warning statements like Markey's, partly because of the earlier Sony/Columbia deal, which probably made opposition seem futile, and perhaps (as Epstein suggests) because of the political clout of Lew Wasserman (MCA's powerful chairman of the board), whose "decades of support for politicians may have taken the edge off any resistance."[17] A serious threat did come, however, when this deal was repositioned within another network of international political economics: the Mideast oil crisis. Matsushita was revealed to be a participant in the Arab-led economic boycott of Israel, and the question arose whether MCA would also be drawn into this arrangement—a situation that would violate not only the U.S. law forbidding any American company (even if foreign owned) from participating in this boycott, but also the political loyalties of Wasserman, who is one of Hollywood's strongest supporters of Israel. Yet economic interests ultimately prevailed, and political loyalties were adjusted. As MCA president Sidney J. Sheinberg put it, his company decided to sell because it needed "a strategic alliance."[18]

A similar justification had been expressed a few weeks earlier by Kirk Kerkorian, the former majority stockholder at MGM/UA Communication Co., which Pathe Communications purchased for $1.36 billion dollars. As if to explain why he was no longer willing to compete with Sony's Columbia Pictures, Kerkorian lamented: "You've got to be in hardware today, you've got to be in satellites, you've got to be in manufacturing home videocassettes and in theaters. That's what it's all about these days."[19] Pathe, a European multinational conglomerate, was founded in 1989 when it took over the independent Cannon Group (formerly run by Israelis Yorum Globus and Menachem Golan).[20] The new MGM-Pathe Communications Co. is co-chaired by Italian financier Giancarlo Parretti and his business partner Florio Fiorini. Parretti (who "was convicted of fraudulent bankruptcy in Naples, Italy this year")[21] had a difficult time putting the financing together for the MGM takeover; his credibility was further strained when he made a surprise bid to Wasserman for the purchase of MCA, only a few hours after the deal had been closed with Matsushita. Ever since his acquisition of MGM, the studio has been struggling to remain solvent.

Within this "game" of ever-expanding systems (that are constantly being restructured into larger networks through intertextuality), there is "an infinite play of difference" to generate new meaning and profit. Even a popular computer journal like *MacUser* informs its readers:

> *Connectivity* is maturing from just a buzzword to the single most important competitive tool of business computing.

As with the uniting of the European Communities, the force driving this coming together of computerdom is not altruism but self-interest. . . . More and more companies will become part of an emerging "GlobalNet"—a United Nations of corporate, academic, and government databases and information networks. . . . The role of the GlobalNet . . . will be to connect users to the rest of the world, regardless of what box they have. This is no mere technological fantasy—it's a revolution in progress.[22]

Within this new global computer/television/cinema hookup, Dutka and Easton insist, one must ask: "Does your TV become your computer, or does your computer become your TV?"—a question that touches on the issue raised at the end of chapter 3 concerning the merger of Nintendo and the TMNT supersystem: that is, which would absorb the other? The answer, Dutka and Easton claim, has "huge implications for global competition, because the Americans dominate the computer arena while the Japanese drive the consumer electronics industry, particularly in the area of HDTV."[23]

At times this restructuring process can be survival-adaptive, as when national boundaries are transcended so that ecological problems can be addressed in a global context or beyond. As a genre, science fiction is particularly well suited for dramatizing the value of such shifts into larger orbital systems. Hence *Star Wars* was the perfect vehicle for launching this merger of systems—as a marketing strategy within the sphere of mass entertainment, and as Reagan's star defense system within the theatrical realm of global politics.

The New World Order

At no time in recent history has this restructuring process been so rapid and pervasive as it is right now at the beginning of the 1990s, with the dismantling of Eastern Europe, the Berlin Wall, and all the familiar Cold War configurations, and with the formation of new structural networks in Europe, the Middle East, and the Pacific Rim. In January 1991, these configurations dramatically shifted again with the outbreak of war in the Persian Gulf. Although in the economic sphere Japan was still ahead and Europe was making great strides, the United States suddenly surged ahead in the political sphere. Drawing on the same restructuring principles that I have described in the foregoing chapters and adapting them as a rhetorical strategy for international power politics, George Bush dubbed this "defining moment" of history a "new world order."

Within this newly defined GlobalNet of the post–Cold War era, Bush has convinced most players at home and abroad that the United States need no longer be seen as a waning economic power, plagued by recession, bank failures, and the homeless and forced to trim its military budget and might—an anachronistic Godzilla without its Rodan. Rather, the "new world order" created a new remilitarized zone, in which the United States was refigured as the lone surviving Superpower—a resuscitated Robocop—capable of leading and policing other united nations and allied networks in a new moral military crusade. Thus, just as World War II provided the context in which the United States first emerged as a major world power, the war in the Gulf provided an arena in which the United States could reverse those optimistic yet threatening historical assessments that were generated at the start of the 1990s: the crediting of Nobel Peace laureate Mikhail Gorbachev and his glasnost policies for bringing an end to the Cold War, the economic success of Japan and West Germany as forward-looking nations wisely diverting their resources from military to consumerist spending, and the celebration of the Pacific Rim and a newly consolidated Europe as the supernetworks of the 1990s. Now, within the warp zones and quick reconfigurations of this new remilitarized global network, Gorbachev was crushing liberation movements in a crumbling Soviet Union on the brink of civil war, West Germany and Japan were defensively contributing billions of marks and yen to the allied cause in compensation for having no troops, and the United States was leading a new alliance that had already absorbed both the Pacific Rim and the European Economic Community.

In the media coverage of the war, a similar scenario was developing. The war immediately stimulated the growth of cable TV, not only here in the United States but also throughout Europe, for everyone wanted to be kept up-to-date on the Gulf crisis. Moreover, the definition of "network news" was almost instantly transformed and globalized by the twenty-four-hour reporting of CNN, Ted Turner's international cable television station headquartered in Atlanta, Georgia—whose broadcasts could be received via satellite in over one hundred nations worldwide. CNN's coverage so far surpassed that of the national American networks (ABC, CBS, and NBC) that anchor Walter Cronkite suggested (on national television) that it was time for these networks to switch their emphasis from mere reporting to analytic commentary; in a similar vein, former NBC president Laurence Grossman claimed that with the combination of CNN and local news, national network news was "becoming an anachronism."[24] Yet CNN's dominance also meant that once again, as with other popular media like movies, TV series, and pop music, the voice of America was the primary mediator of world events—and now a new channel for international diplomacy as well.

In covering the Gulf war, CNN and other stations frequently used the game metaphor—juxtaposing the war coverage with sporting events like the Super Bowl, tallying downed scud missiles and planes or captured prisoners like competitive scores, or interviewing young pilots who claimed that on bombing missions they felt as they did in high school just before the big game. In his press conference on the final day of the war (February 27, 1991), while giving a detailed description of the allied forces' military strategy, General Schwarzkopf also used the football analogy—then, a few sentences later, as if acknowledging both the popular appeal and the disturbing moral implications of the game metaphor, he disavowed it by reminding us (as so many other officials and journalists had done) that this was "not a Nintendo game!" Apparently such reassurances were necessary because the computerized precision of the military equipment and the media's emphasis on the hardware had made the video game analogy so powerful and pervasive.

The Teenage Mutant Ninja Turtles myth was also brought to mind on February 9, 1991, when CNN broadcast a special assignment called "Shell Shock"—on the psychological damage done to Iraqi ground forces by constant bombardments from American B52s. Although the illustrative footage was drawn from World War II (when the syndrome was called "combat fatigue"), the name of the mental disturbance was drawn from World War I. CNN probably chose "shell shock" as the title of the show not only because it is more dramatic and alliterative than "combat fatigue," but also because in the Teenage Mutant Ninja Turtles video games being played in arcades across America, "shell shock" is a well-known euphemism for death.

As political and economic lines are redrawn, multinational mass media like CNN will play an increasingly important role in helping citizens to assimilate and accommodate themselves to these new geopolitical formations. At least equally important will be the role played by the new multinational

Hollywood. For decades we students of film have been writing about the so-called invincible hegemony of Hollywood over global film and video markets—a hegemony that all other national cinemas seemed always to be struggling against and that showed every sign of holding fast, even in the post–Cold War era and in the face of America's economic decline. Yet Europe and Japan have already begun to undermine Hollywood's hegemony from within, at a pace rivaling that of the Eastern European revolutions, and this merger seems strangely compatible with the myth of those successful multinational transformers, Teenage Mutant Ninja Turtles.

Like those heroic mutants, together we are becoming a new global force that is accelerating the mass reproduction of postmodernist players. That is, players who are skillful at forestalling obsolescence, castration, and death through a savoring of transmedia referentiality, fluid movement between cinematic suture and interactive play, and (as Beverle Houston wrote of television) "an extremely intense miming of the sliding and multiplicity of the signifier."[25] Together we are also helping to accelerate the redefinition of movies, television programs, commercials, compact discs, video games, computer programs, interactive multimedia, corporations, nations, politicians, superstars, and toys as amphibious software—any one of which can be used to promote the other in a gigantic network of commercial intertextuality. This process of transformation helps to explain why a Mutant Ninja like Michelangelo, in the midst of martial arts combat on the mean streets of New York, can shriek with *jouissance*, "I love being a Turtle!" As advertised, we are the multinational team that is "playing with power."

Appendixes

The following appendixes describe two empirical studies carried out in July 1990 in conjunction with this project. I chose to interview children from two sites in Los Angeles that were part of my son Victor's ordinary social network: his summer daycare program, and his favorite video arcade (he is a subject only in the latter study). In making these choices I hoped to contextualize the data from the case study of Victor in chapter 1 (that is, to determine whether his responses were idiosyncratic), as well as to capture some of the rich ethnic and racial diversity of Los Angeles.

Because these studies involve only a small number of subjects, they provide neither a solid basis for the ideas expressed in this book nor an adequate test of them. Rather, these interviews are exploratory: they raise new issues (such as the effect of ethnic, racial, class, and gender differences on children's entrance into supersystems like the Teenage Mutant Ninja Turtle network), ones that could become the focus of more thorough and systematic research in the future. In both studies I was aided by two research assistants, Walter Morton and Michael Sinclair, who documented the interviews on video.

APPENDIX 1

PROCEDURE

On July 18, 1990, I showed a thirty-minute videotape titled "April Foolish" (the episode of the animated "Teenage Mutant Ninja Turtles" television show discussed in chapter 4, and one of four episodes sold at Burger King in conjunction with the release of the movie) to a group of eighteen "school-age" students in the summer day-care program at the Anna Arnold Bing School, University of Southern California, which is available to children of students, faculty, and staff.

After introducing myself as a USC professor and as Victor Bautista's mother, I told the children that I was going to show them a videotape of a TV show that some of them might already have seen, that we were going to film them while they were watching it, and that then we were going to ask them some questions. I assured them that this was not a test; there were no right or wrong answers. We merely wanted to find out how they responded to the tape.

As soon as the tape started, the children spontaneously started singing along with the theme song, and they remained attentive throughout the entire episode. Following the screening, we interviewed eleven children between the ages of five and nine (with a median age of six and a half)—five girls and six boys. (Originally there were to be twelve subjects; however, the Asian-American girl we selected decided she did not want

174

to be interviewed.) We purposely selected children who represented the multicultural and racial diversity of Los Angeles: there were four black or mulatto African-Americans (subjects a, c, e, f), three Caucasians (b, h, g), one Latino (i), one Asian-American (k), one Indian-American (d), and one Iranian-American (j). Four spoke a foreign language in the home (d, i, j, k—Tamil, Spanish, Persian, and Korean respectively). We interviewed one subject at a time in a separate room so that the children would not be influenced by each other's answers.

PLOT SUMMARY OF "APRIL FOOLISH"

In this adaptation of "The Prince and the Pauper," television reporter April O'Neil is invited to a masquerade ball at a foreign embassy. Substituting a princess costume for her traditional unisex yellow jumpsuit, she is immediately mistaken for Princess Mallory, who has left the embassy disguised as a commoner so that she can enjoy some freedom. Thus, when Shredder and his henchmen come to kidnap Princess Mallory in order to obtain her father's lidium 90 ("the most valuable element on earth"), they inadvertently capture April. In search of their friend April, the Turtles crash the party, chase Shredder to an art museum, where they fight the villains and save the captive, but fail to recapture the lidium 90. Fortunately for the heroes and humanity, this valuable but dangerous substance loses its power and deconstructs when exposed to atmospheric variables.

QUESTIONS AND ANSWERS

About the Children and Their Family Households

1. What is your age and grade?

Girls	Boys
a. 7 yrs, 2d	f. 9 yrs, 5th
b. 7 yrs, 2d	g. 8½ yrs, 3d

c. 6 yrs, 2d   h. 5 yrs [claimed he was 3], K
d. 6 yrs, 1st   i. 6 yrs, 2d
e. 6 yrs, 1st   j. 6 yrs, 2d
            k. 6 yrs, 1st

2. Do you have any brothers or sisters? How many? What age?

    Yes—6 (3 [b,e,i] had one younger sister; 2 [a,h] had one older sister; 1 [k] had one brother)

    No—5 (c,d,f,g,j)

3. Do you live at home with both your mother and father?

    Yes—9 (b,c,d,f,g,h,i,j,k)

    No, only with my mother—2 (a,e)

4. Do you have a Nintendo entertainment video game system at home?

    Yes—6 (a,c,e,f,h,k)

    No—5 (b,d,g,i,j)

5. Do you have a VCR that plays video tapes like this?

    Yes—9 (a,b,c,e,f,g,h,i,j)

    No—2 (d,k)

6. Do you have a TV set in your home?

    Yes—11

    No—0

7. Is there a computer in your home? Do you ever get to use it?

    Yes/Yes—6 (a,b,d,e,f,g)

    Yes/No—2 (h,i)

    No—3 (c,j,k)

Discussion

The fact that these families are connected with the university as faculty, staff, or students may explain in part why they deviate from national norms (for example, why they have only one or two children, and why so many have personal computers).

About Their Reaction to "April Foolish"

1. Have you ever seen this show before? How many times?
   Yes—7 (4 once [a,b,e,j]; 2 twice [c,k]; 1 many times [h])
   No—4 (d,f,g,i)

2. If so, did you see it on TV or did you get your tape from Burger King?
   TV—4 (a,b,e,k)
   Tape—3 (c,h,j)

3. Did you like this tape? Why or why not?
   Yes—10
   a: I liked the part where they thought April was the princess.
   b: It's neat.
   c: I liked when April goes in the window and when Shredder says go and blast them.
   e: I liked when they were climbing on the roof.
   f: Lots of bad guys and funny parts, Turtles got their job done and Shredder got away.
   i: I liked when April hit them with the door.
   j: I liked the fighting.
   d,h,k: I don't know.
   Somewhat—1
   g: Some parts were stupid, like when there just happened to be a window there when they needed it.

Discussion
   Two girls and one boy mention April in their reasons for liking the tape—a response that may be specific to this particular story, in which April is named in the title and has a leading role. Three boys and two girls mention action—a response that may be more typical for all episodes in the series. The two oldest boys showed some ironic distance either by finding fault

with the tape (g) or by enjoying the humor and rooting for Shredder, the villain (f).

4. Do you think girls or boys would like it better? Why?
    Boys—6
        a: Boys like Ninja Turtles, and girls like Barbies.
        f: Boys like Turtles, girls like April.
        g: Boys like fighting.
        i: Boys like to see the Turtles fighting and getting Shredder.
        h,k: I don't know
    Girls—1
        e: I don't know.
    Both—4
        b,c,d,j: [no reason cited]

Discussion

Five boys said "boys," and two of these mentioned "fighting" as the reason. Only one girl (a) said "boys" and then cited Barbies as the alternative preferred by girls, yet without making it clear whether she herself preferred Turtles or Barbies; on following questions she named Michelangelo as her favorite character, yet said she wanted to wear a princess costume. The other girls who said "girls" or "both" gave no reasons for their answer; neither did the one boy who answered "both."

5. Which character do you like best? Why?
    April—3
        c: She always covers stuff.
        d: She writes about things I like to read.
        e: I don't know.
    The Turtles—1
        b: [no reason cited]
    Leonardo—2
        h: The blue turtle.
        j: Because he's the leader.
    Michelangelo—3
        a: [no reason cited]

g: I like the name.

k: He has a blue mask [it is actually orange].

Donatello and Raphael—1

i: They don't say words like "dude" so much.

Shredder—1

f: He tells the others what to do.

Discussion

Three girls chose April and two gave definite reasons linked to her active role as a reporter. The other two girls violated cultural gender coding by picking a male turtle as their favorite character but gave no reasons for their preference. All of the boys picked male characters, and when one of the older boys (f) violated traditional moral coding by picking Shredder, his reason was linked to power.

6. If you were going to a costume party, what costume would you like to wear? Why?

Princess—2

a: 'Cause I can go to the tower and to the princess's room.

b: I already have a fairy princess costume and I think it's pretty.

Ninja Turtles—3

h: Leonardo [no reason cited]

j,k: [no reason cited]

Tiger—2

e: [no reason cited]

i: I like tigers.

Horsey—1

c: [no reason cited]

Black Arrow—1

f: [describes the costume—mask, black cape, and sword]

Freddy Krueger—1

g: I like him.

Discussion

The girls either chose the princess (for her possessions or prettiness) or a nongendered animal outside the Turtle network (a tiger or horsey). Five of the boys chose definitely male costumes—the three youngest chose the Turtles, the two oldest found more formidable male media costumes from outside the Turtle network. The boy who previously said that the tape appealed both to girls and boys (g) chose a nongendered animal costume, the tiger.

7. Did you like April better in her jumpsuit or when she was dressed like a princess? Why?

Princess—9

a,b,c,d,e,g,h,i: She looks prettier/better.

k: [no reason cited]

Jumpsuit—2

f: Then I know who she is.

j: [no reason cited]

Discussion

Only boys preferred her in the jumpsuit, and the one older boy who gave a reason explicitly saw gendered clothing as a key indicator of identity, even though the unisex jumpsuit violated traditional gender boundaries. Perhaps he preferred the jumpsuit because it disavowed differences in gender, which may start to become threatening to a nine-year-old.

About Their Experience with the Teenage Mutant Ninja Turtles (TMNT)

1. How did you first find out about TMNT?

Television—5 (a,d,f,g; i specifically mentioned TV advertising)

Tapes—2 (c,h)

Movie—1 (e)

From my friend—1 (j)

From my mom—1 (b)

Don't remember—1 (k)

2. Did you see the movie? How many times?

Yes—8 (4 once [a,c,f,g]; 2 twice [b,h]; 1 ten times [e]; 1 twelve times [k])

No—3 (d,i,j)

3. Have you played the home video game?
   Yes—5 (c,e,f,g,h: 3 boys, 2 girls)
   No—6 (a,b,d,i,j,k: 3 boys, 3 girls)

4. Have you played the arcade game?
   Yes—5 (a,f,g,h,j: 4 boys, 1 girl)
   No—6 (b,c,d,e,g,i,k: 4 girls, 2 boys)

5. Have you read any of the TMNT comic books?
   Yes—6 (c,d,e,g,h,j: 3 girls, 3 boys)
   No—5 (a,b,f,i,k: 2 girls, 3 boys)

6. Which do you like best—the movie, TV show, comic book,
   video game, or arcade game? Why?
   The movie—2
      b: 'Cause it's longer.
      k: Because it has color.
   The arcade game—1
      f: It's big and for a quarter you can be Leonardo.
   The movie and the arcade game—1
      g: They are designed to be fun, and I liked the way they
         made the turtles in the movie.
   The TV show—1
      j: 'Cause I like to watch TV.
   The tapes—1
      a: 'Cause there are no commercials.
   The comics—1
      h: [no reason cited]
   The cards—1
      e: 'Cause they show pictures.
   I don't know—2 (d,i)

Discussion

The answers are totally spread out on preference, yet there
are gender differences in experience for the arcade game and
to a lesser extent for the home video game, but not for the

movie or comic books, which appear to be equally accessible to both genders.

7. Do you have any TMNT toys? Any clothes? Which ones?
   Toys:
   Yes—5 (f,h,i,j,k: all boys)
   No—6 (a,b,c,d,e,g: 5 girls, 1 boy)
   Clothes:
   Yes—4 (a,h,j,k: 3 boys, 1 girl)
   No—7 (b,c,d,e,f,g,i: 3 boys, 4 girls)

8. Do you eat TMNT cookies or cereal or drink the juice?
   Yes—6 (b,e: cookies; c: cereal; h,j: juice; k: cookies and juice: 3 girls, 3 boys)
   No—5 (a,d,f,g,i: 2 girls, 3 boys)

Discussion

On these products, which are primarily purchased by parents, there is, surprisingly, even heavier gender coding on toys than on clothes and, not surprisingly, little or no gender coding on the food. This finding supports Susan Willis's claim that "in today's toy market there is a much greater sexual division of toys defined by very particular gender traits than . . . has ever existed before."[1]

9. Which is your favorite Turtle? Why?
   Michelangelo—6
      a: I like him better.
      b: 'Cause orange is one of my favorite colors.
      c: He's the funniest.
      e: [no reason cited]
      g: I like the name.
      k: He has a blue mask [actually orange].
   Leonardo—2
      h: [no reason cited]
      j: He's the leader.
   Raphael—1
      f: He has those little swords.

Raphael and Donatello—1
   i: They don't use words like *dude* so much.
No favorite—1 (d)

Discussion

Four girls preferred Michelangelo and the other girl had no favorite; all of the reasons cited (both by girls and boys) for preferring Michelangelo had nothing to do with power, fighting, or weapons.

10. How do you tell them apart?
   The colors of their masks and bands—4 (a,b,g,i)
   Their names or initials on their belts—2 (e,j)
   I don't know—5 (c,d,f,h,k)

11. What does *mutant* mean?
   f: A kind of animal.
   h: Turtle powers.
   i: Let's go.
   j: Ninja.
   I don't know—7 (a,b,c,d,e,g,k: 5 girls, 2 boys; one girl [b] said, "My father told me but I forgot")

12. What does *ninja* mean?
   a: A guy wearing a black costume.
   c: When you wear a mask.
   f: A guy who knows karate, Chinese or Japanese.
   g: Karate-type thing.
   h: Ninja turtles.
   i: Fight.
   j: Like karate.
   I don't know—4 (b,d,e,k: 3 girls, 1 boy)

Discussion

On the question concerning "how you tell the Turtles apart" (which was in no way linked to gender), the gender split was precisely equal both for those who knew and those who did not know the answer. However, on the questions concerning the definition of *mutant* and *ninja* (words that were associated by many of the children, either correctly or erroneously, with martial arts power), the girls were much more willing than the boys to admit they did not know the answer. Indeed, no one really knew the definition of *mutant*, yet four of the boys guessed or thought they knew, whereas all of the girls (and only two of the boys) admitted they did not know. When asked for the definition of *ninja*, the girls either admitted they did not know or gave a definition that focused on costuming or masquerade, whereas all but one of the boys gave an answer that stressed the link with fighting or karate. At least two answers (one from a boy, the other from a girl) implied that a ninja is a male or "guy"—though historically ninjas included both genders (a fact that is not acknowledged in the TMNT narratives).

13. How do you know they are teenagers?
    a: If they were older, their voices would be deeper.
    b: By the name.
    c: 'Cause they're younger.
    e: Because they're big.
    f: The game says they're fifteen or sixteen.
    g: I'm not sure they are.
    i: By how old they are.
    j: [retells the plot of how Splinter found them when they were babies]
    I don't know—3 (d,h,k: 1 girl, 2 boys)

Discussion

At least four of the answers were relative, comparing this stage of adolescence with either earlier or later stages of growth and implying that being a teenager is a transitional or liminal stage. Also, two of the girls gave what Piaget would call a centralized answer that may have related to their own situation: (c), a six-year-old who is younger than most other second-graders, said, "'Cause they're younger"; whereas (e), a tall six-year-old who is probably bigger than most other youngsters in her first-grade class, said, "Because they're big."

14. Why do you think they are so popular?
   a: They fight and like to help.
   b: The movie and the turtle are neat.
   e: Because they're green.
   f: They save the day and find April and take her where she should be.
   g: Maybe they like the names because they were sculptors and artists.
   i: Kids like how they do tricks.
   j: Because they're ninjas, they fight.
   k: Because they fight.
   I don't know—3 (c,d,h: 2 girls, 1 boy)

Discussion
   Five of the answers (from four boys and one girl) concern action (fighting and/or doing good). The other three answers (two from girls and one from an older boy) concern nonaggressive qualities—being neat, their color, their link with famous artists. Almost all of the answers point to characteristics in the Turtles; none acknowledges any cultural or marketing factors such as how they are commercially promoted. These answers may support Susan Willis's claim that "children have difficulty conceiving of their toys as having been made."[2]

GENERAL DISCUSSION

   Two of the children who speak a foreign language in their home (d,i) showed the least engagement with the Turtle network (in terms of owning commodities like the Nintendo system, a VCR, TMNT toys or clothes, or being exposed to the food, movie, or video tapes). While the girl (d) tended to say "she didn't know" or that she had no favorites among the Turtles, the boy (i) gave answers that challenged the cultural gender coding (for instance, answering that the tape was liked by both girls and boys, and choosing a nongendered tiger costume) or challenged the Turtles themselves (preferring Raphael and Donatello because they didn't use words like *dude* so much, as if implying that they were the least offensive of the Turtles rather than the best). The other two children from homes where a foreign language is spoken seemed more plugged in to the Turtle network in terms of commodities and exposure; one of them (k), however, had the second highest number of "I don't know" responses (8), whereas the other child (j) gave only three such responses. Since both children are six, this difference cannot be accounted for by age, but may be due to the different proficiencies in speaking English ([k] is in the first grade, [j] in the second) or to other cultural differences from their respective Korean and Iranian ethnic backgrounds.

In further research, it might be interesting to explore the various kinds of cultural resistance waged by different ethnic groups from various economic brackets to determine whether such resistance decreases with time spent (in this case) in an American urban culture or is deliberately adhered to as alternative cultural expression within the home. Does resistance differ according to ethnic background—that is, whether the family comes from India, Asia, Latin America, Africa, or Europe?

Age differences also appeared to be a significant factor in the children's responses. While the two oldest male subjects (f and g, one black, the other Caucasian) created some ironic distance from the Turtle network by calling it humorous, stupid, or unrealistic or by preferring other more mature popular heroes (like Freddy Krueger, the popular villain from the *Nightmare on Elm Street* film and TV series, and Black Arrow, an identity temporarily adopted by D.C. comic book hero Green Arrow and passed on to his girlfriend in the "Black Arrow Saga"), one wonders whether a similar resistance would be found in girls of the same age or in boys from different class or ethnic backgrounds? The youngest child (h, age five) tended to say yes to every question, even if that answer was improbable (as was his claim that he was only three, not five) and to answer simply "because" whenever he was asked "why." Yet he did not hesitate to define both *mutant* and *ninja* when several of the older children said they did not know the answer. Would a five-year-old girl or a five-year-old boy from a different class, ethnic, or racial background respond in a similar way? There were not enough subjects in this study to answer such questions; at least six subjects in each category or "cell" would be needed to obtain statistically significant results.

Particularly interesting was the frequency with which some of the girls answered "I don't know," in contrast to the boys, who usually guessed or assumed they knew. While this response was undoubtedly more candid than that of the boys on the definition of *mutant*, when asked to define *ninja* the boys did tend to know the answer, whereas the girls (both those who gave a definition and those who said they did not know the answer) tended to disavow the violence—a pattern that is observable as well in their reasons for preferring the character of Michelangelo and on the final question about popularity. When a girl (a) did directly confront the violence and the cultural gender coding of the Turtles network in contrast to Barbie dolls, her answers were contradictory: she chose Michelangelo as her favorite character (instead of April O'Neil, whom most of the other girls picked), yet wanted to wear a princess costume ("so I can go to the tower and the princess's room")—a response that may involve an awareness of class difference and buying power as much as differences in gender.

This study made me want to spend more time interviewing children like (a), (g), (f), (i), (j), and (k) to find out more about how they negotiate the meanings of cultural production and how they are being formed as gendered subjects by supersystems like Barbie dolls and Teenage Mutant Ninja Turtles.

APPENDIX 2

PROCEDURE

On July 22, 1990, a sunny day in Los Angeles, I went to the Playland Arcade on the Santa Monica Pier, an arcade that draws players from all parts of the city, and videotaped interviews with twelve children who were playing at one of two Teenage Mutant Ninja Turtles arcade machines. My crew was there for five hours (11:00 A.M. to 4:00 P.M.), during which time some forty-five children played with these two game machines. All of these children were males; approximately 40 percent were black (18), 30 percent Caucasian (13), 15 percent Latino (7), and 15 percent Asian (7).

We tried to select subjects who would reflect the racial representation of the players; however, all of the Asian players declined to be interviewed, as did many of the Caucasian children (or their parents). We interviewed ten boys, three of whom we had brought with us—my son, Victor (H), and two male friends from his class (F and J). Since no girls were playing Teenage Mutant Ninja Turtles, we requested interviews with one black girl (B) who was playing a nearby machine and with a Latino girl (A) who was not playing any arcade games but was wearing a TMNT t-shirt. In all, then, we conducted twelve interviews with children aged six to fourteen (with a median age of eight and a half). Five of the children were black (B,D,I,K, L), four Caucasian (C,F,G,J), and three Latino (A,E,H). Three spoke a foreign language in the home: one Hebrew (C) and two Spanish (A,E).

THE TMNT ARCADE GAME

In this arcade game, produced by Konami, four players can play at once. Each player occupies a separate playing post with its own control panel containing two buttons, marked "Attack" and "Jump," and a knob for controlling directional movements. Each player identifies with and controls the moves of one of the four color-coded Turtles, each feeds quarters into a separate slot, and each has a separate tally indicating the current point total and the number of remaining lives.

Regardless of how many players are playing, the Turtle(s) encounter the same enemies in their quest to free their friend April O'Neil and their rat guru, Splinter, who occasionally appear in bondage as static images on screen. Both are being held captive by the villainous Shredder and his henchmen—the Stone Warriors, the evil scientist Baxter Stockman, Rock Steady, Bebop, and Krang—and their fleet of anonymous Foot soldiers, mousers, and robots. The more Turtles in action, the greater their chances of defeating the enemy; thus there is a narrative (as well as an economic) incentive to have all four playing posts occupied.

The game is structured in five "scenes" of nonstop combat, each with its own explicit mission (for example, scene 1, "Fire, we gotta get April out!"; scene 4, "We gotta save Splinter"; and scene 5, "We gotta find the Technodrome") and its own settings and enemies (battling Rock Steady in a burning high rise; fighting in the sewers against a helicopter piloted by Baxter; skateboarding down city streets while confronting enemies on motorcycles, skateboards, and helicopters; seeking out Krang, Shredder, and the latter's masked double for the final showdown in the Technodrome; and so on). If a Turtle is hit by Shredder in this climactic battle, he turns into an ordinary turtle and loses a life.

Each Turtle begins the game with two lives and gains new

energy whenever he eats a pizza. When a Turtle kills Bebop, the Turtle Van drives up to take the amphibious warriors to the next scene, and April appears on screen, kisses a Turtle, and says, "I owe you one." When a Turtle kills one of the Stone Warriors in scene 4, he frees Splinter, who says, "Thank you, my Turtles." In battle, the Turtles receive nasty messages from the enemy, which help to strengthen the players' identification with their heroes. For example, Rock Steady says, "Say your prayers, Toitles"; Bebop taunts, "You're dead, shell brain," or "Watch your mouth, slime ball"; and Shredder mocks, "Tonight I dine on turtle soup." In addition to being printed on the screen like dialogue in comic books, most of these remarks are also spoken as part of the soundtrack—along with the music, explosions, and *cowabunga*'s; however, because of the noise level in most arcades, they are usually difficult to hear.

Whenever a Turtle is defeated in battle, the words *Shell Shock* appear on the screen and he loses one of his lives. When a Turtle loses both lives, the suturing identification is broken, for a series of messages appears that directly addresses the player: *Game Over, To Continue, Insert Coin*. If a player rapidly inserts another coin, he can continue from where he left off and retain his previous score, which is the only way ever to "win" the game. If the player waits too long, the message *Game Is Over* is repeated in big red letters in the center of the screen and he has to start all over from the beginning of scene 1. Thus, the structure of the game motivates players to come prepared with plenty of quarters (or tokens).

QUESTIONS AND ANSWERS

About the Children and Their Family Households

1. What is your age and grade?

Girls	Boys
A. 10 yrs, 4th	C. 14 yrs, 9th
B. 8 yrs, 3d	D. 12 yrs, 7th
	E. 10 yrs, 5th

F. 8 yrs, 2d
G. 7½ yrs, 3d
H. 7½ yrs, 2d
I. 7 yrs, 2d
J. 6½ yrs, 2d
K. 6 yrs, 1st
L. 6 yrs, 1st

2. Do you have any brothers or sisters? How many? What age?

Yes—10 (1 [A] had five sisters, older and younger; 2 [B,D] had three younger sisters and brothers; 2 [I,K] had two younger brothers; 1 [C] had one younger sister; 2 [H,J] had one older sister; 1 [E] had one younger brother; 1 [F] had one older brother)

No—2 (G,L)

3. Do you live at home with both your mother and father?
Yes—8
No, only with my mother—4 (B,C,I,L)

4. Do you speak another language besides English at home?
Yes—3 (Hebrew [C] and Spanish [A,E])
No—9

5. What do your father and mother do for a living?

Mother	Father
A. Works at my school	I don't know
B. [no response]	[no response]
C. Works in office	
D. Works in bank at UCLA	Works on cars
E. Stays at home	Sells things
F. Lawyer	I don't know [marketing exec]
G. Usually reads her book	Does guitar
H. They work [professor]	[makes neon/painter]
I. She cleans up	

J.	Lawyer	A scientist and a teacher
K.	Goes to school	Works on pier
L.	I don't know	I don't know

6. Do you have a Nintendo video game system at home?
   Yes—6 (E,F,G,H,K,L)
   No—6 (A,B,C,D,I,J)

7. Do you have a VCR?
   Yes—11
   No—1 (L)

8. Do you have a TV set?
   Yes—11
   No—1 (I)

9. Is there a computer in your home? If so, do you ever get to use it?
   Yes/Yes—4 (C,F,J,K)
   Yes/No—3 (D,G,H)
   No—5 (A,B,E,I,L)

Discussion

It immediately became clear that the responses of the children were not always reliable. Some subjects were too young to understand some of the questions or to know some of the answers. Others wanted (either consciously or unconsciously) to have their answers reflect their desire rather than reality. Or for whatever reason (class, pride, embarrassment, disavowal), they simply did not want to divulge certain information. These denials and evasions became most obvious in the responses of my own son (H), who claimed that he had no siblings (he has an older sister) and who said that his mother and father "work," without specifying what they do. When I later inquired why he gave these answers, he said that he didn't realize I was asking him what kind of jobs his parents had and that his sister didn't live with us anymore (which is true). Similar omissions or distortions were also present in the responses of his friends (F and

J), whose family situations and experience I know about from other sources. For example, (J) said his mother is a lawyer, yet actually she works with lawyers but is not one herself.

Discrepancies were also detectable in the interviews with two of the children from the lowest economic bracket (B and I), who, before the interview, introduced themselves as sister and brother, but whose responses were frequently contradictory. For example, although the girl (B) presumably was counting him as one of her younger brothers, he claimed he had only brothers, no sisters. When asked what their mother did for a living, she gave no reply, but he said, "She cleans up." When asked whether they had a TV set, she said yes and he said no.

Children from higher economic brackets were also reluctant to admit that they did not possess certain hardware, like the Nintendo Entertainment System. For example, (J) (whose parents intentionally bought him a more expensive computer instead) gave a pained expression, and (L) added (a few questions later), "No, but I'm gonna get one." Unlike the Bing school (the site of the investigation described in appendix 1, where, despite ethnic and racial diversity, the economic and educational status of the families were more similar), here the range was considerably wider. Thus this section of the interview was apparently a painful reminder to some subjects of what they did not or could not have.

About Their Experience with the Arcade Games

1. Have you ever played the TMNT home video game?
   Yes—7 ("Yes, I have it" [G,H])
   No—5 ("No, but I'm gonna get one" [L])

2. If so, which do you like better, the home video game or the arcade game? Why?
   Arcade game—6
   C: Everybody gets to play, it's not as hard.
   D: You can play all four men and get help.
   E: It has bigger men and they fight outside.
   F: It has better graphics.

G: It's more funner.

H: I like the graphics better.

Home game—1

K: It's more fun.

3. How many times have you played this arcade game?

Lots or quite a few times—3 (D,G,H)

About 100 times—1 (F)

40 times—1 (C)

10 times—1 (E)

7 times—1 (J)

4 or 5 times—1 (L)

Twice—2 (B,I)

Never—1 (A)

I don't know—1 (K)

4. Which Turtle do you like to be? Why?

Leonardo—5

C: He has the longest reach.

D: His stick reaches to the victims and kills them better.

I: I like how swift his sword is.

J: He has swords and can chop down metal.

L: I like the way he got those swords . . . I wish I been him.

Michelangelo—3

A: He's cool.

E: He's a party dude.

F: He has the best weapon—nunchucks.

Raphael—2

G: He's funny.

H: He can roll.

Donatello—2

B: I think he's fresh and neato.

K: He hits people with a stick.

Discussion

No matter which Turtle they pick, the reason given by the girls for their preference is an adjective reflective of their own judgment or feeling ("he's cool," "he's fresh and neato") rather than describing his weapons or his actions, which is what the boys tended to focus on. This difference may be explained in part by the fact that the boys know the game better because they play it more frequently, but this same pattern was also observed in the previous study at the Bing school.

5. Do you like to stick with one Turtle or to switch from one to the other? Why?

Switch — 7

D: If I don't like one, I can change.

F: It's easier.

G: I just like to change.

H: Some Turtles are better for some things.

I: I like it.

J: Then I get more practice on all of them.

K: Because.

Stick — 2

B: I don't know why.

C: I get used to their maneuvers.

I like both, it doesn't matter — 2

E, L

I don't know — 1

A (has never played the game)

Discussion

Subjects either gave a strategic reason for switching Turtles (D,H,J,C) or merely expressed an intuitive preference (F,G,I, K,B). Despite the varied reasons cited, apparently most children like to shift identification and become a sliding signifier, or, as (G) puts it, they "just like to change."

6. Why can't you choose to be Splinter or April?

Splinter	*April*
A: [Doesn't know because she hasn't played the game]	A: [Doesn't know because hasn't played the game]
B: He's too old, he's thirty.	B: I don't know.

C: He's just their teacher, he's not one of them.

C: She's a reporter, she's not a Turtle, she's just reporting.

D: Splinter's a bad guy. . . no, because he's a rat, not a Turtle.

D: She's not a Turtle, she's a girl.

E: He doesn't do nothing, he stays at home in the sewer.

E: She's a girl.

F: I don't know, that's the way it's made.

F: She can't fight that well.

G: I always want to be Splinter but this other kid says there is no Splinter in the game.

G: Because I'm a boy.

H: Splinter is captured.

H: April is captured, too.

I: He too old.

I: I don't know.

J: There is no Splinter in it.

J: There is no April in it.

K: I like Splinter too, but he gets caught.

K: You gotta save her.

L: I don't care if I be Master Splinter.

L: Well, I ain't no girl.

7. Do you think this arcade game is made for both boys and girls, or just boys?

    Both boys and girls—11

    Just boys—1 (J: Because boys like Turtles and girls don't, girls won't play them, they like Barbies . . . disgusting!)

Discussion

With the exception of (J), all subjects disavowed the masculine orientation of the arcade game—even though not a single girl was seen playing it all day and even though on the previous question (which dealt with the gender issue more indirectly) many answers did acknowledge gender difference. Except for (A) (a female subject who admittedly has never played the game), all subjects gave a reason for why Splinter could not be picked: because of structural reasons in the game (F,G,J), or because of his role in the narrative as teacher (C) or captive (H,K), or because of his personal characteristics—age (B,I), species (D), or passivity (E).

With regard to April, in contrast, two subjects (B and I, sister and brother) said they did not know why she could not be picked. Of those who did give reasons for her exclusion, four boys (D,E,G,L) mentioned gender, while five others mentioned some structural reason in the game that may or may not relate to gender ("You gotta save her," "She is captured," "She can't fight that well," "She's a reporter," "There's no April in it"). Not surprisingly for this age group, no one criticized or questioned the structure of the game and its treatment of gender difference.

The two oldest boys came close to a kind of parity by explaining that neither Splinter nor April is a Turtle, yet (D) elaborated by naming their species and gender as the respective reasons for their exclusion while (C) (who lives with a single mother) disavowed the gender issue by referring to their respective roles as teacher and reporter. Only two boys (H and J) gave the same structural reason for both Splinter and April ("They are captured," "They are not in it"); interestingly, both these boys have mothers who are career women. Yet on the following question (where children were asked whether the arcade game was made for both boys and girls or just boys), (J) was the only subject who directly confronted the gender issue by answering "boys." Moreover, his response ("Because boys like Turtles and girls don't, girls won't play them, they like Barbies . . . disgusting") was the most overtly negative remark about females in both sets of interviews; instead of stating that the Turtles were designed for boys and Barbies designed for girls (as the question implied), he explicitly *blamed* the girls for willfully choosing dolls over video games. Like the other children, he denied the responsibility of the manufacturers or the media for this difference and accepted them uncritically as a benevolent force. These answers seem to support Susan Willis's contention that most children merely accept the world of the toys and all of its ideological assumptions without "conceiv[ing] of such a universe as having been produced."[1]

While all the explanations of the older children (from age eight to fourteen) referred only to the characters (Splinter, April, and the Turtles), three of the younger children also described themselves—their own preferences ("I like Splinter too"), desires ("I always want to be Splinter"), and gender ("Because I'm a boy"). This pattern is consistent with Piaget's observation that decentration occurs with cognitive development. Yet interestingly, the youngest child (L), who gave subjective reasons for the exclusion of *both* figures and who lives with a single mother, was the most emphatic about excluding April on the basis of gender ("Well, I ain't no girl"). The ambiguity about whether he wanted to be Splinter, though, had more to do with the character's role as a teacher/authority ("I don't care if I be Master Splinter"), as in the more intellectualized explanation of the oldest child (C).

8. Do you think this game is very violent? Do you like that aspect of the game—the fighting? Why or why not?

   Is the game violent?
   Yes—4 (B,F,I,K)
   No—6 (C,D,E,G,H,J)
   I don't know—2 (A,L)

   Do you like this aspect, the fighting?
   Yes—11   (3 [B,G,L] try to justify the violence morally):
             B: Yes, they can beat them up cause Shredder is the one what told them to get him.
             G: Yes, because the foot soldiers are just robots.
             L: I like to watch the Turtles fight Shredder's men.

   5 (C,D,E,F,I) give no justification beyond "it's just fun/action":
             C: I like fighting, it's fun, it's action!

D: It's exciting.
E: I like the action.
F: It has lots of action.
I: It's fun.
  3 (H,J,K) give no reason

9. After playing the game, do you feel like fighting with someone in real life?
    Yes—0
    No—11 (L: "No, I don't like fighting")

Discussion

All eleven subjects who answered these questions claimed that they liked the fighting in the arcade game, yet after playing the game they had no desire to fight in real life. This apparent contradiction could be interpreted to mean (in part or in combination) that the children are disavowing the violence because they know it is socially disapproved behavior, that they are using the games to channel their aggression, or that their disavowal reflects that of the culture as a whole. The contradictions are most obvious in the responses of the youngest subject (L), perhaps because he is still too young to perceive them. Although he says he does not know whether the game is violent, he nevertheless admits that he likes to watch the Turtles fight Shredder's men, and then he insists, "I don't like fighting." He could be distinguishing between fictional fighting (which he likes, particularly when it is morally justified by being against bad guys) and fighting in real life (which he dislikes because his family and society claim to condemn it).

Interestingly, only four subjects (B,F,I,K) admitted the game was violent—three of whom were black and from a low economic bracket; the other subjects denied it or said they didn't know whether it was violent or not. Only three subjects (B,G,L) tried to justify the violence on moral grounds; the others replied that it was fun, or redefined it euphemistically as "action" as if they were inseparable, or simply gave no reason for why they liked the fighting. The only subject who both acknowledged the violence and tried to justify it morally was (B), a black female.

10. When you are playing TMNT, do you ever talk to the other players? What kinds of things do you say?
    Yes—5
    B: Like the water, Our mom, School.
    C: Get him, Look out, Hurry up.
    D: Get that guy, Go after him.
    F: Do you have any quarters left?
    H: I try to tell them that something's coming—like a Foot soldier is going to jump out of the sewer and throw the sewer top.
    Sometimes—2
    E: How do you beat this guy? What level does this go up to?
    J: Hello, Why do the Turtles jump in without your making them?
    No—4 (G,I,K,L)
    G: I just pay attention to the game.
    L: But when we went to Pizza Hut with my cousin, I was talking to her to show her how to play it.

11. Why do you think they made the game so that four players can play at the same time?
    C: So it would be easier to play.
    D: Because they have all these men attacking you at once.
    E: So other people can get a chance to play with their friends and family.
    F: They thought it was easier for little kids to play.
    G: So it can be more funner.
    H: Because it would be harder for just one player.
    I: 'Cause.
    J: So they can beat the bad guys.
    K: 'Cause there are four Turtles.
    I don't know (B,L)

12. When you come to the arcade, whom do you usually come with?

   Friends—5 (C,D,F,I,J)

   Family—7 (B,E,G,H,I,K,L: cousins and brother; family; my dad; mom and dad; sister and friend; dad, brother, and sister; mother, father, cousins, aunties and uncles)

Discussion

All of the subjects said that they usually came to the arcade with friends or family (which may not be the case for older players). Most of them appreciated that four players could play TMNT at the same time, and most enjoyed talking to other players, even if they didn't know them. These responses, which were corroborated by the video taping of the action in the arcade, challenge the claim that video games foster alienation.

Subjects reported three kinds of verbal interaction: to tell other players what to do (C,D); to seek help, information, or money (F,E,J); and to offer assistance to others (H,L). The idiosyncratic response of (B) ("Like the water," "Our mom," "School") may indicate that she has not really played the game. All other responses focus on developing cognitive skills to improve one's ability to play the game, which may suggest the kind of interaction that helps players move across Vygotsky's zone of proximal development.

13. How often do you come to the arcade?

   Lots of times—1 (G)

   Three times a week—1 (F)

   Every weekend—2 (D,K)

   Twice a month—2 (C,E)

   First time today—2 (I,L)

   Not much—1 (J)

   I don't know—2 (B,H)

14. How much money do you usually spend in the arcade? How much have you spent so far today?

   B: $50; today a quarter

   C: $5; today $1.25

D: Once I spent $15; today only $1
E: $5–$6; today $5
F: $10; today around $20 [he actually spent $25]
G: Lots; not much because we just got here
H: $5 or something; today, I don't know [he spent $25]
I: I don't know; today fifty cents
J: Not much; today, about a hundred cents [he spent $25]
K: $100; today $2
L: I don't know; I don't know

Discussion

Some subjects tended to exaggerate the frequency of their visits (such as J, who was actually there for the first time, and F), and several simply didn't know. Most subjects were similarly unreliable in reporting how much money they were spending. There were large discrepancies between the reported average (which seemed highly exaggerated) and the amount they had spent that day (which seemed more realistic), particularly for youngsters in the lower economic brackets (B: $50 versus a quarter, K: $100 versus $2); in contrast, middle-class subjects (F,H,J) tended to underestimate what they had spent both for the average and that day. These findings may support Willis's claim that the erasure of production within commodity fetishism helps to keep children ignorant of how money works in a consumerist culture.[2]

15. What other arcade games do you like to play?
     Double Dragon—4 (E,F,H,L)
     Cars and motorcycle games—3 (B,E,I)
     Final Fight and After Burner—1 (C)
     Super Mario and Motor Cross—1 (D)
     Robo Cop—1 (E)
     Super Contra—1 (F)
     Off Road—1 (G)
     Skeeter Ball—1 (J)
     Castle Vania—1 (L)

All the games—1 (K)

16. Which is your favorite arcade game? Why?
    Teenage Mutant Ninja Turtles—10
    It's fun (C,D,G)
    Lots of action (C,F)
    I like the Turtles (H,I,L; I: They're cool; L: I wish I
        been one of those 'cause they like to eat pizza and I
        like to eat pizza, too)
    They fight (B: They fight, and you get more than three
        turns, you can have four people play; J: It does a lot
        of fighting and I really like them)
    All of them are my favorites—1 (K)

Discussion

Clearly "Teenage Mutant Ninja Turtles" falls in the category
of fast-paced action games, which were favored by most subjects
because they're "fun," but it is distinguished from other games
by allowing four players to play at the same time and by its
distinctive heroes, who apparently are more appealing sites of
identification than most other video game heroes.

About Their Experience with TMNT

1. How did you first find out about TMNT?
    The movie—2 (A,D; D: I saw the movie and then went
    to the arcade and it was there)
    Cartoons—3 (E,K,L; L: I saw a game and a cartoon)
    The store—2 (B,I; B: At the liquor store I saw the cook-
    ies)
    My friend—2 (F,J)
    Arcade—3 (C: I went to an arcade and it was there; D
    and L also mention the game, along with the movie [D]
    and cartoons [L])
    TV commercial—1 (H)
    I forgot—1 (G)

2. Did you see the movie? How many times?
    Yes—8 (6 once [A,D,E,G,J,K]; J: But I haven't seen *Tur-
    tles II*; 2 twice [F,H])

No—4 (B,C,I,L)

3. Do you watch the TV show?
    Yes—7 (A,D,E,F,J,K,L; J: Sometimes, but sometimes I sleep late and miss it)
    No—5 (B,C,N,H,I; H: I don't know what channel it's on)

4. Do you have any of the tapes?
    Yes—6 (B,E,F,H,J,L; J: All four from Burger King, plus two others)
    No—6 (A,C,D,G,I,K)

5. Have you read any of the TMNT comic books?
    Yes—10 (B,C ["a little"], D,E,F,G,H,J ["only one"], K)
    No—2 (A,L)

6. Which do you like best—the movie, TV show, comic book, video game, or arcade game? Why?
    Arcade game—5
        G: It's fun.
        H: I just like it.
        J: Because you can move the guys yourself and in the movie and the tapes, you can just see them.
        C, I: [no reason cited]
    Movie—4
        D: It shows them in person.
        E: They show how it all began and how Splinter throws Shredder off the building.
        F: It's more real.
        A: [no reason cited]
    Comics—1
        B: They're funny.
    Cartoons—1
        K: They're fun.
    Game and cartoon—1
        L: [no reason cited]

7. Do you have any TMNT toys? Any clothes? Which ones?
Toys:
Yes—7 (E,F,G,H,J,K,L)
No—5 (A,B,C,D,I)
Clothes:
Yes—5 (A,E,G,H,L; A,E,G,H were wearing TMNT t-shirts)
No—7 (B,C,D,F,I,J,K)

8. Do you eat TMNT cookies or cereal or drink the juice?
Yes—4 (E,H,J,K)
No—8 (A,B,C,D,F,G,I,L; C: Yuck!)

Discussion

At least two subjects explicitly mentioned a combination of two exposures (movie and arcade game, or game and cartoon) as their entry point into the network, which may indicate that the perception of the transmedia tie-in was part of the appeal. Most subjects in the lower economic brackets had as their entry point the arcade and the store. Thus, all classes may have access to this supersystem but with a different combination of entrances. Some subjects were quite perceptive in distinguishing among the different modes of image production, especially when describing the movie as more realistic (D,F) and the arcade game as more interactive (J).

9. Which is your favorite Turtle? Why?
Leonardo—6
   C: He has the longest reach.
   D: He's more active.
   F: He's the oldest and the best one.
   H,I: He's cool.
   J: He's just my favorite.
Michelangelo—2
   A: He's cool.
   E: He's a party dude and says a lot of weird things.
Leonardo and Donatello—2

K: They're fun.

L: [after a long pause, he added Michelangelo] They fight better.

Donatello—1

B: He's fresh and neato.

Raphael—1

G: He's funny.

10. How do you tell them apart?

Colors—5 (D,E,F,G,H; G: Different colored masks; H: Donatello is purple, Leonardo is blue, Michelangelo is orange, Raphael is red)

Language—2 (E,J; E: Colors and the way they talk; J: 'Cause they don't say the right things, Michelangelo thinks about dudes, Raphael thinks about pizza, Donatello thinks about fighting, and Leonardo thinks about Splinter)

Weapons—1 (C)

Their belts—1 (K)

Don't know—4 (A,B,I,L)

Discussion

As in the study at the Bing school, regardless of which Turtle is chosen, the reasons that girls give for their preference have nothing to do with action or weapons but single out adjectives (or semes) that express their approval ("He's cool," "He's fresh and neato"), whereas several boys give reasons connected with action and weapons (C,D,E,L). Neither of the girls knew how to tell the Turtles apart (probably they are less familiar with the game); the two boys who did not know were the youngest (L) and one of the most economically disadvantaged (I). All the other boys knew, and two gave highly detailed answers concerning colors (H) and language (J).

11. What does *mutant* mean?

C: Not human, a cross between two things.

G: They used to be regular turtles but some slime hit them and they turned into big turtles with muscles.

I: Teenagers.

I don't know—9 (A,B,D,E,F,H,J,K,L; D: I'm not sure; E: I have no idea)

12. What does *ninja* mean?
    C: A form of martial arts.
    D: Just plain ninjas.
    E: Karate person who fights.
    F: A Chinese fighter.
    G: Like someone who kicks and has weapons.
    H: Someone who fights.
    I: Ninja turtles.
    J: They fight.
    L: Some man's karate.
    I don't know—3 (A,B,K)

Discussion

Unlike the study at the Bing school, here only three subjects (C, G, and I, all males) tried to define *mutant,* and all of them were at least on the right track (even the boy who said "teenagers"—which are natural transformers). The rest of the subjects readily admitted that they did not know what the word meant. Perhaps these subjects were more willing (than those in the other study) to admit this because they were in a setting linked to leisure and play rather than in a school environment, where lack of knowledge is interpreted more negatively.

Only three subjects did not try to define *ninja*—both girls and one boy. Most of the boys offering definitions mentioned fighting or karate, and two (D and I) gave tautological answers, merely repeating the phrase ("just plain ninjas" and "ninja turtles"). The youngest boy (L) was the only subject who mentioned gender ("some *man's* karate").

13. How do you know they are teenagers?
    A: I don't know.
    B: One is fifteen, the other is sixteen.
    C: I don't.
    D: They were young at first and then they just grew up.

E: I have a poster that shows they're fifteen and six-teen.

F: They act like teenagers—saying "cowabunga" and things like that.

G: Because they speak and act like them.

H: At the arcade game it tells their age.

I: One is sixteen, the other is fifteen.

J: Because they're not that big.

K: They're fifteen or sixteen.

L: 'Cause they're so young.

Discussion

Only one subject (A, a female who has never played the arcade game) did not know how we know the Turtles are teenagers. Five subjects (B,E,H,I,K) merely stated the specific ages and/or the source of this information (the poster or arcade game). As in the Bing study, those subjects who mentioned teenage characteristics tended to draw attention to qualities that described themselves: (J), who is very big for his age, said, "Because they're not that big"; (L), the youngest, said, "'Cause they're so young"; and (D), who is a very tall twelve-year-old just on the verge of his teens, said, "They were young at first and then they just grew up." With considerable epistemological sophistication, (C) (the only teenage subject in the group) denied that he actually *knew* they were teenagers.

14. Why do you think they are so popular?

B: 'Cause they fight, they beat people, they beat Shredder and save the world.

C: Because they're different, they're not ordinary, people like that.

D: Because everybody likes them.

E: They are selling a lot of stuff in stores and usually I buy things like that.

F: Everybody knows about them and they have lots of stuff.

G: Because they're really funny and lots of people like them.

I: Because they do all kinds of stuff.

L: Because they're cool.

I don't know—4 (A,H,J,K; J: Don't know, they just like them)

Discussion

Unlike the Bing school study, here only two children (B and I, sister and brother) mentioned action when explaining the Turtles' popularity. Others (C,G,L) mentioned nonaggressive qualities (they're "different," "funny," or "cool"). Two subjects (D,G) said, "Because everybody likes them," defining what popular means instead of citing a reason for their popularity. Four (A,H,K,J) claimed they didn't know why the Turtles are so popular. Most interestingly—and again, in contrast to the Bing study—here two subjects (E and F, a ten-year-old Latino and an eight-year-old Caucasian) mentioned the Turtles' commodification—the fact that stores sell lots of goods that carry their image. Both boys seemed to regard this phenomenon as positive.

GENERAL DISCUSSION

Although this study involved too few subjects (particularly females and Latinos) to draw conclusions about gender, class, and racial differences, nevertheless some provocative issues are raised.

Gender difference is even more pronounced in the TMNT arcade game than on the "April Foolish" tape, for in the TV drama (and movie) at least April is one of the main characters, whereas here she is merely a passive captive; moreover, a flat, static image of April in a sexy pose adorns the outside of the machine. This subordination may have led to some of the male subjects' negative comments—particularly on the questions about whether the game was designed for both boys and girls and why April and Splinter were excluded from the action.

As in the study at the Bing school, here we find a black female subject (B) who (like [a]) has contradictory responses to the representation of gender in the Turtle network. On the one hand, she, like most girls in the Bing study, cites nonaggressive qualities as the reason for preferring Donatello over the other Turtles ("He's fresh and neato") and for preferring the comics over other modes of image production ("Because they're funny"). Yet of all the subjects in both studies, she confronts the violence most directly, both admitting that the game is violent and attempting to justify the fighting on moral grounds. She also says she prefers the TMNT arcade game because of the fighting and thinks the fighting is what makes them so popular. Moreover, she likes other fast-action video games like cars and motorcycles. No wonder she has no idea why April O'Neil is excluded.

Although all the subjects were cooperative, some of the questions (particularly about possessions) may have aroused anxiety in those youngsters who could not afford much, possibly even provoking them to lie or exaggerate. This dynamic was particularly true in subjects from lower economic brackets, who were certainly aware of the TMNT network but may have exaggerated the degree of their own participation.

Yet the subjects universally showed little understanding of money—of how much they or their parents spend on the games, or of the manufacturers' economic motives. For example, no one mentioned that one reason for having four players play at the same time is to quadruple profits. In contrast, at least two children acknowledged that the great number of goods carrying the Turtles image contributed to their popularity, a dynamic that they seemed to approve. The subjects apparently all viewed consumerism positively—even if it aroused some unconscious anger or resentment in the have-nots. These findings support Susan Willis's arguments about the toy industry. She states: "Not too many generations ago, children were brought into capitalist production as workers when they were ten or eleven years old. Today the situation is different. Now capitalism seeks to incorporate children as the reproducers of society. Children learn and want to be consumers at an ever earlier age."[3]

I argue throughout this book—and it is an argument consistent with the answers in these two sets of interviews—that children's television, video games, and the intertextual supersystems in which they are positioned function as the primary means by which children are interpellated as interactive consumers, and that physical, emotional, and cognitive growth and the ability to read and generate narratives are appropriated as forms of expanded consumption. In this way, our postmodernist consumer culture guarantees its own reproduction.

Notes

1. FOREPLAY AND OTHER PRELIMINARIES

1. Beverle Houston, "Viewing Television: The Metapsychology of Endless Consumption," *Quarterly Review of Film Studies* 9, no. 3 (Summer 1984): 185.

2. Mikhail Bakhtin, "Discourse in the Novel" (1934–35), in *The Dialogic Imagination*, trans. Caryl Emerson and Michael Holquist (Austin: University of Texas Press, 1981), 281. See also Julia Kristeva, "Poésie et négativité," in *Séméiotikè: Recherches pour une sémanalyse* (Paris: Editions du Seuil, 1969), 246–77.

3. Robert Stam, "Mikhail Bakhtin and Left Cultural Critique," in *Postmodernism and Its Discontents*, ed. E. Ann Kaplan (London: Verso, 1988), 138.

4. Jean Piaget, "Piaget's Theory," in *The Process of Child Development*, ed. Peter Neubauer (New York: Meridian, 1976), 165, 170, 182. Piaget defines *accommodation* as "any modification of an assimilatory scheme or structure by the elements it assimilates" and *assimilation* as "the integration of external elements into evolving or completed structures of an organism."

5. Elaine Dutka and Nina J. Easton, "Hollywood's Brave New World," *Los Angeles Times*, December 23, 1990, "Calendar" sec., 77.

6. Andrew Pollack, "New Interactive TV Threatens the Bliss of Couch Potatoes," *New York Times*, June 18, 1990, C7.

7. Arthur Applebee, *The Child's Concept of Story: Ages Two to Seventeen* (Chicago: University of Chicago Press, 1978), 16. Although Applebee's description of these modes as a "subjective" poetic discourse (that demands spectator response), on the one hand, and an "objec-

tive" transactional discourse (requiring interactive participation), on the other, is somewhat problematic, the modes are useful for distinguishing between two complementary types of spectatorship that develop along with the child's cognitive abilities.

8. Ibid., 125.

9. Not only does Applebee observe that "many traditional theories of language development would certainly imply that . . . the earliest functions of language are interactive, even imitative, rather than detached and personal in the ways characteristic of the spectator role," but he also claims that during the preoperational stage (which lasts until about age six or seven) the child typically "relies on poetic techniques, reexperiencing the story in the process of retelling it" (i.e., on the spectator mode), whereas "with the advent of concrete operations," the older child (of seven or eight) has the "new ability to categorize," which "leads to the first relatively extended discussions of stories using transactional techniques" (i.e., the interactive participant mode) (ibid., 105). Moreover, these analytical techniques of "formal operational thought" are further expanded in two stages of adolescence: "During the earliest of these, probably corresponding to the twelve-to-fifteen-year-old age span during which Piaget asserts that these mechanisms are in the process of being acquired, response is formulated as analysis. . . . The second stage of formal operational thought represents the most mature mode of response. . . . Here, readers begin to generalize about the meaning of a work . . . and can analyze in support of their generalizations; they can categorize and summarize; and they can retell in whole or in part, depending on their purpose" (124–25).

10. Jean Piaget, *The Psychology of Intelligence* (1947), trans. Malcolm Piercy and D. E. Berlyne (Totowa, N.J.: Littlefield, Adams, 1981), 123.

11. Piaget, "Piaget's Theory," 200–202.

12. Jean Piaget, *Judgment and Reasoning in the Child*, trans. Marjorie Warden (Totowa, N.J.: Littlefield, Adams, 1976), 171–72.

13. Jean Piaget, *The Development of Thought: Equilibration of Cognitive Structures*, trans. Arnold Rosin (New York: Viking Press, 1977), 3.

14. Susan Willis, "Gender as Commodity," *South Atlantic Quarterly* 86, no. 4 (Fall 1987): 404.

15. Lynne Joyrich, "Individual Response," *Camera Obscura*, nos. 20–21 (May–September 1989): 193 (special issue entitled "Spectatrix," edited by Janet Bergstrom and Mary Ann Doane).

16. See David Bordwell's *Making Meaning: Inference and Rhetoric in the Interpretation of Cinema* (Cambridge, Mass.: Harvard University Press, 1989), xiv. See also *Narration in the Fiction Film* (Madison: Uni-

versity of Wisconsin Press, 1985); and Edward Branigan's *Point of View in the Cinema: A Theory of Narration and Subjectivity in Classic Film* (New York: Mouton, 1984).

17. Louis Althusser, "Freud and Lacan," in *Lenin and Philosophy and Other Essays*, trans. Ben Brewster (New York: Monthly Review Press, 1971), 207, 209, 211, 212, 215, 216.

18. Louis Althusser, "Ideology and Ideological State Apparatuses (Notes Towards an Investigation)," in *Lenin and Philosophy*, 174.

19. Christian Metz, "Story/Discourse: Notes on Two Kinds of Voyeurism," in *Movies and Methods*, ed. Bill Nichols, vol. 2 (Berkeley and Los Angeles: University of California Press, 1985), 545.

20. Applebee, *Child's Concept of Story*, 138. The study that he cites is Evelyn Goodenough Pitcher and Ernst Prelinger, *Children Tell Stories: An Analysis of Fantasy* (New York: International University Press, 1963).

21. Seymour Papert, *Mindstorms: Children, Computers, and Powerful Ideas* (New York: Basic Books, 1980), 157–58, 166. Papert also compares his computational "patchwork theory" of theory building with Claude Lévi-Strauss's notion of *bricolage* (defined in *Totemism*, trans. Rodney Neeham [Boston: Beacon Press, 1963] and *Structural Anthropology* [New York: Basic Books, 1976]). Papert writes: "Learning consists of building up a set of materials and tools that one can handle and manipulate. Perhaps most central of all, it is a process of working with what you've got. We're all familiar with this process on the conscious level, for example, when we attack a problem empirically, trying out all the things that we have ever known to have worked on similar problems before. But here I suggest that working with what you've got is a shorthand for deeper, even unconscious learning processes. Anthropologist Claude Lévi-Strauss has spoken in similar terms of the kind of theory building that is characteristic of primitive science. This is a science of the concrete, where the relationships between natural objects in all their combinations and recombinations provide a conceptual vocabulary for building scientific theories. Here I am suggesting that in the most fundamental sense, we, as learners, are all *bricoleurs*" (173). Papert observes that, like so-called primitive *bricoleurs*, "computer scientists have devoted much of their talent and energy to developing powerful descriptive formalisms" (100)—which, one might add, sometimes equal, if not surpass, in formalist rigor and detail, the close textual analysis performed by critics of film and television like myself.

22. Mary Ann Spencer Pulaski, *Understanding Piaget: An Introduction to Children's Cognitive Development* (New York: Harper and Row, 1971), 224.

23. Papert, *Mindstorms*, 170.

24. Katherine Nelson, ed., *Narratives from the Crib* (Cambridge, Mass.: Harvard University Press, 1989).

25. Jerome Bruner and Joan Lucariello, "Monologue as Narrative Recreation of the World," in Nelson (ed.), *Narratives from the Crib*, 75.

26. John Dore, "Monologue as Reenvoicement of Dialogue," in Nelson (ed.), *Narratives from the Crib*, 231–60.

27. See B. F. Skinner, *Verbal Behavior* (New York: Appleton-Century Crofts, 1957); and Noam Chomsky, *Aspects of the Theory of Syntax* (Cambridge, Mass.: MIT Press, 1965).

28. See Gregory Bateson, *Steps to an Ecology of Mind* (New York: Ballantine Books, 1972).

29. Dore, "Monologue as Reenvoicement," 234, 232.

30. Ibid., 239, 237, 240.

31. L. F. Alwitt et al., "Preschool Children's Visual Attention to Attributes of Television," *Human Communication Research* 7 (1980): 52–67. Here is how the results of their experiment are summarized in *Television and Behavior: Ten Years of Scientific Progress and Implications for the Eighties*, the influential study by the National Institute of Mental Health (Washington, D.C.: Government Printing Office, 1982): "Children also are attracted to television by specific features of the programs, not by just what they see and hear in general. They more often look, and continue to look, at such features as women characters, activity or movement, and camera cuts, and not to look when there are extended zooms and pans, animals, and still pictures. Auditory cues turn out to be more important than expected; women's and children's voices, auditory changes, peculiar voices, sound effects, laughing, and applause all attract and hold attention, but male voices do not" (1:21).

32. Kaja Silverman, *The Acoustic Mirror: The Female Voice in Psychoanalysis and Cinema* (Bloomington: Indiana University Press, 1988), 100.

33. L. S. Vygotsky, *Mind in Society: The Development of Higher Psychological Processes*, ed. Michael Cole, Vera John-Steiner, Sylvia Scribner, and Ellen Souberman (Cambridge, Mass.: Harvard University Press, 1978), 86.

34. Ibid., 99–100.

35. Roland Barthes, "Structural Analysis of Narrative," in *Image—Music—Text*, ed. and trans. Stephen Heath (New York: Noonday Press, 1977), 124.

36. Sigmund Freud, *Beyond the Pleasure Principle*, trans. James Strachey (New York: Norton, 1961), 17.

37. Peter Brooks, *Reading for the Plot: Design and Intention in Narrative* (New York: Vintage Books, 1984), 101.

38. Ibid., xi.

39. Ibid., 21, 216.

40. Dore, "Monologue as Reenvoicement," 239.

41. National Institute of Mental Health, *Television and Behavior* 1:69.

42. Jerome Bruner and Joan Lucariello, "Monologue as Narrative Recreation of the World," in Nelson (ed.), *Narratives from the Crib*, 96.

43. Earlier versions of this text include a paper read at the Annual Meeting of the Society for Cinema Studies, Washington, D.C., 1990, called "Animal Masquerade and Transmedia Intertextuality: or, Why I Love Being a Turtle"; and an essay, "Playing with Power on Saturday Morning Television and on Home Video Games," *Quarterly Review of Film and Video* 13, nos. 3–4 (1991) (edited by Nick Browne).

44. Houston, "Viewing Television," 185.

45. Gregory Ulmer, *Teletheory: Grammatology in the Age of Video* (New York: Routledge, 1989), vii.

46. Willis, "Gender as Commodity," 405.

47. Sigmund Freud, "Little Hans," in *The Pelican Freud Library*, vol. 8: *Case Histories I: "Dora" and "Little Hans"* (Harmondsworth: Penguin Books, 1977).

48. Susan Rubin Suleiman, "Writing and Motherhood," in *The (M)other Tongue*, ed. Shirley Nelson Garner, Claire Kahane, Madelon Sprengnether (Ithaca: Cornell University Press, 1985), 355–56.

49. Ibid., 364.

50. Ruth Weir, *Language in the Crib* (The Hague: Mouton, 1962); Nelson (ed.), *Narratives from the Crib*.

51. Patricia Anne Robertson and Peggy Henning Berlin, *The Premature Labor Handbook* (New York: Doubleday, 1986), "Marsha's Story," 136–41.

52. This intertextual network can also be extended to include the TV series "Heart Beat" (which premiered on ABC in spring of 1988 and is now in syndication on HBO), a fictionalized melodrama based on the group of obstetricians (the Women's Medical Group in Santa Monica, California) who made it possible for Victor to be born.

53. In this book, I use the term *paradigm* in two ways. In the semiotic sense (as in this instance), it refers to a list or menu of a particular class or category of words, objects, images, or other signifiers, from which one can select an individual member and combine it (syntagmatically) with similarly selected members from other paradigms to

create some form of discourse—such as a sentence, a story, or a meal. In a more general sense, it also means a pattern or model, as in the phrase "the psychoanalytic paradigm."

54. Jacques Lacan, "The Mirror Stage as Formative of the Function of the I," in *Ecrits: A Selection*, trans. Alan Sheridan (New York: Norton, 1977), 1–7.

55. Piaget, "Piaget's Theory," 166.

56. National Institute of Mental Health, *Television and Behavior* 1:6.

57. According to *Television and Behavior*, "When children are a year old, they watch about 12 percent of the time that the set is on. Between ages 2 and 3 comes a dramatic jump in viewing, from 25 to 45 percent of the time. . . . By age 4, children are watching about 55 percent of the time, often even in a playroom with toys, games, and other distractions" (ibid., 21).

58. Piaget, "Piaget's Theory," 166.

59. Applebee, *Child's Concept of Story*, 16.

60. Ibid., 123.

61. National Institute of Mental Health, *Television and Behavior* 1:22.

62. D. S. Hayes and D. W. Birnbaum, "Pre-Schoolers' Retention of Televised Events: Is a Picture Worth a Thousand Words?" *Developmental Psychology* 16, no. 5 (September 1980): 410–16.

63. National Institute of Mental Health, *Television and Behavior* 1:88.

64. Roland Barthes, *S/Z*, trans. Richard Miller (New York: Hill and Wang, 1974), 19, 29.

65. Applebee, *Child's Concept of Story*, 51.

66. Nelson (ed.), *Narratives from the Crib*, 20.

67. Barthes, *S/Z*, 16.

68. Brooks, *Reading for the Plot*, 99–100.

69. Applebee, *Child's Concept of Story*, 52.

70. This distinction might help to explain the controversy over the recent comedy *Problem Child* (1990), which was attacked by outraged parents, animal rights groups, adoption agencies, and child abuse specialists for portraying in live action the kind of violence that is typically found in cartoons; and for the recent commercial success of *Home Alone* (1990), essentially a second-grader's version of *Straw Dogs*. Perhaps the latter was less controversial because the primary targets of the violence were adult burglars rather than kiddies or pets. The distinction might also help account for the creative tension in *Who Framed Roger Rabbit*, where two kinds of violence are played off against each

other—the exaggerated animated frenzy of the cartoon, and the pervasive evil of live action noir. I develop this argument at greater length in my essay "Back to the Future in the 80s with Fathers and Sons, Supermen and PeeWees, Gorillas and Toons," *Film Quarterly* 42, no. 4 (Summer 1989): 2–11.

71. According to Piaget, "As imitation becomes differentiated and interiorized in images, it also becomes the source of symbols and the instrument of communicative exchange which makes possible the acquisition of language" ("Piaget's Theory," 188).

72. D. W. Winnicott, *Playing and Reality* (London: Routledge, 1971), 5–6.

73. Ibid., 41–47.

74. Patricia Marks Greenfield, *Mind and Media: The Effects of Television, Video Games, and Computers* (Cambridge, Mass.: Harvard University Press, 1984), 101–2.

75. Althusser, "Ideology and Ideological State Apparatuses."

76. See, for example, Ralph Cohen's essay "Do Postmodern Genres Exist?" in *Post-modern Genres*, ed. Marjorie Perloff (Norman: University of Oklahoma Press, 1989), 11–27.

77. Althusser, "Ideology and Ideological State Apparatuses," 148–52.

2. SATURDAY MORNING TELEVISION

1. Beverle Houston, "Viewing Television: The Metapsychology of Endless Consumption," *Quarterly Review of Film Studies* 9, no. 3 (Summer 1984): 183–95.

2. For an excellent analysis of the complex relations among television programs, commercials, and toys, see Howard Gardner with Leona Jaglom, "Cracking the Codes of Television: The Child as Anthropologist," in *Transmission*, ed. Peter D'Agostino (New York: Tanam Press, 1985), 92–102.

3. Observing that "television is watched by children about three hours each day on average," the Children's Television Act of 1990 concludes that "special safeguards are appropriate to protect children from overcommercialization on television." More specifically, it mandates that "each commercial television broadcast license shall limit the duration of advertising in children's television programming to not more than 10.5 minutes per hour on weekends and not more than 12 minutes per hour on weekdays." Also acknowledging that television "can be effective in teaching children," the act establishes a National

Endowment for Children's Educational Television, which will offer grants ($2 million in 1991, $4 million in 1992) to persons who propose to create educational television programming for children who are sixteen years of age or younger. For the full text of this act, see *U.S. Code Congressional and Administrative News*, no. 9 (December 1990): 104 Stats. 996–1000.

4. Mimi White has provided one of the best analyses of "intramedium referentiality" in her excellent and influential essay "Crossing Wavelengths: The Diegetic and Referential Imaginary of American Commercial Television," *Cinema Journal* 25, no. 2 (Winter 1986): 51–64. See also John Fiske, *Television Culture* (London: Methuen, 1987). For the 1990 fall season there were more new series based on successful movies than ever before, including spinoffs from *Harry and the Hendersons, Big, Parenthood, Canine, Look Who's Talking, Ferris Bueller's Day Off,* and *True Believer.* Susan King reports that in the case of the season's new children's shows, "because of the competition from syndication, cable, home video and video games," the networks augmented their usual intertextuality with the use of celebrities, primarily as voices for animated characters—a technique that has proved successful in animated features. Examples include Roseanne Barr doing the voice of "Little Rosey" on ABC and, on the new Fox network, Howie Mandel doing the voice of Bobby on "Bobby's World" and Whoopi Goldberg doing Mother Earth on "Captain Planet." See Susan King, "Big Stars, Little Fans," *Los Angeles Times TV Times*, September 2–8, 1990, 1.

5. Althusser, "Ideology and Ideological State Apparatuses," 161–63.

6. Applebee, *Child's Concept of Story*, 3–4. In *Perceptions and Representations: The Theoretical Bases of Brain Research and Psychology* (New York: Macmillan, 1978), 138, Keith Oatley similarly argues that we should see human behavior "not simply as reacting to stimulus patterns from the outside world, but of using internal models of that outside world to interact purposefully, and appropriately with it." He claims that "the richness of the possible representations an animal or person might have . . . of our world (its layout in space, the potentialities of various objects in it, the plans we can make for some course of action) . . . comes close to what we mean by intelligence."

7. Applebee, Child's Concept of Story, 100–101, 105.

8. Dore, "Monologue as Reenvoicement," 249.

9. Ibid., 255.

10. Willis, "Gender as Commodity," 406, 411.

11. Martin Rubin, "Intertextuality in Warner Bros. Cartoons, ca. 1940," paper presented at the Annual Meeting of the Society for Cinema Studies, Washington, D.C., 1990.

12. Fiske, *Television Culture*, 108.

13. Ibid., 109.

14. For a lucid and influential description of "suturing" and "the structure of the gaze" in classical Hollywood cinema, see Daniel Dayan, "The Tutor Code of Classical Cinema," *Film Quarterly* 29, no. 1 (1974): 22–31.

15. Althusser, "Freud and Lacan," 205.

16. Mary Ann Doane, "Film and the Masquerade: Theorising the Female Spectator," *Screen* 23, nos. 3–4 (September–October 1982): 87.

17. Willis, "Gender as Commodity," 409.

18. Lacan, *Ecrits*, 2, 3, 5.

19. Ibid., 289. This series of commercials also features pretty young girls, whose developing curves are intended to impress their older brother or some other older male object of desire. In another of these ads (which could be read as a gay parody of the straight version), a cute young redhead, a sort of contemporary Huck Finn, stands on a bare black-draped stage in t-shirt and jeans, holding a glass of milk and talking to the viewer in direct address about the virtues of this wholesome product. In a chain of images linked by dissolves we see his malleable body undergo a series of transformations that rupture his imaginary unity and deconstruct his masquerade as a growing boy. These comic images raise a double set of questions for two generations and for two groups with different sexual orientations: a brief glimpse of a skeleton (will milk make his bones grow? will he die of AIDS?), the comic inflating of bulging biceps (will milk give him muscles? will he become a body builder with homoerotic appeal?), and the inflation of his head until it pops off like a balloon (blowing his mind, or deflating his egotism and his fear of castration) and lifts him up out of the frame (carrying him away on an all-time high, as he sells both this desirable product and himself as a great "pick-me-up").

20. Houston, "*King of Comedy*: A Crisis of Substitution," *Framework* 24 (Spring 1984): 75–76.

21. *Standard and Poor's Industry Surveys*, March 15, 1990, sec. 3: Toys, 44.

22. Raul Ruiz, as quoted by David Ehrenstein in "Raul Ruiz at the Holiday Inn," *Film Quarterly* 40, no. 1 (Fall 1986): 7.

23. Fiske, *Television Culture*, 114.

24. Dore, "Monologue as Reenvoicement," 255.

25. Fiske, *Television Culture*, 110.

26. Perry W. Thorndyke, "Cognitive Structures in Comprehension and Memory of Narrative Discourse," *Cognitive Psychology* 9 (1977): 77.

27. Ibid., 103.

28. Jean M. Mandler and Nancy S. Johnson, "Remembrance of Things Parsed: Story Structure and Recall," *Cognitive Psychology* 9 (1977): 111, 141–42.

29. Patricia Marks Greenfield et al., "The 30-Minute Commercial: A Study of the Effects of Television/Toy Tie-Ins on Imaginative Play," *Psychology and Marketing*, December 1990, 16.

30. Ibid., 10, 32, 2.

31. Fredric Jameson, "Postmodernism and Consumer Society," in *The Anti-Aesthetic: Essays on Postmodern Culture*, ed. Hal Foster (Port Townsend, Wash.: Bay Press, 1983), 114–15. For other influential discussions of the postmodern aesthetic, see also Jean Baudrillard, *Simulations*, trans. Paul Foss, Paul Patton, and Philip Beitchman (New York: Semiotext[e], 1983); and Jean-François Lyotard, *The Postmodern Condition: A Report on Knowledge* (Minneapolis: University of Minnesota Press, 1984).

32. Vygotsky, *Mind in Society*, 88.

33. Greenfield et al., "30-Minute Commercial," 31–32.

34. Umberto Eco, *The Limits of Interpretation* (Bloomington: Indiana University Press, 1990), 97–98.

35. Ibid.

36. See, for example, Kinder, "Back to the Future in the 80s"; Rob Winning, "PeeWee Herman Un-Mascs Our Cultural Myths About Masculinity," *Journal of American Culture* 2, no. 2 (Summer 1988): 57–63; and Constance Penley, "The Cabinet of Dr. Pee-Wee: Consumerism and Sexual Terror," *Camera Obscura*, no. 17 (May 1988): 133–55 (special issue entitled "Male Trouble"); Ian Balfour, "The Playhouse of the Signifier", ibid., 155–69; and Henry Jenkins III, "Going Bonkers!: Children, Play, and Pee-Wee," ibid., 169–93.

37. Winnicott, *Playing and Reality*, 11–12.

38. Ibid., 50.

39. Joyrich, "Individual Response," 193.

40. Doane, "Film and the Masquerade."

41. Hélène Cixous, "Castration or Decapitation," *Signs* 7, no. 11 (1981): 41–55.

42. One need only consider the success of an adult feature like *Who Framed Roger Rabbit?* (which generated short cartoons that helped both *Honey, I Shrunk the Kids* and *Dick Tracy* in their opening weekends at the

box office and whose own sequel is now in preproduction); the commercial triumph of children's films like *An American Tale, The Land Before Time, Oliver and Company,* and *The Little Mermaid;* the surprising popularity of an animated TV series like "The Simpsons" in prime time; and the revival of the old Warner Brothers cartoons, which the AMC theater chain is now screening with its features in sixteen hundred theaters.

43. Fiske, *Television Culture,* 111.

44. Roland Barthes, *Writing Degree Zero and Elements of Semiology,* trans. Annette Lavers and Colin Smith (Boston: Beacon Press, 1970), 86. This catalogue (or extension of a paradigm onto the syntagmatic plane) is precisely the kind of structure that controls the second episode of "Muppet Babies," broadcast on September 30, "Twinkle Toe Muppets." In order to mediate a quarrel between Piggy and Skeeter over whether dancing should be beautiful or fun, Nanny gives the muppets a videotape with a montage of dance sequences that vary not only in the mode of enunciation (color versus black-and-white, video versus film, animation versus live action), but also in gender, race, generation, culture, period, costume, music, dance style, number of dancers, and so on. As a form of narrative closure, the tape presents Fred Astaire as the ultimate mediator of beauty and fun; like the VCR itself, he also mediates between high art and pop culture.

45. Brooks, *Reading for the Plot,* 108.

46. Houston, "Viewing Television," 184.

47. Lévi-Strauss, *Totemism,* 93.

48. Althusser, "Freud and Lacan," 205, 208.

49. Nancy A. Boyd and George Mandler, "Children's Responses to Human and Animal Stories and Pictures," *Journal of Consulting Psychology* 19, no. 5 (1955): 367–71.

50. Donna Haraway, "A Manifesto for Cyborgs: Science, Technology, and Socialist Feminism in the 1980s," *Socialist Review* 80 (1985): 68.

51. Brooks, *Reading for the Plot,* 100.

52. Houston, "Viewing Television," 189, 184. This state of anxiety is also central to the recent fad of attaching a stuffed Garfield doll to a car window, as if to express the raw terror that motorists feel but are forced to repress as they drive on perilous urban streets and freeways, particularly in Los Angeles with its freeway snipers and drive-by gang shootings. This toy became a populist means of expressing a topic that is omitted from the official industry and advertising discourses on the automobile—another consumerist medium (like television) that prom-

ises empowerment and freedom while in fact fostering greater dependency on complex multinational systems.

53. Winnicott, *Playing and Reality*, 50.

54. Houston, "Viewing Television," 188.

55. For an analysis of the struggle over gendering television, see my essay "Phallic Film and the Boob Tube: The Power of Gender Identification in Cinema, Television, and Music Video," *Onetwothreefour*, no. 5 (Spring 1987): 33–49 (special issue on music video).

56. Walter Benjamin, "The Work of Art in the Age of Mechanical Reproduction" (1935), in *Film Theory and Criticism*, 3d ed., ed. Gerald Mast and Marshall Cohen (New York: Oxford University Press, 1985), 690.

57. Lynn Spigel, *Installing the Television Set: Television and Family Ideals in Postwar America* (Chicago: University of Chicago Press, 1991).

58. Stuart Hall, "Encoding/Decoding," in *Culture, Media, Language*, ed. Stuart Hall et al. (London: Hutchinson, 1980), 128–39.

59. Martin M. Klein ("The Bite of Pac-Man," *Journal of Psychohistory* 2, no. 3 [Winter 1984]: 395–401) argues that the primitive oral and sadistic themes in video games center on the fear of engulfment and on an accompanying compensatory aggression, a combination particularly common in adolescence. The heavy emphasis on oral symbolism, he claims, helps to account for the popularity of Pac-Man, which provides a site of temporary displacement for the adolescent's struggle with the world. For the behaviorist argument, see Geoffrey R. Loftus and Elizabeth F. Loftus, *Mind at Play: The Psychology of Video Games* (New York: Basic Books, 1983), chap. 2.

60. Friedrich von Schiller, "13th and 15th Letters on the Aesthetic Education of Man," in *Critical Theory Since Plato*, ed. Hazard Adams (New York: Harcourt Brace Jovanovich, 1971), 421–22, 426.

3. THE NINTENDO ENTERTAINMENT SYSTEM

1. See Robert McGough, "Passing Fancy? Video Games May Peak This Christmas, but Nintendo's Grip on Toys Remains Unshaken," *Financial World*, November 28, 1989, 39.

2. Craig Kubey, *The Winners' Book of Video Games* (New York: Warner Books, 1982), 80–83, 249–51.

3. Ibid., xiv.

4. Fumio Igarashi, "The Video Game with Media Potential," *Japan Quarterly* 33 (July–September 1986): 297–98.

5. S. Rushbrook, "Messages of Video Games: Socialization Implications" (Ph.D. diss., University of California, Los Angeles, 1986). This study showed that in 1985, 95 percent of all ten-year-old children in Orange County, a densely populated region of Southern California, had played video games.

6. On the proposed joint venture, see, for example, Matt Kramer, "The Next Nintendo 'Game' May Be Brainchild of AT&T," *PC Week*, July 24, 1989, 57; Jeff Shear, "AT&T Likely to Call Others as It Sets Up for a New Game," *Insight*, September 4, 1989, 41; Jason Rich, "Nintendo to Introduce Online Network: The Home Unit Will Become More Than a Toy," *Link-Up*, November–December 1989, 1; and Jason Rich, "The Nintendo Link: A New Way to Play the Market?" *Barron's*, December 4, 1989, 56.

7. Robert W. Casey, "Toy Companies' Tidings of Joy," *New York Times*, December 24, 1989; and "Nintendo Co.: Pretax Profit Climbed 23%, Sales Were Up 40% in Year," *Wall Street Journal*, October 17, 1989, A25.

8. "The Nintendo Kid," *Newsweek*, March 6, 1989, 67.

9. David Sheff, "Nintendo Isn't Playing Games," *San Francisco Chronicle*, December 2, 1990, "The World" sec., 8–9.

10. Kevin McKinney, "Captains of Video," *Omni*, October 1988, 46.

11. Martin Shao, Amy Dunkin, and Patrick Cole, "There's a Rumble in the Video Arcade," *Business Week*, February 20, 1989, 37.

12. For more information about these lawsuits, see Mark Starr, "A Game of Legal Punch-Out," *Newsweek*, January 2, 1989, 50; Ken Rankin, "Antitrust Subcommittee Targets Nintendo," *Discount Store News*, January 29, 1990, 36; Shao, Dunkin, and Cole, "There's a Rumble," 37.

13. Sheff, "Nintendo Isn't Playing Games," 9.

14. Mark Crispin Miller, "Hollywood: The Ad," *Atlantic*, April 1990, 41–68.

15. "The Wizard Behind the Scenes," *Pocket Power*, n.d., 4, 5. Published in New York by Nintendo of America, Inc., in association with EMCI, Ltd., this "pocket-size" journal is described as "a sample of *Nintendo Power*," the 8″ × 11″ magazine that is "the real thing."

16. *Game Player's Buyer's Guide to Nintendo Games* 2, no. 5 (1989): 78, 126 (published in Greensboro, N.C., by Signal Research, Inc.).

17. At the 1990 Annual Meeting of the Society for Cinema Studies, Scott Bukatman gave an excellent paper, "There's Always Tomorrowland: Disney's Phenomenology of Progress," in which he argued that

the entire theme park was structured as an interactive movie experience.

18. Mary Ann Galante, "Disney Proposes New $1 Billion Theme Park," *Los Angeles Times*, January 13, 1990, A1, 30.

19. Susan Scheibler, a film scholar who once worked at Disneyland, has elaborated on the theme park structure in a paper she read at the Ohio Film Conference, November 1989, called "Documentary Spectatorship in Consumer Society."

20. "Nintendo Kid," 65, 68.

21. Of course, I do not mean to suggest that games featuring violence are restricted to the U.S. market. For example, one study conducted in Mexico City showed that 44 percent of arcade games featured violent action. Surprisingly, in this study the oldest subjects were from the upper classes, whereas the youngest were from the lower classes and played more frequently than upper-class subjects. See Patricia Rodriguez, Rolando Medina, and Hector Perez-Rincon, "La conducta lúdica y los nuevos juegos electrónicos: Comunicación preliminar" (Game behavior and the new electronic games: Preliminary report), *Salud mental* 6, no. 3 (Fall 1983): 22–34.

22. See, for example, S. J. Kaplan, "The Image of Amusement Arcades and Differences in Male and Female Videogame Playing," *Journal of Popular Culture* 17, no. 1 (Summer 1983): 93–98; John W. Trinkaus, "Arcade Video Games: An Informal Look," *Psychological Reports* 52, no. 2 (April 1983): 586; Robert F. McClure and Gary F. Mears, "Video Game Players: Personality Characteristics and Demographic Variables," *Psychological Reports* 55, no. 1 (August 1984): 271–76; Henry Morlock, Todd Yando, and Karen Nigolean, "Motivation of Video Game Players," *Psychological Reports* 57, no. 1 (August 1985): 247–50; Claude M. Braun, Georgette Goupil, Josette Giroux, and Yves Chagnon, "Adolescents and Microcomputers: Sex Differences, Proxemics, Task and Stimulus Variables," *Journal of Psychology* 120, no. 6 (November 1986): 529–42; and Claude M. Braun and Josette Giroux, "Arcade Video Games: Proxemic, Cognitive, and Content Analyses," *Journal of Leisure Research* 21, no. 2 (1989): 92–105.

23. Gita Wilder, Diane Mackie, and Joel Cooper, "Gender and Computers: Two Surveys of Computer-related Attitudes," *Sex Roles* 13, nos. 3–4 (1985): 215–28. For my own conversations with children about video games, see appendixes 1 and 2.

24. Patricia Marks Greenfield, "Representational Competence in Shared Symbol Systems," in *The Development and Meaning of Psycholog-*

ical Distance, ed. R. R. Cocking and K. A. Renninger (Hillsdale, N.J.: Erlbaum, forthcoming).

25. Greenfield, *Mind and Media*, 105–6.

26. Edna Mitchell, "The Dynamics of Family Interaction Around Home Video Games," *Marriage and Family Review* 8, nos. 1–2 (Spring 1985): 121 (special issue entitled "Personal Computers and the Family").

27. Sheff, "Nintendo Isn't Playing Games," 10.

28. "Nintendo Kid," 66.

29. Quoted in Shao, Dunkin, and Cole, "There's a Rumble," 37.

30. Quoted in Jason R. Rich, "Say Goodbye to WHAM! ZAP! POW! Video Games Are Getting Less Violent, More Brainy," *TV Guide*, March 2–8, 1991, 31.

31. Greenfield, "Representational Competence in Shared Symbol Systems."

32. Two studies had very interesting findings on this issue. Dianne Tice, Jane Buder, and Roy Baumeister ("Development of Self-Consciousness: At What Age Does Audience Pressure Disrupt Performance?" *Adolescence* 20, nos. 7–8 [Summer 1985]: 301) found that "children under 12 years generally improved under audience pressure; Ss age 14–19 years showed substantial drops in performance; and Ss aged 20 years or older showed moderate drops in performance." In a study that examined game behavior in subjects fourteen and older, McClure and Mears ("Video Game Players") found that the key issue was class rather than age; they observe: "Strangely enough, the higher the socio-economic status, the more anxiety about computers was shown," and conclude: "perhaps these people are more likely to have actually the opportunity to use them than people of lower status and to consider implications for their use" (271). For other studies considering the importance of the age variable, see Robert F. McClure, "Age and Video Game Playing," *Perceptual and Motor Skills* 61, no. 1 (August 1985): 285–86; and William Strein, "Effects of Age and Visual-motor Skills on Preschool Children's Computer-Game Performance," *Journal of Research and Development in Education* 20, no. 2 (Winter 1987): 70–72.

33. Greenfield, *Mind and Media*, 107–8.

34. According to linguist Jacquelyn Schachter, who specializes in second language acquisition: "Adults no longer have access to a parameterized Universal Grammar and . . . such knowledge of the constraints upon target language movement rules (i.e., subjacency) that they do have occurs only as instantiations of the constraint via their

native languages" ("Testing a Proposed Universal," in *Adult Second Language Acquisition: A Linguistic Perspective*, ed. S. Gass and J. Schachter [Cambridge: Cambridge University Press, 1989], 73).

35. Piaget, *Judgment and Reasoning in the Child*, 209.

36. Piaget, "Piaget's Theory," 177.

37. Piaget, *Psychology of Intelligence*, 123, 142.

38. Piaget, "Piaget's Theory," 190.

39. Applebee, *Child's Concept of Story*, 135.

40. Vygotsky, *Mind in Society*, 89, 102, 86–87.

41. See Greenfield, *Mind and Media*, 107, 115; and Greenfield, "Representational Competence in Shared Symbol Systems," 19, 25.

42. Papert, *Mindstorms*, 96.

43. Piaget, "Piaget's Theory," 192.

44. Greenfield et al., "30-Minute Commercial," 8.

45. Papert, *Mindstorms*, 176, 26, 37.

46. See Betsy Carpenter, "On the Trail of Nintendo's Magic," *U.S. News and World Report*, July 16, 1990, 56–57.

47. Greenfield, "Representational Competence in Shared Symbol Systems," 23.

48. Greenfield et al., "30-Minute Commercial," 33–34.

49. *Standard and Poor's Industry Surveys*, 18.

50. Willis, "Gender as Commodity," 47.

51. Quoted in Sheff, "Nintendo Isn't Playing Games," 11.

52. Greenfield, "Representational Competence in Shared Symbol Systems," 24.

53. For studies of the cognitive value of video games, see, for example, Jerry Griffith, Patricia Voloschin, Gerald Gibb, and James Bailey, "Differences in Eye-Hand Motor Coordination of Video-Game Users and Non-Users," *Perceptual and Motor Skills* 57, no. 1 (August 1983): 155–58; Marshall B. Jones, "Video Games as Psychological Tests," *Simulation and Games* 15, no. 2 (June 1984): 131–57; James W. Hull, "Videogames: Transitional Phenomena in Adolescence," *Child and Adolescent Social Work Journal* 2, no. 2 (Summer 1985): 106–13; D. Gagnon, "Videogames and Spatial Skills: An Exploratory," *Educational Communication and Technology* 33, no. 4 (Winter 1985): 263–76; Steven B. Silvern, "Classroom Use of Video Games," *Educational Research Quarterly* 10, no. 1 (1985–86): 10–16; Michel Dorval and Michel Pepin, "Effect of Playing a Video Game on a Measure of Spatial Visualization," *Perceptual and Motor Skills* 62, no. 1 (February 1986): 159–62; Marshall Jones, William Dunlap, and Ina Bilodeau, "Comparison of Video Game and Conventional Test Performance," *Simulation and*

Games 17, no. 4 (December 1986): 435–46. For studies that dispute the harmful effects of video games, see T. Panelas, "Adolescents and Video Games Consumption of Leisure and the Social Construction of the Peer Group," *Youth and Society* 15, no. 1 (September 1983): 51–65; Eric Egli and Lawrence Meyers, "The Role of Video Game Playing in Adolescent Life: Is There Reason to Be Concerned?" *Bulletin of the Psychonomic Society* 22, no. 4 (July 1984): 309–12; Daniel Graybill, Janis Kirsch, and Edward Esselman, "Effects of Playing Violent Versus Non-violent Video Games on the Aggressive Ideation of Aggressive and Nonaggressive Children," *Child Study Journal* 15, no. 3 (1985): 199–205; Gary Creasey and Barbara Myers, "Video Games and Children: Effects on Leisure Activities, Schoolwork, and Peer Involvement," *Merrill-Palmer Quarterly* 32, no. 3 (July 1986): 251–61; Daniel Graybill, Maryellen Strawniak, Teri Hunter, and Margaret O'Leary, "Effects of Playing Versus Observing Violent Versus Nonviolent Video Games on Children's Aggression," *Psychology* 24, no. 3 (1987): 1–8. For more general studies about violence and media, see also Nancy Signorelli and George Gerbner, *Violence and Terror in the Mass Media: An Anno-tated Bibliography* (New York: Greenwood Press, 1988); Geoffrey Barlow and Alison Hill, eds., *Video Violence and Children* (New York: St. Martin's Press, 1985); and Edward L. Palmer and Aimée Dorr, *Children and the Faces of Television: Teaching, Violence, Selling* (New York: Academic Press, 1980).

4. TEENAGE MUTANT NINJA TURTLES

1. Stacy Botwinick, "Nintendo Edges Barbie in '89 Best Seller Survey," *Playthings*, December 1989, 29.

2. Not only does the rock group New Kids on the Block have its own Saturday morning animated TV series on ABC, but it is also being marketed in TV commercials as a fivesome that, in contrast to Teenage Mutant Ninja Turtles, might appeal more to girls. As if trying to construct precocious groupies, these ads urge young female consumers to compete with each other to be "the best fan" by collecting the plastic figures for all five members of the group as well as all five sets of matching paraphernalia. Thus, in a sense, the group is being marketed as a cross between Barbie dolls and Ninja Turtles.

3. Willis, "Gender as Commodity," 404, 406.

4. See Kathleen Doheny, "Turtle Trouble," *Los Angeles Times*, August 27, 1990, E1–2.

5. This relativity of age, size, and growth is also apparent in the reception of the various incarnations of the TMNT myth. For example, in *TV Guide*'s special "Parents' Guide to Children's Television" (March 2–8, 1991), the TMNT animated television series is judged the "worst" show in the age-two-to-five category ("a grotesque mix of marketing and manipulation," 7), whereas the videotape of the first TMNT live-action movie is the top choice for ages eight and up ("the reliance on the martial arts appeals to young boys more than any other toy or comic book," and "how can a parent ignore the popularity of these terrific terrapins?" 17). By some strange logic, it is as if once a child reaches the stage of operational thought, parents no longer have to be concerned with commercial manipulation.

6. Sheila Benson, "When Comics Click on Film," *Los Angeles Times*, June 15, 1990, F14–15.

7. Barthes, *S/Z*, 24.

8. Quoted in Will Murray, "Teenage Mutant Ninja Movie Stars," *Comics Scene*, ser. 23, 4, no. 12 (April 1990): 32.

9. Ibid., 10.

10. Piaget, *Judgment and Reasoning in the Child*, 177, 179.

11. Willis, "Gender as Commodity," 415–16.

12. In the sequel *Teenage Mutant Ninja Turtles II: The Secret of the Ooze*, Shredder is outraged when his infantile monsters mistake him for their mother, as if that is the ultimate insult. And April is stripped both of her love interest (who is replaced by an Asian American martial arts wizard) and her androgyny: she becomes merely the Turtles' prissy "straight man."

13. Papert, *Mindstorms*, 11.

14. Willis, "Gender as Commodity," 416.

15. Papert, *Mindstorms*, vii.

16. In the original comic book, which parodies other comic book superheroes, the violence is quite bloody and the Turtles much meaner. They explicitly tell their enemies, "Yes, we can bleed!"

17. Some of Tsuburaya's techniques from the Godzilla series are adapted in the TMNT movie: the transformation of the "monster" into comical yet superheroic good guys, the use of humans in super-realistic motorized animal masquerade, and the positioning of these superheroes in constant combat where they defeat bad monsters (like Shredder) and rescue or redeem lost boys and girls (like Danny).

18. Quoted by Nina J. Easton in "Behind the Scenes of the Big Deal," *Los Angeles Times*, December 31, 1989, "Calendar" sec., 6.

5. POSTPLAY IN GLOBAL NETWORKS

1. Karl Schoenberger, "Ad Giant in Japan Sells Clout," *Los Angeles Times*, June 14, 1990, A20.

2. Teresa Watanabe, "Japan Sets Sights on Creativity," *Los Angeles Times*, June 10, 1990, A1.

3. See Leslie Helm, "Japan's Labs Open at Last," *Los Angeles Times*, November 11, 1990, D7.

4. Quoted in ibid.

5. Noël Burch, *To the Distant Observer: Form and Meaning in Japanese Cinema* (Berkeley and Los Angeles: University of California Press, 1979), chap. 5.

6. Charles Champlin, "The Oscars Go Global," *Los Angeles Times*, March 27, 1990, F2.

7. Karl Schoenberger, "Japanese Film: The Sinking Sun," *Los Angeles Times*, April 4, 1990, F7.

8. Kevin Thomas, "Last Picture Show in Little Tokyo," *Los Angeles Times*, October 31, 1990, F1.

9. Michael Cieply and Alan Citron, "The Poker Game to Win MCA," *Los Angeles Times*, November 30, 1990, A22.

10. Dutka and Easton, "Hollywood's Brave New World," 77, 84, 85.

11. Robert Epstein, "The Dream Factory May Never Be the Same," *Los Angeles Times*, November 10, 1990, F20.

12. A. G. Hawn, "HDTV—The 'Even Playing Field' Gets Muddy: An Inside Report on the Future of High Definition Television," *Video Times*, Winter 1990, 33.

13. Epstein, "Dream Factory," F20.

14. Dutka and Easton, "Hollywood's Brave New World," 84.

15. Hawn, "HDTV," 32–33, 38.

16. Quoted in Cieply and Citron, "Poker Game to Win MCA," A22.

17. Epstein, "Dream Factory," F20.

18. Quoted in Michael Cieply and Leslie Helm, "Matsushita to Buy MCA—$6.5 Billion, *Los Angeles Times*, November 27, 1990, A25.

19. Quoted in Alan Citron and Michael Cieply, "Pathe Closes Long-delayed MGM/UA Deal," *Los Angeles Times*, November 2, 1990, A1.

20. Michael Cieply and Alan Citron, "Parretti Makes Surprise Offer to Purchase MCA," *Los Angeles Times*, November 28, 1990, A19.

21. Jube Shiver, Jr., "The Bidding for MCA," *Los Angeles Times*, November 29, 1990, D13.

22. John Rizzo and Jon Zilber, "How I Learned to Stop Worrying and Love Connectivity: Networking the '90s," *MacUser*, January 1991, 92–93.

23. Dutka and Easton, "Hollywood's Brave New World," 84.

24. Quoted in Jane Hall, "Network News: An Endangered Species?" *Los Angeles Times*, February 16, 1991, F1.

25. Houston, "Viewing Television," 185.

APPENDIX 1

1. Willis, "Gender as Commodity," 404.
2. Ibid.

APPENDIX 2

1. Willis, "Gender as Commodity," 405.
2. Ibid.
3. Ibid., 406.

Works Cited

Althusser, Louis. "Freud and Lacan." In *Lenin and Philosophy and Other Essays,* translated by Ben Brewster, 189–219. New York and London: Monthly Review Press, 1971.

———. "Ideology and Ideological State Apparatuses (Notes Towards an Investigation)." In *Lenin and Philosophy and Other Essays,* translated by Ben Brewster, 127–86. New York and London: Monthly Review Press, 1971.

Alwitt, L. F., D. R. Anderson, E. P. Lorch, and S. R. Levin. "Preschool Children's Visual Attention to Attributes of Television." *Human Communication Research* 7 (1980): 52–67.

Applebee, Arthur. *The Child's Concept of Story: Ages Two to Seventeen.* Chicago: University of Chicago Press, 1978.

Bakhtin, Mikhail. *The Dialogic Imagination.* Translated by Caryl Emerson and Michael Holquist. Austin: University of Texas Press, 1981.

Balfour, Ian. "The Playhouse of the Signifier." *Camera Obscura,* no. 17 (May 1988): 155–69 (special issue entitled "Male Trouble").

Barlow, Geoffrey, and Alison Hill, eds. *Video Violence and Children.* New York: St. Martin's Press, 1985.

Barthes, Roland. *Image—Music—Text.* Edited and translated by Stephen Heath. New York: Noonday Press, 1977.

———. *S/Z.* Translated by Richard Miller. New York: Hill and Wang, 1974.

————. *Writing Degree Zero and Elements of Semiology*. Translated by Annette Lavers and Colin Smith. Boston: Beacon Press, 1970.

Bateson, Gregory. *Steps to an Ecology of Mind*. New York: Ballantine Books, 1972.

Baudrillard, Jean. *Simulations*. Translated by Paul Foss, Paul Patton, and Philip Beitchman. New York: Semiotext(e), 1983.

Benjamin, Walter. "The Work of Art in the Age of Mechanical Reproduction" (1935). In *Film Theory and Criticism*, 3d ed., edited by Gerald Mast and Marshall Cohen, 848–70. New York: Oxford University Press, 1985.

Benson, Sheila. "When Comics Click on Film." *Los Angeles Times*, June 15, 1990.

Bordwell, David. *Making Meaning: Inference and Rhetoric in the Interpretation of Cinema*. Cambridge, Mass.: Harvard University Press, 1989.

————. *Narration in the Fiction Film*. Madison: University of Wisconsin Press, 1985.

Botwinick, Stacy. "Nintendo Edges Barbie in '89 Best Seller Survey." *Playthings*, December 1989, 29.

Boyd, Nancy A., and George Mandler. "Children's Responses to Human and Animal Stories and Pictures." *Journal of Consulting Psychology* 19, no. 5 (1955): 367–71.

Branigan, Edward. *Point of View in the Cinema: A Theory of Narration and Subjectivity in Classic Film*. New York: Mouton, 1984.

Braun, Claude M., and Josette Giroux. "Arcade Video Games: Proxemic, Cognitive, and Content Analyses." *Journal of Leisure Research* 21, no. 2 (1989): 92–105.

Braun, Claude M., Georgette Goupil, Josette Giroux, and Yves Chagnon. "Adolescents and Microcomputers: Sex Differences, Proxemics, Task and Stimulus Variables." *Journal of Psychology* 120, no. 6 (November 1986): 529–42.

Brooks, Peter. *Reading for the Plot: Design and Intention in Narrative*. New York: Vintage Books, 1984.

Bruner, Jerome, and Joan Lucariello. "Monologue as Narrative Recreation of the World." In *Narratives from the Crib*, edited by Katherine Nelson, 73–97. Cambridge, Mass.: Harvard University Press, 1989.

Bukatman, Scott. "There's Always Tomorrowland: Disney's Phenomenology of Progress." Paper delivered at the Annual Meeting of the Society for Cinema Studies, Washington, D.C., 1990.

Burch, Noël. *To the Distant Observer: Form and Meaning in Japanese Cinema*. Berkeley and Los Angeles: University of California Press, 1979.

Carpenter, Betsy. "On the Trail of Nintendo's Magic." *U.S. News and World Report*, July 16, 1990, 56–57.

Casey, Robert W. "Toy Companies' Tidings of Joy." *New York Times*, December 24, 1989.

Champlin, Charles. "The Oscars Go Global." *Los Angeles Times*, March 27, 1990, F1–2.

"Children's Television Act of 1990." In *U.S. Code Congressional and Administrative News*, no. 9 (December 1990), 104 Stats. 996–1000.

Chomsky, Noam. *Aspects of the Theory of Syntax*. Cambridge, Mass.: MIT Press, 1965.

Cieply, Michael, and Alan Citron. "Parretti Makes Surprise Offer to Purchase MCA." *Los Angeles Times*, November 28, 1990.

———. "The Poker Game to Win MCA." *Los Angeles Times*, November 30, 1990.

Cieply, Michael, and Leslie Helm. "Matsushita to Buy MCA— $6.5 Billion." *Los Angeles Times*, November 27, 1990.

Citron, Alan, and Michael Cieply. "Pathe Closes Long-delayed MGM/UA Deal." *Los Angeles Times*, November 2, 1990.

Cixous, Hélène. "Castration or Decapitation." *Signs* 7, no. 11 (1981): 41–55.

Cohen, Ralph. "Do Postmodern Genres Exist?" In *Post-modern Genres*, edited by Marjorie Perloff, 11–27. Norman: University of Oklahoma Press, 1989.

Creasey, Gary, and Barbara Myers. "Video Games and Children: Effects on Leisure Activities, Schoolwork, and Peer Involvement." *Merrill-Palmer Quarterly* 32, no. 3 (July 1986): 251–61.

Dayan, Daniel. "The Tutor Code of Classical Cinema." *Film Quarterly* 29, no. 1 (1974): 22–31.

Doane, Mary Ann. "Film and the Masquerade: Theorising the Female Spectator." *Screen* 23, nos. 3–4 (September–October 1982): 74–87.

Doheny, Kathleen. "Turtle Trouble." *Los Angeles Times*, August 27, 1990.

Dore, John. "Monologue as Reenvoicement of Dialogue." In *Narratives from the Crib*, edited by Katherine Nelson, 231–60. Cambridge, Mass.: Harvard University Press, 1989.

Dorval, Michel, and Michel Pepin. "Effect of Playing a Video Game on a Measure of Spatial Visualization." *Perceptual and Motor Skills* 62, no. 1 (February 1986): 159–62.

Dutka, Elaine, and Nina J. Easton. "Hollywood's Brave New World." *Los Angeles Times*, December 23, 1990, "Calendar" sec.

Easton, Nina J. "Behind the Scenes of the Big Deal." *Los Angeles Times*, December 31, 1989, "Calendar" sec.

Eco, Umberto. *The Limits of Interpretation*. Bloomington: Indiana University Press, 1990.

Egli, Eric, and Lawrence Meyers. "The Role of Video Game Playing in Adolescent Life: Is There Reason to Be Concerned?" *Bulletin of the Psychonomic Society* 22, no. 4 (July 1984): 309–12.

Ehrenstein, David. "Raul Ruiz at the Holiday Inn." *Film Quarterly* 40, no. 1 (Fall 1986): 2–7.

Epstein, Robert. "The Dream Factory May Never Be the Same." *Los Angeles Times*, November 10, 1990.

Fiske, John. *Television Culture*. London: Methuen, 1987.

Freud, Sigmund. *Beyond the Pleasure Principle*. Translated by James Strachey. New York: Norton, 1961.

————. *The Interpretation of Dreams* (1900). Vols. 4 and 5 of *The Standard Edition of the Complete Psychological Works of Sigmund Freud.* Edited by James Strachey. London: Hogarth Press and the Institute of Psychoanalysis, 1962.

————. "Little Hans." In *The Pelican Freud Library*, vol. 8: *Case Histories I: "Dora" and "Little Hans."* Harmondsworth, Eng.: Penguin, 1977.

Gagnon, D. "Videogames and Spatial Skills: An Exploratory." *Educational Communication and Technology* 33, no. 4 (Winter 1985): 263–76.

Galante, Mary Ann. "Disney Proposes New $1 Billion Theme Park." *Los Angeles Times*, January 13, 1990.

Gardner, Howard, with Leona Jaglom. "Cracking the Codes of Television: The Child as Anthropologist." In *Transmission*, edited by Peter D'Agostino, 92–102. New York: Tanam Press, 1985.

Gibson, William. *Neuromancer.* New York: Ace Books, 1984.

Graybill, Daniel, Janis Kirsch, and Edward Esselman. "Effects of Playing Violent Versus Nonviolent Video Games on the Aggressive Ideation of Aggressive and Nonaggressive Children." *Child Study Journal* 15, no. 3 (1985): 199–205.

Graybill, Daniel, Maryellen Strawniak, Teri Hunter, and Margaret O'Leary. "Effects of Playing Versus Observing Violent Versus Nonviolent Video Games on Children's Aggression." *Psychology* 24, no. 3 (1987): 1–8.

Greenfield, Patricia Marks. *Mind and Media: The Effects of Television, Video Games, and Computers.* Cambridge, Mass.: Harvard University Press, 1984.

————. "Representational Competence in Shared Symbol Systems: Electronic Media from Radio to Video Games." In *The Development and Meaning of Psychological Distance*, edited by R. R. Cocking and K. A. Renninger. Hillsdale, N.J.: Erlbaum, forthcoming.

Greenfield, Patricia Marks, Emily Yut, Mabel Chung, Deborah Land, Holly Kreider, Maurice Pantoja, and Kris Horsely. "The 30-Minute Commercial: A Study of the Effects of

Television/Toy Tie-ins on Imaginative Play." *Psychology and Marketing*, December 1990, 32.

Griffith, Jerry, Patricia Voloschin, Gerald Gibb, and James Bailey. "Differences in Eye-Hand Motor Coordination of Video-Game Users and Non-Users." *Perceptual and Motor Skills* 57, no. 1 (August 1983): 155–58.

Hall, Jane. "Network News: An Endangered Species?" *Los Angeles Times*, February 16, 1991.

Hall, Stuart. "Encoding/Decoding." In *Culture, Media, Language*, edited by Stuart Hall et al., 128–39. London: Hutchinson, 1980.

Haraway, Donna. "A Manifesto for Cyborgs: Science, Technology, and Socialist Feminism in the 1980s." *Socialist Review* 80 (1985): 65–107.

Hawn, A. G. "HDTV—The 'Even Playing Field' Gets Muddy: An Inside Report on the Future of High Definition Television." *Video Times*, Winter 1990, 32–38.

Helm, Leslie. "Japan's Labs Open at Last." *Los Angeles Times*, November 11, 1990.

Hayes, D. S., and D. W. Birnbaum. "Pre-Schoolers' Retention of Televised Events: Is a Picture Worth a Thousand Words?" *Developmental Psychology* 16, no. 5 (September 1980): 410–16.

Houston, Beverle. "*King of Comedy*: A Crisis of Substitution." *Framework* 24 (Spring 1984): 74–92.

———. "Viewing Television: The Metapsychology of Endless Consumption." *Quarterly Review of Film Studies* 9, no. 3 (Summer 1984): 183–95.

Hull, James W. "Videogames: Transitional Phenomena in Adolescence." *Child and Adolescent Social Work Journal* 2, no. 2 (Summer 1985): 106–13.

Igarashi, Fumio. "The Video Game with Media Potential." *Japan Quarterly* 33 (July–September 1986): 295–98.

Jameson, Fredric. "Postmodernism and Consumer Society." In *The Anti-Aesthetic: Essays on Postmodern Culture*, edited by Hal Foster, 111–25. Port Townsend, Wash.: Bay Press, 1983.

Jenkins, Henry. "Going Bonkers! Children, Play, and Pee-Wee." *Camera Obscura*, no. 17 (May 1988): 169–95.

Jones, Marshall B. "Video Games as Psychological Tests." *Simulation and Games* 15, no. 2 (June 1984): 131–57.

Jones, Marshall, William Dunlap, and Ina Bilodeau. "Comparison of Video Game and Conventional Test Performance." *Simulation and Games* 17, no. 4 (December 1986): 435–46.

Joyrich, Lynne. "Individual Response." *Camera Obscura*, nos. 20–21 (May–September 1989): 190–94 (special issue entitled "Spectatrix," edited by Janet Bergstrom and Mary Ann Doane).

Kaplan, S. J. "The Image of Amusement Arcades and Differences in Male and Female Videogame Playing." *Journal of Popular Culture* 17, no. 1 (Summer 1983): 93–98.

Kinder, Marsha. "Back to the Future in the 80s with Fathers and Sons, Supermen and PeeWees, Gorillas and Toons." *Film Quarterly* 42, no. 4 (Summer 1989): 2–11.

———. "Music, Video, and the Spectator: Television, Ideology, and Dream." *Film Quarterly* 38, no. 1 (Fall 1984): 2–15.

———. "Phallic Film and the Boob Tube: The Power of Gender Identification in Cinema, Television, and Music Video." *Onetwothreefour*, no. 5 (Spring 1987): 33–49 (special issue on music video).

King, Susan. "Big Stars, Little Fans." *Los Angeles Times TV Times*, September 2–8, 1990, 1.

Klein, Martin M. "The Bite of Pac-Man." *Journal of Psychohistory* 2, no. 3 (Winter 1984): 395–401.

Kramer, Matt. "The Next Nintendo 'Game' May Be Brainchild of AT&T." *PC Week*, July 24, 1989, 57.

Kristeva, Julia. "Poésie et négativité." In *Séméiotikè: Recherches pour une sémanalyse*, 246–77. Paris: Editions du Seuil, 1969.

Kubey, Craig. *The Winners' Book of Video Games*. New York: Warner Books, 1982.

Lacan, Jacques. "The Mirror Stage as Formative of the Function I." In *Ecrits: A Selection*, translated by Alan Sheridan, 1–7. New York: Norton, 1977.

Lévi-Strauss, Claude. *Structural Anthropology*. New York: Basic Books, 1976.

———. *Totemism*. Translated by Rodney Neeham. Boston: Beacon Press, 1963.

Loftus, Geoffrey R., and Elizabeth F. Loftus. *Mind at Play: The Psychology of Video Games*. New York: Basic Books, 1983.

Lyotard, Jean-François. *The Postmodern Condition: A Report on Knowledge*. Minneapolis: University of Minnesota Press, 1984.

McClure, Robert. "Age and Video Game Playing." *Perceptual and Motor Skills* 61, no. 1 (August 1985): 285–86.

McClure, Robert F., and Gary F. Mears. "Video Game Players: Personality Characteristics and Demographic Variables." *Psychological Reports* 55, no. 1 (August 1984): 271–76.

McGough, Robert. "Passing Fancy? Video Games May Peak This Christmas, but Nintendo's Grip on Toys Remains Unshaken." *Financial World*, November 28, 1989, 39.

McKinney, Kevin. "Captains of Video." *Omni*, October 1988, 46, 216.

Mandler, Jean M., and Nancy S. Johnson, "Remembrance of Things Parsed: Story Structure and Recall." *Cognitive Psychology* 9 (1977): 111–51.

Metz, Christian. *The Imaginary Signifier: Psychoanalysis and the Cinema*. Translated by Celia Britton, Annwyl Williams, Ben Brewster, and Alfred Guzzetti. Bloomington: Indiana University Press, 1982.

———. "Story/Discourse: Notes on Two Kinds of Voyeurism." In *Movies and Methods*, edited by Bill Nichols, 2:543–49. Berkeley and Los Angeles: University of California Press, 1985.

Miller, Mark Crispin. "Hollywood: The Ad." *Atlantic*, April 1990, 41–68.

Mitchell, Edna. "The Dynamics of Family Interaction Around Home Video Games." *Marriage and Family Review* 8, nos. 1–2 (Spring 1985): 121–35 (special issue entitled "Personal Computers and the Family").

Morlock, Henry, Todd Yando, and Karen Nigolean. "Motivation of Video Game Players." *Psychological Reports* 57, no. 1 (August 1985): 247–50.

Murray, Will. "Teenage Mutant Ninja Movie Stars." *Comics Scene*, ser. 23, 4, no. 12 (April 1990): 9–12, 32.

National Institute of Mental Health. *Television and Behavior: Ten Years of Scientific Progress and Implications for the Eighties.* Vol. 1. Washington, D.C.: Government Printing Office, 1982.

Nelson, Katherine, ed. *Narratives from the Crib.* Cambridge, Mass.: Harvard University Press, 1989.

"The Nintendo Kid." *Newsweek*, March 6, 1989, 64–65.

Oatley, Keith. *Perceptions and Representations: The Theoretical Bases of Brain Research and Psychology.* New York: Macmillan, 1978.

Palmer, Edward L., and Aimée Dorr. *Children and the Faces of Television: Teaching, Violence, Selling.* New York: Academic Press, 1980.

Panelas, T. "Adolescents and Video Games: Consumption of Leisure and the Social Construction of the Peer Group." *Youth and Society* 15, no. 1 (September 1983): 51–65.

Papert, Seymour. *Mindstorms: Children, Computers, and Powerful Ideas.* New York: Basic Books, 1980.

Penley, Constance. "The Cabinet of Dr. Pee-Wee: Consumerism and Sexual Terror." *Camera Obscura*, no. 17 (May 1988): 133–55 (special issue entitled "Male Trouble").

Piaget, Jean. *The Development of Thought: Equilibration of Cognitive Structures.* Translated by Arnold Rosin. New York: Viking Press, 1977.

———. *Judgment and Reasoning in the Child.* Translated by Marjorie Warden. Totowa, N.J.: Littlefield, Adams, 1976.

———. "Piaget's Theory." In *The Process of Child Development*, edited by Peter Neubauer, 164–212. New York: Meridian, 1976.

———. *The Psychology of Intelligence* (1947). Translated by Malcolm Piercy and D. E. Berlyne. Totowa, N.J.: Littlefield, Adams, 1981.

Pollack, Andrew. "New Interactive TV Threatens the Bliss of Couch Potatoes." *New York Times*, June 18, 1990.

Pulaski, Mary Ann Spencer. *Understanding Piaget: An Introduction to Children's Cognitive Development*. New York: Harper and Row, 1971.

Rankin, Ken. "Antitrust Subcommittee Targets Nintendo." *Discount Store News*, January 29, 1990, 36.

Rich, Jason. "Nintendo to Introduce Online Network: The Home Unit Will Become More Than a Toy." *Link-Up*, November–December 1989, 1.

———. "The Nintendo Link: A New Way to Play the Market?" *Barron's*, December 4, 1989, 56.

———. "Say Goodbye to WHAM! ZAP! POW! Video Games Are Getting Less Violent, More Brainy." *TV Guide*, March 2–8, 1991, 31.

Rizzo, John, and Jon Zilber. "How I Learned to Stop Worrying and Love Connectivity: Networking the '90s." *MacUser*, January 1991, 92–97.

Robertson, Patricia Anne, and Peggy Henning Berlin. *The Premature Labor Handbook*. New York: Doubleday, 1986.

Rodriguez, Patricia, Rolando Medina, and Hector Perez-Rincon. "La conducta lúdica y los nuevos juegos electrónicos: Comunicación preliminar" (Game behavior and the new electronic games: Preliminary report). *Salud mental* 6, no. 3 (Fall 1983): 22–34.

Rubin, Martin. "Intertextuality in Warner Bros. Cartoons, ca. 1940." Paper presented at the Annual Meeting of the Society for Cinema Studies, Washington, D.C., 1990.

Rushbrook, S. "Messages of Video Games: Socialization Implications." Ph.D. diss., University of California, Los Angeles, 1986.

Schachter, Jacquelyn. "Testing a Proposed Universal." In *Adult Second Language Acquisition: A Linguistic Perspective*, edited by S. Gass and J. Schachter, 73–88. Cambridge: Cambridge University Press, 1989.

Scheibler, Susan. "Documentary Spectatorship in Consumer Society." Paper presented at the Ohio Film Conference, November 1989.

Schiller, Friedrich von. "13th and 15th Letters on the Aesthetic Education of Man." In *Critical Theory Since Plato*, edited by Hazard Adams, 421–26. New York: Harcourt Brace Jovanovich, 1971.

Schoenberger, Karl. "Ad Giant in Japan Sells Clout." *Los Angeles Times*, June 14, 1990.

———. "Japanese Film: The Sinking Sun." *Los Angeles Times*, April 4, 1990, "Calendar" sec.

Shao, Martin, Amy Dunkin, and Patrick Cole. "There's a Rumble in the Video Arcade." *Business Week*, February 20, 1989, 37.

Shear, Jeff. "AT&T Likely to Call Others as It Sets Up for a New Game." *Insight*, September 4, 1989, 41.

Sheff, David. "Nintendo Isn't Playing Games." *San Francisco Chronicle*, December 2, 1990, "This World" sec.

Shiver, Jube, Jr. "The Bidding for MCA." *Los Angeles Times*, November 29, 1990.

Signorelli, Nancy, and George Gerbner. *Violence and Terror in the Mass Media: An Annotated Bibliography*. New York: Greenwood Press, 1988.

Silverman, Kaja. *The Acoustic Mirror: The Female Voice in Psychoanalysis and Cinema*. Bloomington: Indiana University Press, 1988.

Silvern, Steven B. "Classroom Use of Video Games." *Educational Research Quarterly* 10, no. 1 (1985–86): 10–16.

Skinner, B. F. *Verbal Behavior*. New York: Appleton-Century Crofts, 1957.

Spigel, Lynn. *Installing the Television Set: Television and Family Ideals in Postwar America*. Chicago: University of Chicago Press, 1991.

Stam, Robert. "Mikhail Bakhtin and Left Cultural Critique." In *Postmodernism and Its Discontents*, edited by E. Ann Kaplan, 116–45. London: Verso, 1988.

Standard and Poor's Industry Surveys, March 15, 1990, sec. 3: Toys.

Starr, Mark. "A Game of Legal Punch-Out." *Newsweek*, January 2, 1989, 50.

Strein, William. "Effects of Age and Visual-motor Skills on Preschool Children's Computer-Game Performance." *Journal of Research and Development in Education* 20, no. 2 (Winter 1987): 70–72.

Suleiman, Susan Rubin. "Writing and Motherhood." In *The (M)other Tongue*, edited by Shirley Nelson Garner, Claire Kahane, and Madelon Sprengnether, 352–77. Ithaca: Cornell University Press, 1985.

Thomas, Kevin. "Last Picture Show in Little Tokyo." *Los Angeles Times*, October 31, 1990, "Calendar" sec.

Thorndyke, Perry W. "Cognitive Structures in Comprehension and Memory of Narrative Discourse." *Cognitive Psychology* 9 (1977): 77–110.

Tice, Dianne, Jane Buder, and Roy Baumeister. "Development of Self-Consciousness: At What Age Does Audience Pressure Disrupt Performance?" *Adolescence* 20, nos. 7–8 (Summer 1985): 301–5.

Trinkaus, John W. "Arcade Video Games: An Informal Look." *Psychological Reports* 52, no. 2 (April 1983): 586.

Ulmer, Gregory. *Teletheory: Grammatology in the Age of Video.* New York: Routledge, 1989.

Vygotsky, L. S. *Mind in Society: The Development of Higher Psychological Processes.* Edited by Michael Cole, Vera John-Steiner, Sylvia Scribner, and Ellen Souberman. Cambridge, Mass.: Harvard University Press, 1978.

Watanabe, Teresa. "Japan Sets Sights on Creativity." *Los Angeles Times*, June 10, 1990.

Weir, Ruth. *Language in the Crib.* The Hague: Mouton, 1962.

White, Mimi. "Crossing Wavelengths: The Diegetic and Referential Imaginary of American Commercial Television." *Cinema Journal* 25, no. 2 (Winter 1986): 51–64.

Wilder, Gita, Diane Mackie, and Joel Cooper. "Gender and Computers: Two Surveys of Computer-related Attitudes." *Sex Roles* 13, nos. 3–4 (1985): 215–28.

Willis, Susan. "Gender as Commodity." *South Atlantic Quarterly* 86, no. 4 (Fall 1987): 403–21.

Winnicott, D. W. *Playing and Reality*. London: Routledge, 1971.

Winning, Rob. "PeeWee Herman Un-Mascs Our Cultural Myths About Masculinity." *Journal of American Culture* 2, no. 2 (Summer 1988): 57–63.

Index

Compositor: Auto-Graphics, Inc.
Text: 10½/14 Baskerville
Display: Baskerville
Printer: Maple-Vail Book Manufacturing Group
Binder: Maple-Vail Book Manufacturing Group